PRAISE FOR *BIKE R...*

M000282668

Bowman thoughtfully recounts her experiences in Afghanistan, Ukraine, and Bangladesh, among others, furnishing perceptive commentary on the various cultures and histories of these nations ravaged by war and impoverishment. She writes with great lucidity and a breezy, anecdotal charm and harbors no idealistic pretensions about the work she does, however important... A splendid and intelligent recollection of an eventful law career.

—*Kirkus Reviews*

In *Bike Riding in Kabul,* Jamie Bowman takes the reader on an even wilder ride where only the bravest travelers would venture. From an explosive assignment in turbulent South Sudan to a narrow escape from an anti-American mob in Bangladesh, to life in a shipping container in terrorist-plagued Kabul with an irrepressible Argentinian boyfriend, her global odyssey is a page turner that lays bare the real life of a resolute and resourceful foreign aid practitioner.

—Olivia Ward, *East-West News Service*

...*Bike Riding in Kabul* is a thing apart. It is a beautifully written account of a lawyer's determination to provide authentic, quality advice to fledgling democracies grappling with legal frameworks in post-conflict settings. The book is one part history and one part development—its stories told with large doses humor and personal reflection.

Bike Riding in Kabul enjoys high scores for its nuanced presentation of large policy issues, but just as importantly for its precise depiction of all the little musings that make up an aid advisor's experience. Cringy colleagues, neglected locals, and misgivings about the brash assumptions of a superpower all feature in the book. It now belongs on my special shelf, the one reserved for...books that really plumb the depths of memoir while surfacing the larger issues of international policy.

—Kimberley Wilson, Sr. Lecturer, International Business and Human Security, The Fletcher School, Tufts University

Bike Riding in Kabul...is a unique take on the travel memoir genre... Unlike many [other] travel memoirs, there is a heavy focus on helping others through the author's travels instead of personal enlightenment. Of course, there were enlightening moments for Bowman as she learns about the world outside of the United States, but that wasn't the focal point. It was a nice change and made me feel like I wasn't reading the same stories from memoirs past.

Bike Riding in Kabul by Jamie Bowman was a delightful read...that I highly recommend. If you're looking for a unique travel memoir or just a profound story, then this is a book you must pick up.

—THOMAS ANDERSON, Editor In Chief, Literary Titan

Jamie Bowman's *Bike Riding in Kabul* is the story of an intrepid, courageous, and endlessly adventurous Western rule of law advisor. She contributes her unrelenting best in confusing and often dangerous settings to support strengthening or rebuilding societies edging themselves away from political earthquakes, war, and conflict. Bowman, unlike the odd author who tries to describe this kind of work with technical descriptions, introduces us to the complexity of her work and how to succeed in navigating the world of both inspired and cynical consultants, international agencies, and the endless cast of heroes and villains in the countries she has served. In doing so, she lays her own life bare and reveals in compelling vignettes how her patience, resilience, empathy, and respect for the people she is really there to serve help to overcome her misgivings, to push for what is right and to preserve her optimism. This is a wholly human story with many lessons for those interested in what happens on the front lines of the development and post-conflict work our countries sponsor, as well as for those of us directly involved in the same kind of efforts. A book that has been a long time in coming.

—WILLIAM (BILL) LORIS, Founder and Executive Director Emeritus, Rule of Law for Development Program, Loyola University Chicago School of Law; Co-Founder and former Director General, International Development Law Organization, Rome

Bike Riding in Kabul

The Global Adventures of a Foreign Aid Practitioner

JAMIE BOWMAN

Boyle
&
Dalton

Book Design & Production:
Boyle & Dalton
www.BoyleandDalton.com
Copyright © 2022 by Jamie Bowman

Paperback ISBN: 978-1-63337-634-2
E-Book ISBN: 978-1-63337-635-9
LCCN: 2022915016

Printed in the United States of America
1 3 5 7 9 10 8 6 4 2

*In celebration of the life of
Walter M. Bowman, MD,
and for Pat.*

Contents

Author's Note

Bike Riding in Kabul recounts my personal and professional adventures working as a legal advisor in post-conflict and emerging market countries. I did not set out to make a political statement regarding the United States' approach to foreign aid or development efforts. That said, I hope some lessons will be learned from the stories provided.

In writing this book, I relied upon old emails, information on the internet, several people who appeared in the book, the *Afghanistan Papers* (prepared by the Special Inspector General for Afghanistan Reconstruction, published by *The Washington Post* in 2019), and my best recollection of the events portrayed. Other participants may have different recollections than mine, and I encourage them to write their own stories.

Due to the strict word count limits of modern publishing, I omitted plenty of wonderful people and I'm sorry about that. I also left out a number of events and even a couple of projects which didn't move the stories forward. The timeline of certain events have been compressed, but only when such changes had no impact on the story's substance. I changed almost all the names and certain descriptions to protect the identity of people I encountered. People change. I know I have. And they shouldn't be put in a position of defending their actions ten years after the fact.

(I have not attempted to expand on my personal experience by adding updates regarding the recent events in Ukraine and Afghanistan.) Some of those events are still unfolding, and it would be premature for me to comment.

Juba, Southern Sudan

2006

The camp was oddly quiet that afternoon. Even the birds had gone silent. Usually there was a playful chorus of cheeps and twitters, but there was barely a peep that day. At the time, I thought it might have something to do with the heat, but thinking back, the birds probably sensed what was coming.

It was early April 2006, and Juba, Southern Sudan, was at the tail end of the annual dry season. The temperature was only in the mid-90s, but it felt more like 110. I had an old fan, but it was useless. So inside my tent, it felt even hotter. It would stay this way until the onset of the rainy season, which was expected in a week or two. After that, it would be cooler but more humid. So at least I had that to look forward to.

Lunch was over, and the other project consultants were back in their offices at their respective ministries. I worked for the Ministry of Legal Affairs, which had limited office space and other issues, so I worked out of my tent in Afex Camp, the main residence of Juba's expat community. Most people saw this as a hardship—no air-conditioning, no coffee maker, no one to talk to—but for me, it was a blessing. With the other consultants gone, the camp was delightfully peaceful. The only sounds were the soft humming of the cleaning ladies, the occasional bleat of a goat, and, of course, the chattering of birds.

Drenched in sweat, I sat at my desk, a locally made table that I had to stabilize with a wedge of a wine cork. I was researching a new assignment. The Minister wanted a memo on recent trends in immunity for politicians. As always, he was pushing for the modern approach. My hands were poised over my keyboard when I heard a series of loud "pops" in the distance. I sat back in my chair and listened. I hoped it was firecrackers, but in this part of the world, it was more likely to be gunfire.

BANG. BANG. BANG. Three successive explosions shattered the peace of the afternoon. The cleaning ladies screamed in unison, and a frantic fluttering of wings made the trees come alive. Then a deep KA-BOOM rumbled through the camp. Whatever it was, it sounded dangerous. Whatever it was, it sounded close.

I found myself on the floor of my tent, with no clear memory of how I got there. I leaned back on my hands and, through the meshed windows of the tent, watched a long line of cooks, servers, cleaning ladies, and other local staff, wide-eyed with fright, run toward the camp entrance.

I heard SPUTTER-WHOOSH, followed by the screaming of a high-pitched whistle. I knew from my time in Kabul it was a missile in flight. On more than one occasion, I'd woken to the shrill pitch of an errant missile overshooting the US Embassy. I felt strangely calm but then realized my right arm was trembling uncontrollably.

Knowing any missile could easily slice through the tent canvas, I frantically looked for a place to take cover. My best option, perhaps my only option, was the three feet of rough masonry that supported the sink in the rear of the tent. I knew it was important to stay low, so I crawled the five or six feet into the toilet area and slid under the counter. Two greenish lizards scrambled out from the damp, dark corner, paused to blink at me, then disappeared.

2

CRACK. SWOOSH. KA-BOOM. KA-BOOM. More loud explosions followed, four or five, at least. I pushed myself as far under the sink as possible and felt the metal collar of the U-shaped pipe dig into my back. Between the explosions I could hear the muffled cries of people not that far away. I prayed no one was seriously hurt.

Then the explosions stopped, and calm returned to the camp. The birds started chirping again, which I took as a sign that the coast was clear. Just as I contemplated venturing out from under the sink, Alex, the bombastic, easily annoyed United Nations intel officer, poked his head through the opening of my tent.

"Yoo-hoo. Sister?" he sing-songed. It was an ongoing joke. As a legal advisor to the Minister of Legal Affairs, I thought it best to dress conservatively. I wore simple T-shirts, knee-length skirts, and loafers, which Alex said made me look like a nun. He always found a way to work in a religious reference. I crawled out from under the sink, and all three hundred pounds of him stepped inside my tent.

"I hope this doesn't mean that vespers will be canceled tonight," he bellowed. Even during a crisis, Alex couldn't forego the opportunity to tease me.

CRACK. CRACK. BANG. We were startled by another round of explosions. I screamed, and Alex threw himself on the ground, prostrate. Then, after a few smaller explosions, the quiet returned.

"You okay?" he asked with unexpected sincerity.

"I think so. Do we know what's happening?"

"It could be the start of the third Civil War," he said, taking a relaxed pose on one elbow. His position gave me an unwanted peek at a wedge of his dimpled beer gut. "I'm waiting to hear from the UN Headquarters."

If Southern Sudan was back at war, our escape options were limited. The airport would be a no-go. It was three and a half miles away, and if the insurgents knew what they were doing, it would be the first thing they would seize. We might be able to get out by the river—the White Nile flowed all the way up to Khartoum—but who knew what would be waiting for us there? Plus, we'd be sitting ducks on the water.

"Just stay where you are for now." Alex stood up, brushing off the dirt and dust. "It might be the safest place in camp." Then he disappeared out the slit in the tent.

Coiled up under the sink, flicking bits of lizard poop off my knees, I thought about my time in Southern Sudan. All projects have their problems, but this one had more than most. In my first month, I had to be evacuated from Rumbek, a rough city up North, because of a stupid misunderstanding. A few weeks later, I contracted malaria and was bedridden for a week. I was at odds with the local lawyers, and now this, whatever *this* was.

I felt a desperate need to call Roberto, my boyfriend of five years. It was Roberto who had encouraged, no, insisted that I take the job in Southern Sudan so we could be together. Then he opted for a better job in Dubai, leaving me in Juba on my own.

"Roberto," I imagined myself yelling through my phone, "this may be the last call I ever make. I just want to say thanks for getting me into this, you asshat."

But maybe it wasn't Southern Sudan. Maybe it was me. After six years of jobs in places like Kosovo, Ukraine, Bangladesh, and Afghanistan, perhaps I had lost my tolerance for working in the difficult places. Perhaps I had burnout from living in tiny hotel rooms, converted shipping containers, and recycled safari tents.

Then again, I would be turning fifty next year, a milestone in anyone's life. Maybe I was just getting too old for this shit.

CHAPTER I

Pristina, Kosovo

2002

From the Tropics to the Taliban

I first learned of the job in war-torn Southern Sudan from a remarkably chipper recruiter who called me from Washington, DC. (At the time, I was finishing up a short-term contract in Kabul, Afghanistan and was looking for a new project.) She explained that an attorney position was opening up in the Ministry of Legal Affairs in Juba. She had seen my resume and thought I might be a good fit. Then she reeled off a long list of eligibility requirements, several of which I had no chance of meeting.

In addition to ten years of development experience, (the ideal candidate needed a law degree (LLM preferred), legislative drafting expertise, fluent English and a familiarity with Swahili and Arabic, experience working in conflicted states, time in sub-Saharan Africa, excellent communications skills, cultural sensitivity, and tolerance for living in a place that "lacked standard amenities.") She didn't specifically mention that I'd be living and working out of a tent and would occasionally have to take cover with the lizards under the sink(But it was a chance to work in Africa, and for personal and professional reasons, I wanted the job.)

"Well, I don't have any sub-Saharan experience," I admitted up front, failing to mention the other areas where I fell short. "But I still want to apply."

"*Seriously?*" she squealed with a combination of delight and disbelief. On reflection, her reaction should have been my first clue that Southern Sudan would not live up to my romantic, Karen Blixenish idea of Africa.

That evening I looked over my resume for ways to improve my chances of being hired for the job in Juba. It had been six years since I left my comfortable life in Southern California to work overseas. In 2000, not long after the world welcomed in the new millennium, I left my job as in-house counsel with one of the giant mortgage lenders for the unpredictability of international work. My mother refused to believe this was a legitimate career and solemnly told friends and family that I was a spy, and that's all she could say about it.

Over the following six years, I covered a lot of ground. I provided legal advice to officials in Oceania, Eastern Europe, as well as Southeast and Central Asia. In some cases, the governments were making the complex transition from communism to a free market economy. Others were trying to update their laws to better compete in the global economy. I usually worked with one of the ministries—Finance, Justice, or Commerce—but occasionally, I landed in the Parliament. I spent my days evaluating antiquated legal frameworks, preparing reform roadmaps, drafting legislation, and doing whatever else it took to move the process forward. There were days when it was the best job in the world, but plenty of others when it was the worst.

But as I reviewed my resume that night, I couldn't help noticing a disturbing downward trajectory in my assignments. My first overseas job was with the Assembly of Micronesia, the legislature of a small island nation in the Western Pacific Ocean. I supported the agendas of two senators, one of whom chaired the Committee on Health, Education and Welfare. When the Assembly was in session, I worked on the reallocation of discretionary funds, rumored to be buying favors. The other months I spent summarizing World Health Organization reports on hookworm, tuberculosis, and teen pregnancy. It wasn't particularly challenging work. And while I liked Micronesia for its friendly people, fantastic weather, and world-class tuna, time on that island should have been counted in dog years. Life moved very, very slowly.

So after eighteen months on Pohnpei, an island that could be circumnavigated by car in less than two hours, I had enough international experience to work on projects funded by the United States Agency for International Development or USAID for short. USAID is the US government agency with primary responsibility for America's foreign assistance programs. I accepted the first job that offered me a ticket off the island and was hired by a firm that was implementing a massive project in the Balkans. From there, I went on to jobs in Kyiv, Dhaka, and Moscow, and at that point, I was working in post-invasion Kabul. So essentially, I'd gone from the Tropics to the Taliban in six short years.

If there was a silver lining, I was sure I had enough time in challenging environments to work just about anywhere—including Juba. So after correcting a couple of typos, I sent my resume off to Washington and crossed my fingers.

Arrival in Pristina

My first long-term contract after leaving Micronesia was with a USAID-funded project in Pristina, Kosovo. I was hired to draft the Law on Mortgage, a high priority for the Office of the Prime Minister, or so I was told. And while I know most people tune out when they hear the words "legislative drafting," I was absolutely thrilled to get the job.

I flew into Pristina on the first Sunday of May 2002. Once part of Yugoslavia, Kosovo is located in the Balkans region of Southeastern

Europe.)According to a Bradt Travel guide from the 1980s, which I skimmed in a used bookstore, Thessaloniki, Greece, was a short four hours away by car, and Rome was a scenic ferry ride across the Adriatic. I was convinced that I was going to a less-traveled part of Europe—all the charm, but fewer tourists. I was so excited about my new job that I (gave little thought to the war that had ravaged the region in the 1990s.)

The plane from Vienna to Pristina was packed with United Nations personnel discussing their roles with the United Nations Mission in Kosovo, known as UNMIK.(From my cramped middle seat, I picked up snippets of conversations about the challenges facing post-conflict Kosovo.)

A plump, dark-haired man sitting just across the aisle spoke in a detached tone about an ongoing weapons collection program.

"Plenty of pistols and automatic rifles," he said, half yawning. "Mostly Zastava and Tokarev." Then with a wry smile, he added, "but also a few Kalashnikovs." In response to a question I couldn't hear, he said, "A swimming pool—an ordinary swimming pool behind the office. Thousands of weapons protected by nothing but a plastic tarp and a poorly paid guard." I looked around to see if anyone else was listening.(Easy access to thousands of weapons didn't strike me as the type of conversation suitable for a plane full of people)

(Just behind me, a couple spiritedly debated the potential effects of the trial of Slobodan Milosevic, the former Yugoslav president, who was facing charges of genocide and other war crimes at the International Criminal Court in the Hague.)

"It will do nothing but reopen old wounds," he insisted in a loud, urgent whisper.

"On the contrary," she countered forcefully. "It will help the whole of the Balkans to face their past. And that will start the healing process."

In the row ahead, two men discussed strategies for dealing with the growing street-dog problem; the previous week, another child in a rural village had been attacked. The man on the right spoke slowly in heavily accented English, "I agree something has to be done, but the Norwegians are simply gunning these animals down."

And as the wheels skidded on the tarmac at the Pristina International Airport, I realized that I was a part of all this. Okay, it was just the mortgage law, but I was there to help the people of Kosovo—*and I absolutely loved it.*

Bajram, the driver who worked for my project, a young man with dark hair, a close-cropped beard, and a villain-worthy scowl, met me outside the terminal. He walked up to me with a furrowed brow, holding a bad photocopy of my passport photo, and asked in a loud voice, "Mrs. Jamie?"

He didn't really need the photo. Everyone else in the vicinity, including the children, wore dark jackets and tight-fitting acid-washed blue jeans. I was dressed in my favorite pastel sweater set, pencil skirt, and low-stacked heels. With my shoulder-length light brown hair, I could have easily walked out of a page of the Brooks Brothers' winter catalog. As a result, I looked comically out of place. A wave of unease washed over me because my suitcase was full of more pastels, some floral prints, and an embarrassing amount of paisley.

Bajram silently hoisted my suitcase into the back of the SUV and directed me to the passenger's side with a jerk of his chin. Still silent, he slid into the driver's seat, started the engine, and gunned out of the parking lot, narrowly missing a horse and cart traveling at slow speed on the shoulder of the road.

Someone mentioned that the ability to speak English in transitioning countries such as Kosovo is a huge advantage for the local staff. It affects both employability and salary. So I thought I'd see if Bajram wanted to practice his conversational English. I asked him some basic questions about his family and education, but his vocabulary was limited, and the discussion didn't go very far.

I changed the subject to movies, hoping he would find talking about new releases more interesting.

"Have you seen any good movies?" I asked. He frowned in my direction. "Harry Potter? Lord of the Rings? Shrek?" I listed the popular movies at the time. When he understood what I was talking about, he smiled for the first time.

"Tare-tino," he whispered cautiously.

"Sorry?" I squinted and leaned in a little closer.

"Tar-an-tino. Do you know his movies?" He was talking about Quentin Tarantino, the young director whose movies were known for violence and gore.

"I've seen *Pulp Fiction*," I said brightly, delighted that we were making a connection.

"*Pulp Fiction. Reservoir Dogs*. Tarantino is great director." Bajram was grinning now. "I have seen his movies many, many times. My friends and I watch." Then he recounted one of the more disturbing scenes from *Reservoir Dogs*, the one where Mr. Blonde slashes the policeman's face and severs his ear. As I listened, I realized that except for some minor difficulties pronouncing the words "assassination" and "blood splatter" (and we worked on that) Bajram was essentially fluent in the languages of death, murder, and mayhem.

As we sped toward the city I got my first look at my new hometown. Pristina sustained surprisingly little damage in the NATO air strikes, but it still wasn't much to look at. Flanking the road was a mishmash of uninspired concrete apartment buildings—brutalist architectural souvenirs of Yugoslavia's communist past. The aesthetics were further degraded by rust-stained satellite dishes that hung like enormous metallic mushrooms off the side of virtually every balcony.

But once I looked past the sad buildings, there was a vibrancy about the city that I hadn't expected in a place that had so recently been at war. New business signs were going up, clothing stores displayed the current fashions in the windows, and families walked down the street laughing and enjoying the weekend.

As we neared the town, Bajram pointed out the enormous portrait of Bill Clinton, the forty-second president of the United States, that hung high on the side of a multi-story building. (Kosovars and ethnic Albanians credit Clinton with the NATO bombing campaign that forced Belgrade to withdraw its troops from Kosovo in 1999.)

My dad had a good Bill Clinton story, but it was too complicated to tell Bajram. When running for president in 1992, Clinton admitted to trying marijuana as a twenty-something Rhodes Scholar at the University of Oxford. But as he "didn't inhale," he argued, his actions did not break the law. Fast forward three or four years, and President Clinton was in my hometown of San Jose, California, raising funds for his reelection campaign. My dad, an anesthesiologist with an exceptional reputation, was selected to serve as a member of the elite medical team that would tend to Clinton in the event of a medical emergency. My father's famous comment was, "How can I give Bill Clinton an anesthetic if he doesn't inhale?"

(Just a few blocks farther, Bajram pulled into the semicircular driveway of the Grand Hotel Pristina.) Despite it being the premier short-term address for international officials and advisors, the Grand was, well, less than grand. Its dilapidated, mustard-colored exterior had all the curb appeal of a large Midwestern prison.

A lanky bellhop, wearing a uniform that was too small for his long arms and legs, escorted me to the fourth floor. The room was basic, at best—just a double bed with a frayed coverlet, a wood vanity that doubled as a television stand, and a well-used armchair with a permanent butt impression in the seat. I wasn't too concerned. (My stay at the Grand would be short-lived. I'd be moving into an apartment soon enough.)

The phone in my room didn't work, there was no internet connection, and it was much too early to go to bed, so I went downstairs to look around. The lounge area had indoor and outdoor areas, and despite the chilly evening, several families sat outside. The parents drank coffee and chain-smoked while the children played a rough game that seemed to involve choking each other.

The harried waiter rushed over and turned his ear toward me to better hear my order.

"Red wine." He repeated it back to me, then pulled out a small dish of peanuts from behind the bar. The peanuts were tempting, but the broken and apparently used toothpick that peeked out from among the nuts put me off.

The only other person at the bar, a red-headed man wearing a cream-colored cable-knit sweater, looked over at me and asked, "New arrival?"

"Brand new," I responded cheerfully. "Just arrived this afternoon." Then thinking I was rather interesting, I volunteered, "I'm working in the Prime Minister's Office for USAID."

"USAID?" He stood up and slipped a five-dollar bill under his empty glass. I nodded proudly. "Best of luck," he smirked. "You're going to need it." Then he disappeared through the patio door without further explanation.

The Conflict

After signing my consulting agreement in late April, I panicked briefly because I had only a limited knowledge of the history of Kosovo and what had precipitated the war that tore the Balkans apart. The Bradt Travel guide spoke of Kosovo's beautiful mountain peaks, Ottoman-era buildings, and medieval fresco paintings but, being an old edition, had nothing about the recent conflict. Luckily, during my layover in Amsterdam, a friend arranged for me to meet a couple of his colleagues, Zivko from Serbia and Flamur from Albania.

12

(I met Zivko, a professor from Belgrade, at a hard-to-find Serbian café not far from Willemspark.) Zivko hustled in, about twenty minutes late, and cheerfully greeted everyone in the café in a combination of English and what I assumed was Serbian. He was tall, well over six feet, with a head of dark wavy hair and stunning blue-green eyes. After dumping his leather satchel on the chair next to me, he went to the bar and spoke to a bald apron-clad man drying glasses, who smiled mischievously.

("The first thing you need to know about working in Serbia..." Zivko paused. "You do know that Kosovo is part of Serbia, right)" I nodded, not knowing enough to disagree. "The first thing you need to know is how to drink Rakija."

Right on cue, the barman placed a tray with water glasses, a small carafe, and two short glasses of clear liquid in front of us.

"Rakija is almost a national drink in Serbia," he said proudly. "It's homemade from fermented fruit, usually plums." He picked up one of the short glasses and indicated that I should do the same. We clinked them together, and he knocked his back in a single gulp. I took a healthy sip.

It was like having gasoline in my mouth. My eyes teared up, my nose began to run, and as I swallowed, I felt a fire-like sensation slide down to my gut. I stifled a wheeze with the back of my hand.

Zivko sucked air through clenched teeth, slapped the table a couple of times, then growled, "It's the good stuff."

"Tasty," I squeaked. Zivko signaled to the barman for two more glasses, even though I hadn't finished the first.

"I'm good. I'm good." I was almost pleading, but two more glasses arrived.

"Okay," he said, settling back in his chair. "Let's talk about what led up to the recent conflict in Kosovo. In the year 1389...)

"Hang on." I stopped him in mid-sentence. "Sorry for interrupting, but don't you mean 1989?"

"Oh no," he said, looking troubled. "If you want to understand the recent conflict, you must go back to 1389, to the Battle of Kosovo when the first Ottoman Sultan Murad defeated the Serbs." I counted the centuries on my fingers.

"Are you saying the current conflict started six hundred years ago?" I asked incredulously.

"Kosovo is the Serbian 'Jerusalem. Some of the holiest shrines of the Serbian Orthodox Church are there. So Kosovo will always be part of Serbia. Time is of no consequence."

Over the next hour and a half, Zivko spoke of wars, conquests, rebellion, flight, and oppression, and he only got as far as World War II. It was fascinating, but unfortunately we both had places to be, so I gave him my card, and he promised to send me articles that would give me more of the "true history" of Kosovo.

I then rushed across town to meet Flamur, the Albanian lawyer, at a restaurant near the Dam Square. He was seated by the window with a small carafe and two glasses of what I suspected to be more Rakija.

"The most important thing about working in Kosovo is learning the Albanian tradition of drinking Rakija. It's almost a national drink." I pretended to be thrilled by this new experience. We clinked glasses, and I took a small sip. The clear, high-octane liquid went down much easier this time.

"Okay." Flamur settled back in his chair. "Let's talk about what led up to the recent conflict in Kosovo. After World War II . . ."

Over the next two hours, I heard how Serbia, with Kosovo as one of its provinces, was absorbed into the newly formed communist federation of Yugoslavia led by President Josip Broz, known as Tito. Tito lived to the ripe old age of eighty-seven, an amazing accomplishment considering he had a very public "ideological dispute" with Joseph Stalin. Under Tito's relaxed communist regime, a diverse Yugoslav population—including Albanians, Bosniaks, Croats, Montenegrins,

Slovenes, Kosovars, and Serbs—lived fairly harmoniously for more than thirty-five years.)

(After Tito's death in 1980 things began to unravel). Over the next few years(ethnic tensions and armed unrest escalated until open conflict erupted throughout the region.(Ultimately an estimated 100,000 people were killed, making the Balkans War Europe's most devastating conflict since World War II)(Finally, the signing of the Dayton Accords, the general framework agreement for peace in Bosnia and Herzegovina in 1995, ended the war in Bosnia.(But issues in Kosovo were left unresolved.)

(Slobodan Milosevic, the president of Serbia, had revoked Kosovo's autonomy and whipped up ethnic hatred,)referring to the events of 1389 and World War II in his propaganda.(Ethnic Albanians lost their jobs and were expelled from the region) After attempts at a diplomatic solution failed,(NATO conducted seventy-eight days of air strikes against Serbia, and Belgrade finally withdrew its armed forces from Kosovo.)

("The Serbs have always been the aggressors," Flamur explained. "It was only Tito that was strong enough to keep them in check.")

I walked back to the hotel a bit loopy from all the Rakija, wondering what I had gotten myself into.

My First Day

On my first morning of work, I was awakened before dawn by a blast of sound. At first, I thought it was an air-raid siren—it had that much force—and I considered diving under the bed.(Then I realized it was a powerful human voice—a long, beautifully sustained note—a call to prayer and a reminder that Kosovo is close to ninety percent Muslim.) I got up and struggled with the window that probably hadn't been opened in a decade. Once it was open, the beautiful sound and brisk air filled the room.

The first call was followed by several others coming from the numerous mosques nestled among the houses and apartment buildings of downtown Pristina. Each call was delayed just a few seconds off the next, so it was an almost continuous chorus of sound. It was a remarkable way to start the day.

After breakfast, a relatively paltry affair of sour cheese, sliced vegetables, and white bread I met the project's SUV on the street in front of the Grand. Brian, my new boss, a young thirty-something with a Kennedy-esque appeal, sat in the back seat with his phone pressed to his ear. As the Chief of Party, Brian was responsible for overseeing the work of thirty international advisors, managing the small local staff, dealing with the home office in Virginia, and liaising with USAID. I'm sure there were days when his job was a complete nightmare.

We drove down the congested street to the main project office and joined a meeting that was already in progress. The large room was full of twenty or twenty-five people sitting around a huge rectangular table. These were the project's advisors who were providing technical support and building the capacity of the local staff in many of Kosovo's ministries and agencies. They were accountants, lawyers, and administrators, most of whom hailed from the United States.

Brian made some project announcements then ceded control of the meeting to Joel, an advisor embedded with the Kosovo Energy Corporation (KEK), the country's sole provider of power Under Tito's communism, utilities such as water and electricity were provided without charge. But as part of the effort to transition to a free market economy, Kosovo's residents were now required to pay for services that had previously been free. As you might imagine, this part of the project wasn't going well.

Joel argued that KEK should be able to disconnect service for nonpayment—a practice that is followed in the United States and other free market economies. Brian mused that a spate of dead Kosovars, frozen to death in their apartments the coming winter, might be bad optics for both the KEK and its advisor, USAID. The point was lost on Joel, who suggested that a few deaths would send a strong message about paying the power bill on time and in full. Some advisors nodded approvingly, but most looked appropriately horrified.

After the meeting, I followed Brian down the street to a large, run-down, but surprisingly elegant structure known as the "Government Building." It served as the temporary headquarters for both the Office of the Prime Minister and the Kosovo National Assembly, the country's new Parliament. Brian passed through a metal detector without incident, but I was held up by a female guard who dug through my computer bag. Seemingly disappointed at not finding anything more dangerous than a hairbrush, she unsmilingly tossed it back at me with some force.

I followed Brian up the stairs to an office that was dark, stuffy, and in need of a really good cleaning. He explained, almost apologetically, that I would be sharing the office with two other project advisors, a local attorney, and the occasional short-term translator. He assured me three or four times that it was only a temporary arrangement.

Brian made quick introductions to Tom, the other expat in the office, and Dardan, the local attorney who welcomed me in English but quickly excused himself so he could get back to work on a rush translation.

"I'll come to pick you up on Thursday afternoon for the weekly briefing at USAID. You'll be meeting Terry Jones," Brian said. I wasn't completely sure, but I thought I heard Tom snort behind his computer screen. Brian threw a sharp look in Tom's direction and continued, "Terry Jones is the USAID project manager, and depending on how the meeting goes, he may want to ask you a few questions about your background." He promised to call Tom later and then slipped out the door.

There weren't enough desks or chairs, so I found a relatively clean spot on the floor and started leafing through a file labeled "mortgage."

There wasn't much to review—just some copies of the old law and a skimpy draft law prepared by another consultant.

"I hope you know something about mortgages," Tom commented in a not entirely friendly way.

For once, I took a moment before responding. (I'd spent fifteen years of my adult life working in the mortgage industry.) I had an intimate knowledge of both the US federal and state laws governing the creation, servicing, sale, and enforcement of mortgages in each of the fifty states, Puerto Rico, and Guam. I also knew about the practical aspects of mortgage lending. I had firsthand experience dealing with serial tax return fraud, wildly inflated property appraisals, forged payment stubs, broker kickbacks, and the alarming regularity with which spouses try to rip off spouses.

I almost said, "Yes, Tom. I know a shitload about mortgages." But it was my first day, and I was trying to make a good impression. So I smiled sweetly and said, "I think I can handle it."

USAID

I was picked up outside the Government Building on Thursday afternoon for my first weekly meeting at USAID. Bajram was at the wheel and gave me a brotherly wink in the rearview mirror. Brian was on the phone, calmly counseling the person on the other end not to make any rash decisions. He promised to speak to Terry and get back with an answer that afternoon. As one call ended, another came in. From what I could hear, it was another unhappy consultant.

We pulled up in front of USAID's offices, which occupied a house on one of the hills overlooking Pristina. I entered the front door, and a local employee curtly directed me up a flight of stairs to a small room where several advisors were waiting. I recognized some from the meeting earlier in the week. There was good-natured banter about political affiliations, ex-girlfriends, and poor life choices. They knew each other well. That much was certain.

The man sitting next to me leaned over and asked, "Is this your first time meeting Terry Jones?" I nodded. "Well, you're in for a real treat," he said sarcastically. "He's fired several consultants since I've been here, and it's only been a couple of months."

"Don't scare her," someone called out from across the room. "Terry hasn't thrown anything at a consultant for several years."

After a ridiculously long wait, we were summoned to the conference room. Brian was speaking to a diminutive, not particularly attractive man seated at the center of the conference table. Trying to hide his exasperation, Brian spoke in the calm, measured tone a person might use when dealing with a toddler acting out in public. Whatever the issue was, Brian gave assurances that it would be taken care of. With that, Terry turned his attention to the advisors, and the berating began as soon as we drew ourselves up to the table.

Terry first went after the accountancy team, deriding them for their inadequate performance, both individually and collectively. The training manuals were poorly written. The scheduling was bad. There weren't enough female attendees. A gray-haired man in a dress shirt and tie stammered the beginnings of an explanation, but Terry talked over him and ridiculed him for "amateurish mistakes."

In a flash, Terry's focus turned to the pension reform advisor, who bolted straight up in her chair at the sound of her name. He demanded estimates on the number of potential participants, and when she took time to refer to her notes, he grew frustrated and wondered aloud why she shouldn't be on the next plane out of Pristina. It was extremely tough to watch.

By the end of the meeting, each of the ten advisors, except me as the new hire, had been singled out for poor performance or some gratuitous rebuke. It was brutal.

19

As we silently filed out of the conference room, I noticed a colorful poster board lying sideways on the floor against the cabinet. It was the iconic USAID logo—the handshake, framed by a red, white, and blue shield, encircled by the words ("United States Agency for International Development.") For me, (the logo had always conjured the laudable values of America's foreign aid—humanity, compassion, and generosity.) How ironic that it lay there on its side, ignored—and what I'd just witnessed was far from humane, compassionate, or generous.

As I stood outside USAID's offices, I felt a little shell-shocked. Someone clapped me on the shoulder and said, "Don't worry, you'll get used to it."

"That's what I'm afraid of," I said quietly, mostly to myself.

Brian stood next to the project vehicle talking on his phone. He stopped briefly to offer me a ride back to the city center, but I decided to walk instead. I needed time to think through what I'd just witnessed.

Back at the Grand Hotel, I went directly to the front desk and asked about monthly discounts. I decided it was best to pass on an apartment and stay at the Grand. It would be more expensive but less humiliating if I turned out to be one of the advisors who was sent home early.

Calling Home

That evening, I called my parents in San Jose, ostensibly to tell them about my first week at the new job. But my real purpose was to hear the results of the battery of tests my father had undergone earlier in the week. He'd experienced bouts of forgetfulness and loss of cognitive functions, and we were hoping for a treatable diagnosis.

I could tell by my mother's muffled voice that she was cupping the receiver. She quietly explained that my dad's scans showed "brain shrinkage," an early indicator of some form of dementia, probably Alzheimer's. It was something we suspected, something we probably already knew, but something we didn't want to know.

Even as a young girl, I knew I had lucked out in the dad lottery. (Intelligent, kind, and considerate, my dad was a successful doctor, loving husband, and supportive father.) His colleagues frequently sought me out to tell stories about my dad's high standard of patient care, strong work ethic, and solid moral principles. At some hospital function, Dr. Lyon, an orthopedist, pulled me aside and told me a story that summed up my dad perfectly.

When Dr. Lyon was starting out, the more established doctors mocked him. "They ridiculed my hair and mimicked the way I spoke. But I was top of my class at Harvard—you'd think that would count for something. But those guys wouldn't give me a break." Dr. Lyon took off his glasses and wiped his eyes. Despite the passage of thirty-odd years and a successful career, it was apparent that that time in Dr. Lyon's life still stung.

"Your dad called out the other doctors for their comments," he said. "He put himself in the line of fire for me. That's the kind of guy your dad is." Such stories set high ethical and moral standards that I always tried to meet.

Having my dad's condition clinically confirmed was tough on everyone. As there were few medical options, it seemed that our role was to watch the man we loved so dearly fade away. I asked my mother if I should come home, half hoping she'd give me a credible excuse for leaving Kosovo. She told me to stay where I was—jobs were tough to come by, and she'd need me more in a few years.

The Sites of Pristina

That first weekend, I wanted to explore Pristina and see its sites of interest. So I approached the young concierge for suggestions. Delighted by my interest, he pulled out an old map of the downtown area.

"Well, you can start at one end of town and visit the statue dedicated to Gjergj Kastrioti Skanderbeg, an Albanian nobleman who led forces against the Ottoman Empire. Then walk through town to the National Library of Kosovo. Unfortunately, it's closed for renovations, but it's an amazing piece of architecture. And end up here," he pointed with his pen, "the famous statue of Mother Theresa. It should take you about a couple of hours, including a stop for coffee."

"What are my other options?" I asked, hoping for something a little more adventurous.

"Well, if you want to hike, you should walk up the Vila Germia, a popular café perched on top of a hill, just outside of town."

I followed the concierge's hand-drawn map. The route took me through the busy downtown area, past the mortar-pocked buildings, through several weedy, garbage-strewn lots, to a large open playing field. Just beyond the field, I could see a quaint dirt path that led through a beautiful wood. Unfortunately, the beginning of the path was blocked by a pack of ten or twelve filthy street dogs congregated around a food truck, hoping for scraps.

They were enormous breeds—Dobermans, Labrador retrievers, and a couple of German shepherds. They stood shoulder-to-shoulder and moved in unison. If I took one step to the left, so did they. If I countered with two steps to the right, they did too. They scared me. The food truck owner saw my plight and distracted the dogs with some cooked meat so I could pass.

As I walked through the wood, I thought about my work situation. The project was designed to help lay the groundwork for a more prosperous Kosovo. It was exciting work that I wanted to be a part of. I convinced myself that the Thursday afternoon meeting at USAID hadn't been all that bad. So with renewed commitment, I spent Sunday evening reviewing the skimpy mortgage file, marking up the existing draft law, and preparing a list of next steps.

Week Two

On Monday morning I marched into the second-floor office full of renewed optimism for my job and what could be accomplished. It didn't take long for my enthusiasm to wane. For one thing, it wasn't just the physical state of the office that was dreary; it was the whole setup. Dardan, the local attorney, reminded me of Bob Cratchit toiling away at his desk for long hours for low pay to support his large family. He sat hunched over his keyboard, painstakingly translating documents full of complex concepts and obscure terminology.

Whether it was USAID's pressure to produce policy and laws or just his personality, Tom was difficult. He discouraged any interaction that might help to make sitting in that office bearable. When I asked Dardan about his weekend, Tom shouted, "He's working. Don't bother him." Dardan felt it too. When Tom left the office, Dardan turned to me and said, "That man is oppressive, and I should know. I've experienced both a communist regime and the brutality of the Serbs."

But by the end of the week, I realized I had a bigger problem than just the office and my office mates. After meeting with other consultants about the mortgage law, it became clear that USAID was aiming for more than just a traditional mortgage industry. By advocating for short notice periods, non-judicial foreclosure, and other pro-lender provisions, its goal was to replicate the go-go approach dominating the mortgage industry in the United States. The same system that drove me to international work in the first place.

Back in the late 1980s when I started my career as in-house counsel for a large reputable mortgage lender, my firm promoted the American dream of homeownership and the accumulation of family wealth. All that changed with the popularization of home equity loans, the type that fueled the subprime industry. Almost overnight, my firm became a top financier of Caribbean vacations, Harley-Davidson motorcycles, and breast augmentations. Pushing these loans seemed unethical. I just couldn't see how it was sustainable—and of course, it wasn't.

Because of my doubts about the new loan programs I tried to find a different job, but for the most part the demand for attorneys was in subprime, the very area I was trying to leave. It was only by chance that I stumbled upon the international job postings that took me to Micronesia. (And now here I was in Kosovo, being paid to draft legislation that would support the same type of system I'd escaped two years previously.)

The Cadaster

Regardless of what type of mortgage industry Kosovo would end up with, I needed a better understanding of the mortgage system that was in place. I needed to investigate a number of key issues, including the application process, how real estate was appraised, and the method for maintaining the registry of land ownership and encumbrances some-times called the "cadaster." Regarding the latter, Dardan assured me that Kosovo kept a cadaster with detailed information on land rights. In fact, he was a bit offended that I had even asked.

I also needed to meet with the banks and other institutions that might rely on the new law. When drafting legislation, it's essential to get input from the private sector, or you run the risk of ending up with a law subject to post-enactment complaints (embarrassing), and in the worst case, a law that doesn't fulfill its intended purpose (career-kill-ing). So I scheduled meetings with the larger banks in Pristina, those most likely to offer a mortgage product. As a bonus, these meetings would give me a valid excuse to get out of my dreary second-floor office.

I received a quick response from the CEO of a Dutch bank who spoke in precise English that might have been better than mine. We discussed the challenges to lending in Kosovo, the rudimentary approach to property evaluation, the large housing stock left vacant by the Serbs who were forced to flee Pristina, and the risks of future conflict.

"So besides a modern law, what else do you need to increase mortgage lending," I asked, trying to be personable.

"A cadaster would be nice," he said ironically.

"I was assured there was a cadaster. A good one, too," I responded.

"Oh, you don't know." He smiled as if prepared to deliver the punch line of a good joke. "When Belgrade's forces pulled out of Kosovo in 1999, they took Kosovo's cadaster book along with them." He leaned back in his chair and waited to see if I understood the significance.

"Oh shit," I said, then quickly apologized for my language.

"Oh shit, indeed," he nodded. "Someone really knew what they were doing."

By taking the cadaster, the Serbs had robbed Kosovo of its official land records, information that was critical to establishing a modern mortgage industry. This one act would hobble Kosovo's economic recovery for years, maybe a generation, and do more damage than a thousand mortar shells.

The Kukri Bar

The other project consultants were visibly appalled when they learned I was staying long-term at the shabby, not-so-Grand, but the hotel had its advantages. I didn't suffer during the strike by the Regional Water Company when the average resident went without water for several days. The Grand Hotel and other state-owned enterprises were exempt, and I happily showered every morning. My colleagues in the second-floor office pointedly complained about going unwashed.

Another bonus of staying at the Grand was the army of short-term advisors who passed through the unloved lobby and wanted to talk about their projects. I met child psychologists who dealt with the effects of war on children, volunteer veterinarians who came to neuter the street dogs, wood specialists hoping to restart Kosovo's furniture industry, and compost advisors, to name a few.

Best of all, the Grand was literally crawling distance from the Kukri Bar, one of Pristina's most popular expat hangouts. Named after the type of utility knife used by the Nepalese Gurkhas recruited by the British army, "Kukri" conjured the more exotic aspects of the British empire. It was owned and operated by a Brit who did his best to replicate a proper English pub experience. They served bacon sandwiches, held a weekly quiz night, and offered a roast beef dinner on Sunday. In addition, there were persistent rumors that soldiers in uniform could get an alcoholic beverage disguised as a cup of tea or mug of coffee, adding to the Kukri's allure.

Peter, a British IT consultant, walked me over to the Kukri that first time. We were about to make the trek up to USAID's offices but were waved off because, once again, Terry was annoyed at the accountancy team and was meeting with them instead of us. We were delighted by the reprieve and decided to celebrate with an early cocktail.

Walking along the fence that surrounded an abandoned construction site, I asked, "Peter, does this make us bad people?"

"You mean that we're ecstatic that the accountants are in trouble instead of us?" he asked. "I can assure you that if the roles were reversed, they would be just as delighted that we were in trouble."

"I don't understand why USAID allows Terry to behave that way," I said.

"The problem with Terry is that he only thinks about managing projects, not people. He doesn't seem to get that good people make good projects. I wonder if he started that way. Some people think that

26

America's approach to foreign aid—the program structure, incentives, and monitoring—have a corrupting influence. Something to keep in mind if you're in development for the long term."

We descended the short flight of stairs into the Kukri and were surprised to find that the bar was fairly crowded despite the early hour; it was exactly five o'clock. Peter introduced me to Lars and Stephan, two advisors from Germany working with one of the banks.

"American?" Lars asked.

"I'm from San Francisco," I smiled smugly, waiting for the usual compliments about California—the glorious weather, the fabulous wine country, and the outstanding beaches.

"Let me ask you," he paused to take a sip of beer. "What do you think about the United States Electoral College? It strikes me as less democratic than a direct popular vote." I didn't know how to answer. To be honest, I never thought about the Electoral College, except when it forms every four years to elect the president and vice president. Luckily, Peter saved me.

"Lars, let us get a drink before we start comparing democracies," he said. I mouthed "thank you" to Peter when Lars couldn't see me.

At the bar, I stood between two men named Louis, one from Belgium and another from Britain. Belgian Louis asked how many guns I owned. When I told him I didn't own any firearms, he responded, "I thought everyone in America had at least one gun. Isn't that your Second Amendment right?"

After a few beers, British Louis was poking me in the arm and complaining about the terms of the Lend-Lease program under which the United States supplied materials to the anti-fascist coalition of countries during World War II. The United Kingdom was still making payments, which according to Louis was patently unfair. "We were fighting the Nazis, for God's sake," he bellowed.

Just about everyone I met zeroed in on the fact I was American.

Some made good-natured jokes. But on my way out, Stephen, the German consultant, was a bit more pointed. Noting that all the world's great empires have failed and that it was only a matter of time until the United States followed suit, he advised me to "enjoy it while it lasts."

Two Visions for Kosovo

Over the following weeks, the situation in the office improved—Tom warmed up a bit—but the Thursday afternoon meetings at USAID did not; in fact, they took a turn for the worse. Terry was constantly on edge, eager to humiliate advisors for minor slipups and for what he perceived as an inferior work product.

It was during those meetings that I realized that there were two visions for Kosovo's future—the US vision and the European vision—and they were very different. The Americans pursued a more pro-market approach, while the Europeans pushed for stronger government intervention. These differences directly affected the policies and laws governing essential areas such as pensions, health care, financial services, utility regulation, and others. As a result, there was ongoing friction between the American advisors supported by USAID and those sponsored by the United Nations and the European Union.

I didn't quite understand the dispute. It was no secret that Kosovo wanted to join the European Union, and for that to happen, it had to enact laws that followed the directives and regulations of that body. It seemed evident that the European consultants were in a better position to advise on policy and draft legislation. But there were complaints about the United Nations' work, or so I was told. As a related matter, USAID was able to respond more quickly to requests. So war-weary Kosovo found itself in a whole new conflict: the one between the Americans and the Europeans.

Parliamentary Process

At the beginning of my second month in-country, I realized I wasn't the only one drafting high-profile legislation. Almost everyone on the project was working on a new law. Terry demanded weekly updates on the Pension Law, the Organic Budget Law, the Accountancy Law, the Telecom Law, and several others. These new laws would replace the old communist rules and form the legal framework necessary to create a free market economy.

Drafting a law is one thing; getting it enacted is another. Under Kosovo's interim constitution, draft legislation known as a "bill" had to be passed by the Assembly and signed into law by the president. It sounds straightforward enough, but in practice it's not so easy. Once a bill is submitted to the Assembly, it's referred to committees for review and possible amendment. A lot can happen in that process. A bill can go into committee saying one thing and come out saying something very different. Terry Jones understood this risk and wanted to post someone in the Assembly to watch over the process and do what they could to ensure that the laws drafted by USAID's advisors didn't get mangled by the committees.

At the close of another difficult Thursday afternoon meeting—the privatization team had been flambéed over their slow (nonexistent) progress—I overheard Brian tell Terry that he had a potential candidate to work in the Assembly, but the consultant wanted a daily fee of $1,000. Terry turned to Brian and said, "Too expensive. Someone on the project has parliamentary experience. I remember seeing it on a resume. Let's hunt that person down."

I figured Terry was talking about me. I thought back to my eighteen months working for the Assembly in Micronesia. If I hadn't broken my two-year commitment, I would still be living the island life, enjoying freshly caught tuna and drinking beers in bars nestled in the mangroves.

I didn't volunteer for the Assembly position in Kosovo. I feared

29

that if I showed any interest, Terry was mean-spirited enough to reject me. So I waited to see what happened. Before the berating began at the next Thursday meeting, Terry leaned across the table, pointed at me, and said, "It's you. You're the one with parliamentary experience." He gave me two choices—go to the Assembly or go home.

Franck

There was a major obstacle to my proposed transfer to the Assembly, and his name was Franck. Franck was on loan from the French Senate and headed up the United Nations' technical support to the Parliament. Small and exceptionally tidy, with closely cropped gray hair and icy blue eyes, Frank was not enthusiastic about a USAID consultant joining the team at the Assembly. But he was kind about it. He softly touched my shoulder and assured me in his heavily accented English, "It's not you, Jamie. It's not you."

He suggested that even with my experience in Micronesia, my placement in the Assembly would be inappropriate. He noted that instead of a congress in the American style, the Assembly would operate as a parliament, the system favored in Europe, and questioned whether I'd feel comfortable under the circumstances. I assured him I would—I had no choice.

In light of Franck's reticence, Brian went over Franck's head and spoke to the president of the Assembly, and after the president's approval was secured, Franck had no choice. But I had to agree to some ground rules before he'd give me an office.

"We expect you to help out as necessary with laws and projects other than those sponsored by USAID." I nodded and made the mistake of adding, "That goes without saying," which led to a ten-minute explanation of what the phrase meant.

Then he broached the real issue.

"Terry Jones. That is the name of your boss, yes?" I nodded and prepared for the worst.

"If you work for the Assembly, he will not be visiting you." I wasn't sure if that was a question or a statement. "You see, Jamie, we will not permit any…" he paused to find the right word, "…discord in the Assembly." There it was. Terry Jones, the most recognizable face of the US effort in Kosovo, was a liability.

The Assembly

My transfer to the Assembly was like getting early parole from prison. For one thing, I had my own office. It was just a tiny forgotten supply closet that smelled like a wet mop, but it was all mine. The small, not quite rectangular window overlooked the massive generators that powered the Government Building when the electricity shut off. Some afternoons I had to work in the stairwell to avoid breathing the generator exhaust, but it was worth it. No one yelled at me for being a few minutes late, and I was free to meet other consultants and talk about ways to collaborate.

I also had an extremely competent counterpart, Kate, the UN's second-in-command, who was on loan from the Australian Parliament. Just over five feet tall, Kate was always well-coiffed and nicely dressed, which put undue pressure on those of us who didn't mind a wrinkled shirt or scuffed shoes now and then. But her petite size and reserved manner were deceptive. She was not one to be messed with. One time I witnessed her telling an especially annoying consultant to essentially "buzz off," but she did it with such finesse that he thanked her on his way out.

If she had any objection to my joining the Assembly staff, she kept it to herself. She made it clear that I was part of the team, and there was no room for friction among consultants in the Assembly. Now, *this* was what I'd signed up for.

The Environmental Law

A new consultant was immediately hired to take my place in the dreary second-floor office. Joe was a retired commercial attorney from Massachusetts who carried himself with the gentle dignity of an aging diplomat. His wife, Peggy, accompanied him, and they looked at Kosovo as an exciting post-retirement adventure they could enjoy together.

Joe had been in-country only a couple of weeks when I received a text from Ned, the project gossip, that Joe had been fired and there was a going-away function at the Kukri at the end of the week. As it was explained to me, one of Joe's first assignments was the review of the Environmental Law drafted by the United Nations Environmental Program. His task was to flag any provisions that might hinder economic growth or lead to so-called "rent-seeking" activities (the collection of bribes). Joe didn't fully understand the nuances of the assignment, and the final draft submitted to the Assembly contained several provisions that Terry deemed unacceptable. So Terry fired him.

That night I called home to check in and was glad when my dad answered. I briefly explained the situation in Kosovo and how difficult it was to work for someone like Terry.

"I've worked with doctors like that," my dad offered. "It's the brain surgeons who behave the worst. They have a reputation for being high-handed and unnecessarily nasty, especially to the nurses. I think it has something to do with the pressure of knowing a large percentage of their patients will come out severely impaired."

Maybe this was part of Terry's problem. He'd worked in foreign aid a long time and knew of the high rates of failure. But in my mind, that still didn't excuse his behavior.

Salted Butter

The walk up to the Vila Germia, the state-owned café, became my weekly pilgrimage. It was good exercise and provided a nice respite from the noise and congestion of downtown Pristina. Of course, each week I had to confront that pack of dogs that panted at me menacingly, but I learned to take slices of meat from the breakfast buffet to distract them as I passed by.

One Saturday morning, I ate breakfast across from Anna, a Polish consultant on a two-week assignment with one of the new banks. Anna was cheerful and outgoing, and when she learned about the Vila Germia walk, she invited herself along.

Anna was a big talker. She talked through town, past the Government Building, past the treacherous dogs, and by the time we reached the playground, I was sure I had heard her whole life story, but there was more.

"When I was a child in Warsaw," she started, "my family received CARE packages from the United States." CARE packages were part of a food relief effort initiated by the United States after World War II. I felt a small flush of pride, expecting to hear how the packages had provided much-needed support when Poland was going through such a difficult time.

"And you know what was in those CARE packages?" Anna's tone took on an unexpected edge. "Salted butter." She repeated it for emphasis. "Salted butter. Jamie, people in Poland do not eat salted butter."

I stopped and turned around so I could face her. "So was that the only thing in those CARE packages? Just salted butter?" I'm sure I looked confused.

"No, it was a big box. There were cans of tinned meat, sugar, cocoa, powdered milk, raisins, coffee, and soap. Maybe a few other things." She stopped to think. "That's all I can remember now. But the ridiculousness of sending a Polish family salted butter has stayed with me all these years."

33

(I wasn't naive about the United States. I knew there were questionable practices that we needed to reckon with. But of all the complaints that could be lodged against my country, providing salted butter in a food CARE package seemed—well, petty.)

"And that's what you remember about those gift packages from the United States, the salted butter?" I asked with more than a hint of disdain.

"Just because it's a gift, Jamie," she explained in her heavily accented English, "it doesn't mean you don't make an effort to give the right size or preferred color, am I right?" I kept walking.

I wanted to turn around and say, "It's just frickin' butter, Anna," but there was a message in what she was saying. If the United States was going to be effective in the Kosovo rebuilding effort, we had to be better prepared to support the right reforms. I refrained from asking any more questions about the CARE package and let Anna have the last word about the butter.

Piro

(The work in the Assembly started to ramp up, and someone realized that if I were to be effective, I needed an assistant.) The ideal candidate would have a legal background, know something about the legislative process, and speak one or more of the local languages. The obvious option was to poach one of the local lawyers from the group already working with the executive branch. I'd have my choice—everyone wanted to get out of the dreary office on the second floor.

Elvira, the project office manager, arranged a full day of interviews. (The last candidate was Piro, a twenty-something American-Albanian from Michigan. He was the only candidate who walked into the interview smiling, which gave him an immediate advantage.)

Piro dressed in thrift-store chic—a blue button-down shirt and a pair of khakis that were a couple of sizes too big for him. He had a head of dark, wavy hair, which he nervously tried to press flat through-out the interview. I liked him immediately, but his resume was a little thin. He didn't have a college degree, and the bulk of his experience was in "hospitality." But he was passionate about the work and opti-mistic about the future of Kosovo. When I asked him about making difficult decisions, he said, "You have to crack a couple of eggs to make an omelet."

The moment Piro signed his employment contract, he started calling me "Boss." It was not my preference, but somehow it worked. It quickly became apparent that I had hired Pristina's "little brother." Everyone knew him and liked him. I never saw him drinking coffee alone in the Assembly's café. There was always someone who implored him to join their table.

As a bonus, he was perfect for the job. When dealing with mem-bers of the Assembly or UN officials, his manners were impeccable. He quickly developed an extensive network of contacts, so we always knew more than everyone else and more than what we let on. Not only did he translate, but he also protected me from my lack of cultural knowl-edge. "Boss, don't hold your fingers like that—it's a Serb sign." "Boss, you need to take notes; it makes them feel important." "Boss, we need another chair so visitors will feel welcome."

With Piro on the team and able to translate, we were invited to attend the committee meetings that dealt with economic and financial laws. This was a big deal because, at the time, committee meetings were closed to outside observers, including the press and other projects.

Appreciating that we were given an extraordinary opportunity, we did our best to make ourselves useful by making sure we had extra copies of the bills under consideration and committee schedules to hand out to the less organized members. We took the lead on tracking down subject matter experts to respond to member questions about policy.

We spent a lot of time with some new members who complained

that they were being treated unfairly by the press. One member asked us to draft legislation that would make it illegal to criticize the work of the Assembly, which led to a long discussion about freedom of speech over several cups of coffee in the Assembly café.

Serbs in the Assembly

Working in the Assembly was hectic but exciting. Piro and I monitored all the economic and financial laws and were involved in drafting amendments as necessary. We reviewed the operational rules for both the Assembly and the committees and participated in legislative working groups. And pursuant to my agreement with Franck, a significant amount of non-USAID work passed through my office. And just when we thought we had a handle on what was expected of us, the Serbs showed up and took things to a whole new level.

I was sitting at one of the small tables in the Assembly café when I noticed concentric ripples in the tall glass of water that came with my espresso. Then I heard the rattling of the window panes followed by a terrific rumbling. If I'd been in California, I would have thought it was a small earthquake. But here in Kosovo, it meant heavy vehicles were moving nearby.

I looked toward the door and watched a convoy of UN vehicles race around the semicircular driveway and careen to a stop in front of the side entrance. These weren't the ubiquitous white SUVs that were parked all over town. They were oversized, angular, heavily armored personnel carriers.

It probably wasn't the wisest move, but I stood up to get a better look. Almost before the vehicles came to a complete stop, the Polish security detail, each one bigger and more muscular than the last, appeared with weapons at the ready and took up strategic defense positions. I feared that something horrible was about to happen.

"Oh, good," I heard just over my shoulder. I jumped. It was Franck who had materialized out of nowhere. He did that all the time. One minute I'd be in the hallway all by myself, and the next, Franck would be at my elbow asking about a particular bill or document. I never got used to it. I jumped every time.

"The Serbs have arrived," he said.

"The Serbs have to be brought to the Assembly by the United Nations Kosovo Force?" I asked incredulously.

"Well, yes. Last year there were reports of Serbs being killed by mobs of Albanian extremists for simply being identified as a Serb or for speaking Serbian in public. So we have to take every precaution." Then he smiled benignly and walked back toward his office.

When the "all clear" was given, the guards opened the rear doors of a personnel carrier, and several elderly Serb members moved quickly into the safety of the building. It struck me that while the Serbian members rushed into the building under heavy guard, no doubt in genuine fear of their lives, we sat just inside sipping lattes and macchiatos in the Assembly café.

Getting the Serbian members to the Government Building was one thing; their meaningful participation in the legislative process was another. Understandably, the memories of the open conflict and war atrocities were still raw for both the Serbs and the ethnic Albanians, and in several cases, they refused to sit in the same room. But there were quorum requirements, and a certain number of members had to be in attendance to transact business.

We tried our best to reason with members from both sides. The long-term goal was for Kosovo to join the European Union, and everyone agreed on that. So we asked the obvious question, "How can you expect to push Kosovo's case in Brussels if you can't sit at the same table here in Pristina?"

"It will be different," we were assured. "It will be different."

Fourth of July Party

With my transfer to the Assembly, and the need to keep a wall between the legislature and the executive branch, I stopped visiting the office on the second floor. Most of my colleagues in the Assembly were European and always seemed to be going on or returning from vacation. As a German consultant explained, "We Europeans do vacation better than the Americans." There may have been something to that. Regardless, I started to feel a bit isolated.

So at the end of June I asked Brian if the project would sponsor a Fourth of July party. I gave him the hard sell, explaining how getting everyone together in a social setting would be good for project morale. He wasn't particularly enthusiastic, but he agreed to fund the party, provided I found an acceptable person to serve as event security. At the time, Pristina had upwards of 26,000 peacekeepers in residence, so I was reasonably confident I could find *someone*.

Walking off my frustration after one of the Thursday afternoon meetings at USAID, I stopped at the tiny convenience store halfway down the hill from the USAID offices. The store abutted a barbershop distinguished by a larger-than-life portrait of the actor Pierce Brosnan from his James Bond days. Standing directly beneath Pierce's picture was a man about sixty, with a muscular build, wearing an immaculately pressed, dust-free uniform. There were UNMIK patches on both shoulders, but I didn't recognize the unit. He was focused on lighting a small cigar but looked up and caught me sizing him up.

"Ma'am." He was a Southerner—someone who'd appreciate the importance of the Fourth of July to a group of American consultants far from home.

"Are you a police officer?" I asked.

"Have been." I love American "cop talk"—no extraneous details to muddy the conversation. He flicked the match out and took a long draw of his cigar. His name was Blaine, and before coming to Kosovo, he had spent twenty-five years as a sheriff in the Outer Banks of North Carolina. I explained the party, trying to make it sound more interesting than I knew it would be, hoping he'd agree to provide security.

As he listened, I noticed a change in his facial expression. He pointed at me with his cigar and asked, "You work for the Assembly, right?" I wasn't wearing my Assembly ID and couldn't figure out how he knew where I worked.

"Yes," I said suspiciously.

"Okay, I'll serve as the event security, provided you let me take you out to dinner. Sound good?" he asked. We shook to finalize our deal, and he nearly crushed my hand with his firm grip.

On the day of the party, Blaine showed up in uniform and did a remarkable job alternating between greeter and bouncer, leaving me free to mingle with my colleagues. I told the salted butter story a few times, mostly to stir up some debate and to gauge whether my original reaction was off the mark. The responses from both the Americans and the few other nationalities in attendance were the same—Anna was an ingrate.

The following Saturday, I met Blaine in the lobby of the Grand Hotel to head out for our dinner date. As we walked down a small side street, almost every person we passed—the shopkeepers, mothers with small children, even young boys riding bikes—silently greeted Blaine with a nod or shy wave. He reciprocated with a smile.

The restaurant was tiny, with only five or six tables. The waiter rushed over and quickly changed the soiled tablecloth. Then he returned with a new candle, which he lit after several tries with a Bic lighter, leaving the faint smell of butane lingering at our table. Blaine nodded appreciatively at the gesture.

As we waited for our meal, Blaine told stories about his life back in the Outer Banks: his favorite arrests and the badly behaved college kids who flooded his town during spring break. Eventually, I asked him about the people who greeted him on the street.

"You seem to be a bit of a celebrity here. How do all those people know you?" I took a small bite of my penne pasta as I waited for his answer.

"I run the jail here in Pristina." I'm sure I laughed out loud. "There's a constant stream of friends and relatives visiting their loved ones in the jail. That's how I learned about this restaurant. The chef's brother has been in one of my cells for several months and receives daily meal deliveries. One of the meat dishes smelled so good I thought we'd give it a try." I dropped my fork, and it clanged against the plate.

"You have the chef's brother locked up in your jail?" I immediately thought about poisoning.

"Don't worry. They won't do anything to me. My deputy is a complete bastard. Enjoy your pasta."

At the end of the meal, Blaine put his elbows on the table, leaned forward, and spoke in a soft tone.

"You know, I had already heard about you that day we met outside the barbershop. A French guy, Franck I think, talked about you joining the team at the Assembly at one of the UN's weekly meetings," he said, holding his unlit cigar between his fingers. "He wasn't so keen on you at first, he didn't want an American in the Assembly, but now he says you're a good addition." I smiled at the compliment.

"My contract is ending in a couple of weeks and I'm going back to the States. I thought I might pass along some old sheriff wisdom before I go. Is that okay with you?" He paused until I nodded.

"From what I hear in those meetings, there's a lot of pettiness between the Americans and the Europeans, and it's negatively affecting what we're trying to do here. You're in a unique position and need to stay above all that because you have a real opportunity to accomplish something in the Assembly. Always remember you want to be a credit to your country."

The idea that I could somehow be a credit to my country made me emotional and I teared up.

40

"Please don't cry," he begged. "It will be all over the jail tomorrow."

Translation Challenges

By the first week of August, the Assembly was functioning surprisingly well. The initial refusal by some members to work with others became less of an issue, and committees began to meet regularly and take their responsibilities seriously. While this was good for the democratic process, it posed a considerable challenge for the translators.

In addition to seats for the Kosovars and the Serbians, a block of seats was set aside for other ethnic minorities, including Romani, Bosniaks, and Turks. Some members spoke Albanian and Serbian, but not English. One spoke Turkish but not Serbian. A couple of others spoke Albanian and refused to speak Serbian. Consequently, there were times when there were as many translators in the room as there were members. But it was necessary to ensure everyone had a voice in the parliamentary process.

It was slow going at first, but a rhythm developed into a kind of multilingual ping-pong. Albanian–Serbian–English. English–Serbian–Turkish. Turkish–English–Albanian. Occasionally, Piro would hold up a hand to signal that one of the translators hadn't finished or that a thread had been lost. He would translate into Albanian, then point to the translator who should speak next, and that person would translate into either Serbian or Turkish. Then things would resume again.

Somehow, despite the translation challenges, points were made, amendments were drafted, and legislation was tailored to the needs of the new country. It was strangely satisfying.

But the translation challenges didn't stop there. As members became more confident in their roles, references to past conflicts became more common. In some cases, discussions in the committees grew hostile, which raised the question, "*Should* everything be translated?"

(This came into sharp focus one afternoon when Piro and I were unexpectedly asked to explain one of the bills to a new committee) The meeting was already in progress, and a female member, sitting at the head of the table, was speaking in Serbian. She was going around the conference table, singling out each of the other members in attendance. Everyone in the room was frozen(It was clear she was saying something unpopular.)

Piro started to translate in a whisper and then stopped. I waited a few seconds and then nudged him with my elbow, but he just shook his head.(He only started translating again when another member began speaking. When the female member responded, Piro went silent again.)

(I leaned close to him and whispered, "What is it? Why aren't you translating?"

He kept his head down. "Boss, I won't translate what she's saying.")

At first, I thought it was because the woman was speaking Serbian, and if that was the case, Piro's unwillingness to translate was unacceptable. But he was not one for being pushed or bullied. I leaned in close to him and said, "You're better than this."

Honestly, I thought he was going to cry.(But it turned out he was taking a stand, "She's spewing nationalist bullshit. I won't translate the ugly words she is speaking."

He was refusing to translate hate speech, and I had to be okay with that.)

Piro good guy

Meeting Roberto

(Despite the heat and dust of summer, I began to enjoy Pristina(Kate and I worked well together) and we socialized outside of work. We went to the movies at the new cinema built by the United Nations and ate dinner under the colorful umbrellas of the many outdoor cafés. Kate was a bit germophobic, and we started each meal with a dab of Purell hand sanitizer, which she kept in her oversized, black handbag. (She must have brought a year's supply with her from Australia.)

One warm evening in mid-August, I joined the infrastructure team for dinner at a nearby Italian restaurant. (These were the consultants who worked on remodeling the airport, improving access to potable water, and implementing other long-term projects funded by USAID.)

I sat next to Clive, a lovely Englishman with one of those hyphenated last names that sound like old money. He told a sweet story about teaching his seventeen-year-old son how to tie a bow tie, over his old Nokia phone. He demonstrated how he cradled the phone between his shoulder and ear and guided his son through the steps while he tied his own tie facing a mirror. (Other consultants offered similar stories about missing little league games and dance recitals while working overseas. The poignancy of the stories made us all a little homesick.)

As the other diners started to leave, Clive waved to a man sitting by himself at the table reserved for the group from Parsons (a USAID implementer primarily responsible for road construction projects) I guessed the man was about fiftyish, but it was hard to tell. He had a wiry build, muscular forearms, and a head of yellow-blond hair that needed cutting. His face was weathered and tanned, which highlighted his unusual light blue eyes.

"This is Roberto." Clive made the introductions. ("Roberto's a particularly talented engineer from Buenos Aires.) There's literally no problem he can't solve. Today he devised an ingenious plan for storing helicopters at the airport. You're both nice people. You should get to know each other."

After asking permission, Roberto sat down in the chair next to me (He explained that he was the senior engineer on a project responsible for upgrading the roads that ran through the Serbian enclaves (these small roads allowed Serbs to access food and supplies without driving into Pristina, where they were still under threat.) I explained the

(problems we were having getting the ethnic Albanians and the Serbs to deal with each other in the Assembly.)

He was fascinated by my job, or at least he pretended to be. He asked a lot of questions. How was the Assembly structured? How did I cope with the different languages? Did I enjoy the work? It felt good to have someone show interest in me. I was delighted when he offered to walk me the few blocks back to my hotel.

On the main road, we came upon a stalled car that was partially sticking out into traffic. The driver was under the hood with a flashlight while his young wife or sister stood on the curb smoking a cigarette and holding a crying infant.

"Come on." Roberto grasped my upper arm. "Let's help this poor guy out. He's in a dangerous situation." I was wearing black patent leather pumps, completely unsuited for pushing cars out of traffic, so I hesitated.

"It's only a Yugo," he said, pulling me across the street. "Think of the poor baby."

As we approached the car, Roberto raised his palms to indicate that we were there to help push. The grateful driver called to the woman with the baby, who crushed her cigarette with the toe of her shoe and climbed into the passenger seat. The driver positioned himself with one hand on the steering wheel and the other on the door. On the count of three, we started to push, but the car barely budged.

Roberto looked at me, wide-eyed, and said, "That's a very heavy baby." I laughed because it was obvious something else was going on. Roberto went up to the driver to make sure the emergency brake was off.

As we tried to push a second time, the trunk popped open, revealing two huge bags of cement.

"Ah, it's not the baby," Roberto said. We both laughed. Fortunately, a teenager appeared on the street, and Roberto cajoled him into helping. At the end of the first block, the driver gestured wildly to the right—we were making a turn.

"Dios mio," Roberto whispered. "This guy wants us to push him all the way to Albania." We continued to push two more blocks and into a driveway where the driver grabbed a brick and put it behind the rear wheel—an emergency brake.

After we bid farewell to the couple, the baby, and the very heavy car, Roberto walked me the rest of the way to the hotel.

"I sure know how to show a woman a good time," he laughed. Roberto was kind and had a sense of humor. I liked him.

At the Grand, I offered Roberto my business card, but before taking it, he gave my hand a firm but tender squeeze, leaving a gritty smudge on the back of my hand.

Employee of the Week

Piro was taking on more and more responsibility. Some days we'd be in meetings all day long, which meant he was working and translating for six or seven hours at a stretch. It must have been exhausting. But I don't remember him ever complaining. He loved being in the middle of all the action. I couldn't give him a raise, but I wanted to show him my appreciation, so I established "Employee of the Week."

I wrote to a few of Piro's friends to ask for photos to use on the award poster. Photos flooded in and gave me some insight into Piro's personal life—Piro sailing, lunching at European cafés, belly dancing, and speaking from a dais. I found a large piece of construction paper and made a poster with the heading "Employee of the Week."

Every Friday morning, I would ceremoniously announce the Employee of the Week, and since I only had one employee, Piro always won. It was a good ongoing joke. Even Franck would pop in to congratulate Piro on his weekly award.

Beautiful Pristina

The first week of September, I was in the project office dropping off my time sheet when my cell phone buzzed at the bottom of my bag. It caught me by surprise because no one ever phoned me. If colleagues or members needed to chat, they'd drop by the Assembly office and sit on the extra chair Piro insisted we procure. When I finally found my phone, I couldn't understand the caller. He either had a heavy accent or was speaking in a foreign language. I handed the phone to Elvira, who sighed audibly at the imposition. She spoke first in Albanian, then in Serbian, and then passed the phone back to me.

"He is speaking English." It was Roberto. Finally. We made arrangements to have dinner that night.

I met Roberto in the lobby of the Grand Hotel in the early evening. He held a single red rose that was well past its prime.

"I stole it from the garden of an abandoned house," he said. "There is no one there to enjoy them, so I thought you would." Considering where we were, the rose was operatically romantic.

We ate at one of Pristina's small family-owned restaurants and enjoyed red wine from Montenegro that cost less than a Euro a glass. (Roberto spoke of his life growing up in Argentina.) His father had been an insurance executive who had personal dealings with Eva Peron, but Roberto had his own history with celebrities. As a teenager, he had a chance encounter with Prince Philip, the Duke of Edinburgh, a guest at one of the large estancias outside of Buenos Aires in 1962.

I told him more about my work in the Assembly and my weekend walks up to Vila Germia. He was particularly interested in my complaints about the menacing dogs that stood next to the food truck. He was a dog lover and wanted to see them for himself.

We had more in common than one might think. (We were both economic refugees of sorts, pushed out of our jobs by changes in circumstance.) He was in Kosovo due to the downturn in the Argentine

Chapter 1: Pristina, Kosovo

economy) I was there because of my doubts regarding the sustainability of the subprime mortgage industry.)

After dinner, we took a slow walk around downtown Pristina. Roberto held my hand and then put his arm around my shoulders. That night, Pristina looked different to me. (I no longer saw the unwashed windows held together by strips of duct or masking tape. The slack cables hanging from rusty poles and makeshift wooden supports simply disappeared) Instead, I saw the brightness of Jupiter and Saturn dominating the night sky. (I noticed the elegant architectural details of the prewar buildings) I heard the faint sounds of an accordion playing an ancient melody. For the first time I saw the beauty of the city.

The Telecom Law

(By the end of September, a number of bills had made their way through the committee process and were coming up for a vote. (Once those bills passed, Piro and I would be involved in the finalization) (I knew from the meetings at USAID that several more bills were about to be submitted, and we would be involved with those) I looked over my legislative matrix, and while it would be a hectic few months, Piro and I were fairly confident that we could handle all the tasks assigned to us. So I wasn't particularly pleased to find a copy of the Law on Telecommunications sitting on my desk when I returned from lunch one day. It had a yellow sticky note on the cover that read ("It's one of yours, Franck," meaning someone at USAID was involved, and I had to review it.)

(A good fifty-plus pages long, the bill contained policy and terms beyond my area of expertise) I took my red ink pen out of the top drawer, sighed heavily, and peeled back the front cover. The problems started on page one and continued with disturbing regularity throughout the document. At the front of the document was a list of definitions,

47

but over a third were not actually used in the law itself. It meant the bill was a sloppy "cut and paste" job from the law of another jurisdiction. To make matters worse, the bill suffered from poor punctuation, unnecessary repetition, and incomplete sentences.

"Jamie." I jumped. It was Franck standing next to my desk.

"There are problems with the telecom law," he said. Franck apparently knew more than he let on, too.

"Yeah," I said, trying to think through how to deal with the situation. "I'll ask the drafter to come in for a chat."

A couple of days later, Arthur, a fellow project consultant, strode into my office, clearly unhappy about having to respond to my concerns about the bill. I strongly suggested that he take the bill back, fix all the problems, and then resubmit at a later date. Arthur was having none of it.

"Look, almost a third of the defined terms don't appear in the law," I noted. "So they need to be removed."

"They're terms that are used in the industry," he argued. "So they should be left in."

"Removing the extra definitions is not up for discussion," I said. "It's a basic principle of legislative drafting: only necessary definitions are in included in the law. But that's just the start. There are more significant problems that must be addressed. There's bad punctuation, repetition, and bad grammar."

Despite my insistence Arthur refused to take the law back or agree to changes. He didn't have to. I learned later that his contract required only that he draft the law and submit it to the Parliament. There were no requirements regarding quality or suitability.

After he left my office, I placed my arms on my desk and laid my head down in complete frustration with what had transpired. (Ordinarily, this kind of lack of cooperation would get your bill put on the bottom of the pile or mysteriously lost.) But it was a USAID product, so I couldn't just make it disappear.

48

incompetence

don't point out incompetent

I thought about drafting a memo listing all the problems with the telecom bill, hoping to force a reckoning. By luck, I ran into Peter, the British IT consultant who was back in town. He seemed to have a better understanding of how everything worked, so I ran the memo idea past him.

"Jamie, I support your thinking," he said. "But it will be the last memo you write for USAID. They pay a lot of lip service to transparency, but they don't encourage it, and they don't reward it. You'll be labeled a 'loose cannon,' and I guarantee you will be sent home."

"You're saying that I should have another job lined up before I submit it."

"Definitely."

I spent the next several days trying to improve the bill, but it was a mess. I didn't change any of the policy; I just removed the unused definitions, made sure all sentences had nouns and verbs, and fixed a number of typos. I returned the draft to Franck, and I hoped I'd never have to hear about the telecom law again.

Franck big mess

Loving Improvements

At the beginning of our relationship, Roberto and I tried to be part of the project's social scene, but it didn't work out. Roberto's English wasn't strong enough for a group setting. He complained that my colleagues talked too fast, too loudly, and used too much slang.

But that wasn't his only criticism. He complained about certain behavior that he saw as being uniquely and annoyingly American. For one thing, we referred to our country as "America" instead of the "United States." Roberto thought that was dismissive of Canada, and all of South America, which he pointed out was 95 percent larger than the United States. I shrugged and noted that technically we *were* "Americans."

49

"You are *North* Americans," he corrected. I could tell this distinction was important to him, and I promised to make the change.

His willingness to overlook these minor faults ended when a consultant I didn't know very well slapped Roberto on the back and said, "After that old green card, eh buddy?" implying that he was only dating me to get access to the United States. It was an insult to us both.

Roberto fumed, "Only an American would be so arrogant to think their country was the only place in the world where people would want to live."

So we enjoyed Pristina on our own. I'd wait for Roberto to return from his road construction project out in the Serbian enclaves, and we'd meet up in the evenings for romantic dinners. Sometimes, he'd hold my hand and kiss my fingertips. Then, when the electricity shut off, which was a frequent occurrence, Roberto would lean over and kiss me in the darkness for the minute or so it took for the generators to kick in.

The more I got to know Roberto, the more I appreciated that he was just a good person—eager to use his engineering skills to help anyone who needed a hand. But I had to be careful. Whatever our relationship was, I couldn't count on anything long-term. Roberto's contract ended at the end of the year, and he would be going back to Argentina. I wasn't against a long-distance relationship but drew the line at dating a man who lived in a different hemisphere.

The Hearing

October arrived, and the days started to cool down. One rainy afternoon, Piro burst into the office and, even before unwrapping his scarf or shrugging off his coat, cried out, "Boss, the chairwoman wants to hold a legislative hearing on the bill. We have to be a part of that." Despite Piro's excitement, it wasn't great news.

Legislative hearings are held to discuss issues and problems related to a particular bill or the need for new legislation. They are a vital part of the democratic process. At that time, the Assembly had only one female chairperson, the striking Kennedy School of Government graduate who headed up the Transportation and Telecommunications Committee. So I figured that the proposed hearing would be on the poorly drafted telecom bill.

I walked down to Kate's office, and she brightly confirmed that the president of the Assembly had approved a hearing on the telecom bill, and a date had been set for the following month to give adequate time to send out the proper notices. I groaned.

"Cheer up," she said. "It's a public hearing, so the press will be there. Maybe you'll get your mug on television."

"But that's not a particularly well-drafted bill," I said. "This could be a very embarrassing exercise."

"Not for you," she said. "You did what you could."

Arthur, the consultant who had drafted the bill, would be called to testify about the bill's origins and the vetting process, and to address comments received from other interested parties, such as the European Union and the United Nations—that much was certain. So I pulled together the draft rules on legislative hearings, and some other guidance, expecting Arthur to drop by the office to ask basic procedural questions and perhaps get some tips on how to prepare. But I heard nothing from him.

On the day of the hearing, the room had to be set up, the audio equipment needed to be tested, agendas had to be printed, and hundreds of other details had to be arranged. Kate was confident that the local staff could take care of most of these tasks, but due to a miscommunication, that's not what happened. Apparently, in Kate's morning pep talk to the local staff she said, "Everyone must look their very best," meaning we needed to make a good impression. Unfortunately, there was a translation error, and most of the staff spent the morning in their offices applying nail polish and makeup. So Kate, Piro, and I ran around making sure everything was ready.

The Government Building had a rather complicated design. It was as if two buildings had been joined together, so it was easy to get lost in its miles of corridors and multiple stairwells. An hour before the hearing was scheduled to start, Kate handed me a stack of paper printed with bold arrows and the word "Hearing" on each of them. She put me in charge of posting them at reasonable intervals to guide attendees from the entrances to the hearing room. Unfortunately, the arrows pointed only in one direction—to the right—so I had to hang some of the pages upside down, which meant the word "hearing" was upside down as well. But I didn't think it mattered. Surely people would simply follow the arrows and disregard the text.

After taping up the last arrow and descending the first flight of stairs, I came across an elderly man, carefully unsticking the arrows from the wall and turning them so the word "hearing" was right side up. As a result, for every two arrows that pointed in the right direction, there were another two or three that guided you the wrong way, making the whole system entirely useless. In the end, Piro and the well-made-up local staff escorted groups of attendees up the stairs.

Whether it's for a meeting of four, a conference of twenty, or a legislative hearing, introductions are notoriously long in the Balkans. So I stayed in my office a full hour until I was confident that testimony had begun. When I slipped into the hearing room, I was pleased to see the high number of attendees. The room was packed with members, staff, consultants, and the press. Getting such a diverse group of people together to discuss new legislation was an exciting achievement. I saw Kate on the opposite side of the room and gave her a very discreet "thumbs up." She deserved it.

As expected, Arthur was the first witness to testify, and the panel was already putting questions to him. He sat hunched over at the large wooden table, with his mouth too close to the microphone, which caused unpleasant audio feedback. The questioning was in English with translations in Albanian and Serbian.

"It's not going well," I heard someone whisper in my ear. I jumped. Franck had materialized out of nowhere again.

"Let me put the question to you again, sir." The panelist was a European telecommunications expert. "Have you read the EU's telecom package adopted just last year? Do you know what it says?"

Arthur smiled and leaned into his microphone and responded to the question. "No. I have not read the package. It was not considered in the drafting of this law." Then he sat back in his chair and smiled again.

Everyone in the room recognized that it was a colossal failure by a USAID consultant. I thought back to the comments made by Anna, the chatty banking consultant from Poland who had deplored the salted butter her family had received in CARE packages. "Just because it's a gift, it doesn't mean you don't make an effort to give the right size or preferred color."

A few weeks ago, I'd had the telecom bill in my hands. I should have done more to avoid this waste of time. I realized that by not writing a memo and alerting USAID of the problems with the telecom bill, I was a part of all this—*and I absolutely hated it.*

Not wanting to stay for the humiliation of Arthur's testimony, I made a discreet exit by following a couple of attendees out of the hearing room and down the stairs. They carried identical document portfolios with the bright blue starred flag of the European Union emblazoned on one corner.

"Tell me, how is it possible that a telecom expert working in Kosovo did not know about the EU telecom package?" one asked sarcastically.

"If you are American, you don't have to be an expert. You just have to get along with the boss," said the other. This was mortifying but accurate.

They followed the trail arrows, not knowing they were utterly use-less. When they came to a particularly critical juncture, which would either lead them to the exit or back into the labyrinth of the building, I let them go the wrong way. It was my petty payback for their delight in Arthur's failure. For all I know, those two might still be wandering around the Government Building, trying to find their way out.

(It would take several months of redrafting, but the Assembly ulti-mately passed a telecommunications law. It was a completely different version, which had been rewritten to take into account the directives and regulations of the European Union.)

The Septic Tank

After the telecom law debacle, I started to think about leaving Kosovo.) The meetings at USAID were still unsettling, and to make matters worse, I would soon lose my support team. Kate was scheduled to fly back to Australia in early November, and Roberto would leave before the end of the year. Pristina wouldn't be the same without them.)

I had enough experience to apply for jobs in other countries, and just by luck, one morning at breakfast I sat across the table from one of the high-level managers from a well-known consulting firm. We agreed to meet up at the Kukri after work for a quick interview.

I called Roberto to break our standing dinner date. He understood but maintained he could not go an entire twenty-four hours without seeing me. He had just finished a quick project, so he came over to the Grand, kissed me in the lobby, and walked me over to the Assembly. Later, when I told Piro, he said, "Boss, that's so romantic."

The interview wasn't what I expected. I handed the guy my resume. He handed me his card and promised to keep me in mind for suitable opportunities. Five minutes, and we were through. So I called Roberto and we met at the bar in the Grand Hotel. I asked about his day.

"Today, I located a missing manhole cover," he said in his lyrical English. "And it wasn't easy."

"How did you find the missing manhole cover?" I asked, taking a sip of wine.

"Do you know what a septic tank is?" he asked. I assured him I did, but he explained it anyway.

"A septic tank is an enormous room full of shit." He stood up, held his arms wide apart, and took a couple of paces right and left to demonstrate the hugeness of a septic tank.

("Well, last year when the roads were resurfaced," his voice took a serious tone, "they didn't consider the manhole cover, and it was lost under the new paving material." I nodded as if this made all the sense to me. ("But now they needed to find it, and they called me in to help.")

"What did you do?" I asked.

"I knew there had to be a pipe connecting the septic tank to the manhole cover. So I opened the door to the septic tank, took a huge breath of air, and put my head inside." I laughed out loud and slapped the bar.

"Then," he continued, "I looked around that room full of shit and located the pipe, which directed me to the lost manhole cover." I laughed again. Only Roberto would have a story like this.

"So after putting your head in that room full of shit," I was still laughing, "and finding the manhole cover, what did you do then?"

"I walked directly to the hotel and kissed you." I put my hands over my face and laughed until I could barely breathe.

Lets European vacations

December

(Pristina cleared out in December. Those Europeans who took frequent vacations in summer also took breaks for the end-of-year holidays.) The days were bittersweet. I'd turned in my resignation, which meant Roberto and I only had a few more weeks together. With fewer people in town, Roberto felt more comfortable going to the Kukri and socializing. One evening Peter, the British IT consultant, walked in with a consultant named Vince, the newest hire in the Prime Minister's Office, and they joined us. We laughed about the dreary second-floor office and the fact that there still weren't enough chairs for the number of people working in that room. Vince commented that there was much speculation about how I had been able to escape.

As Vince went to the bar to get a drink, (Peter explained that it had been a rough afternoon meeting at USAID, and Vince had unfairly borne the brunt of Terry's anger over another consultant's work.)

"Well, the end justifies the means, right?" Vince commented good-naturedly as he rejoined the group.

("Bullying and tearing people down never justifies the means," Roberto responded, which surprised me because Roberto rarely spoke in these situations. The world looks to the United States for strong leader-ship, and that's not what you have here. Instead, you have a tyrant sitting up there in that office.) Everyone stayed quiet for a few moments.

"So why don't you leave?" Vince asked, looking at me.

"I am leaving," I said. "I've handed in my resignation. This just isn't the right job for me (By staying, I feel as if I'm giving tacit approval to the bullying and bad management. I don't want to be a part of that." I thought about my dad's reputation for civility and added, "I wasn't raised that way."

The Street Dogs

The Saturday before my departure, the weather turned cold and the forecast called for snow flurries in the early afternoon. Despite the weather, Roberto insisted we take the walk up to the Vila Germia. He was keen to see the pack of vicious street dogs that had menaced me every Saturday since the first week of my arrival. So we left the Grand early, hoping to complete the walk before the first snowflake.

We walked hand in hand past the Government Building, through a weedy, garbage-strewn field, and as expected, just beyond the food truck, we came upon the pack of dogs. There were ten of them at least, standing in a group, panting in their usual threatening manner.

Roberto studied the dogs in silence. Then he turned toward me and asked, "Are these the terrifying street dogs you've been talking about?"

"Yeah," I replied. "They're scary, aren't they?"

Roberto looked back at the dogs, then gave me a bit of side-eye. He slapped his hand against his upper thigh and called out something in Spanish. The entire pack—all ten—bounded at full speed in our direction. I was knocked over in the furry stampede, and when I reached up for a helping hand, Roberto was too busy to help. He was scratching the neck of one of the Shepherds with one hand and patting a Doberman with the other.

"Jamie, these aren't street dogs." He looked down at me, laughing. "They're somebody's pets. Family dogs that were abandoned when their owners fled Pristina. Poor guys. They just need a little affection."

As predicted, snow started to fall. Roberto spread his arms wide and slowly turned while trying to catch some of the large, fluffy flakes on his tongue. Being from Argentina, this was only the second time he'd seen snowfall. As I watched him enjoy the snow, I realized that despite living in different hemispheres, I wanted to try and find a way for our relationship to work.

Leaving Pristina

My last morning in Kosovo, I stopped by the Government Building to finish some notes for my successor, drop off the office keys, and post the last Employee of the Week photo—Piro, of course, holding a plastic glass of champagne and smiling directly into the camera.

Piro had a full morning of meetings, so we said a frantic good-bye in the office, and I watched him scurry down the hallway with a folder under his arm. About halfway down, he turned around and said, "Thanks, Boss." It was better that way. I would miss Piro; we'd made a good team, and I had no doubt he would flourish in the Assembly and whatever he chose to do after his time in Kosovo. Eventually he returned to the States, finished college, and went on to earn a PhD.

On my walk back to the Grand Hotel, I thought about the preceding ten months. My time in Kosovo gave me a front-row seat to how the United States provided financial and technical support to a post-conflict country, and I was left with more questions than answers. We played a major role in establishing policy and drafting the necessary laws and regulations, but we did it without the "heart" that I thought made us uniquely American. And while I wanted to continue to work internationally, I didn't want to do it in an environment that required I cast off the strong values I'd been raised with.

Bajram drove me to the airport and talked the entire way. Tarantino's *Kill Bill Vol I* had been released in October, and he insisted on describing some of the more memorable assassinations, including the ninja decapitations.

Many of the internationals who worked in Kosovo during those early post-conflict years look back at their experience with a nostalgic tear. I know I do. It was a rare combination of fascinating work, interesting counterparts, and learning about new cultures. And while it's easy to fixate on the dust, noise, and frustration, I also remember it for the roses picked from abandoned gardens, the romantic walks in the moonlight, and the long candlelit dinners.

Despite all that, I couldn't get out of there fast enough.

CHAPTER 2

Kyiv, Ukraine

2003

Our Neighbor

In early January 1972, Mr. Yerfest, our elderly neighbor who lived two doors down from us in California, stopped by to drop off some misdelivered mail. Elfin-like in his old age, Mr. Yerfest handed me the PG&E bill and a women's clothing catalog then turned to my dad and proudly announced, "Today I am celebrating fifteen years as an American citizen."

"Isn't that something," my dad responded with a smile and a handshake.

"Would you like to hear the story of how my family came to live in the United States of America?" Mr. Yerfest asked in heavily accented English.

"Absolutely," my dad answered, genuinely interested.

"The four of us, Mrs. Yerfest, Bohdan, Perla, who was just a baby in arms, and me—we all escaped from Ukraine in 1952 when it was still under the control of the Soviet Union," he said with more than a bit of defiant pride. Then, speaking directly to me, he added, "It was the stuff of Hollywood movies."

Mr. Yerfest began by detailing the many hardships of living in

59

Ukraine after the end of World War II. Retreating forces did their best to destroy Kyiv, and much of the city was uninhabitable. Food was scarce, and what was available was almost inedible. The Russians had retaken control of the country, and the secret police were back in operation. A minor misstep could mean years in Siberia and even a death sentence.

"Whatever you've heard about the suffering of Ukrainians," Mr. Yerfest said, "multiply it fifty—no, a hundred times—and you'll start to get an idea of how bad it really was."

Mr. Yerfest was placed in a compulsory labor program and worked on the immense, Soviet-sponsored construction projects in Kyiv. "I must have laid two million bricks," he said. He was good at his job, and the precision of his work caught the attention of a high-ranking official visiting from Moscow. When Mr. Yerfest stepped up to the dais for recognition, his clothes were so threadbare that his bare bottom was visible through the back of his coveralls.

"You see," Mr. Yerfest explained, again speaking to me directly, "the sight of my backside was humiliating not only for me, but for the Russian officials as well."

As recompense, Mr. Yerfest received a new set of coveralls and a small monetary award. The money was enough to hire a guide to help the family escape to Western Europe.

"It was a terrible decision to have to make," he said with eyes glistening with emotion. "We were leaving our family and loved ones behind. We didn't know if we'd ever see or hear from them again. But I was determined that my children would have a different life."

"On the first attempt," Mr. Yerfest continued, "We got as far as the border. So close I could see it. And in the excitement, the baby slipped from my arms and started to cry. We had to go back."

My dad rubbed his forehead the way he did when he was nervous.

"On the second attempt, I held baby Perla tight in my arms. Like this." (He brought his arms up against his chest. "And that time, there was no slipping. We made it out.")

(Three decades later, in early 2003, just a few months after I left Kosovo, I accepted a short-term contract on a USAID-funded commercial law project in Kyiv, Ukraine. USAID and the World Bank were co-sponsoring a new mortgage law. In addition to finalizing a draft law, I'd be providing training on free market concepts to a team of Ukrainian lawyers. I was replacing a Canadian advisor who was leaving early, so his young Ukrainian bride could start her new life in Alberta. Marrying a Westerner, I would learn, was the twenty-first century way of escaping from Ukraine.)

When I told my mother I was going to Kyiv, she frowned. "The place Mr. Yerfest had to escape from?" she asked. "You must be joking."

Arrival in Kyiv

(My door-to-door travel time from San Jose to Kyiv was over twenty hours, and I felt it—)I was tired, hungry, and severely jet-lagged. My new firm's logistics assistant had booked me into the Theodosius, a small hotel located at the less desirable end of Khreshchatyk Avenue, Kyiv's main thoroughfare. (The exterior of the hotel was drab and off-putting, but the lobby was surprisingly nice. Several massive columns supported a dramatically high ceiling, making the room appear larger than it really was.)

Two jowly middle-aged men, sporting dark, poorly fitting suits and identical crew cuts, sat side by side on a worn couch, keeping a close watch on the front door. I paused to look for the reception desk, and one of the two men mechanically raised his hand and pointed to the far end of the room. I smiled and nodded appreciatively, but there was no response.

Svetlana, the clerk on duty, a short, squat woman with an unpleasant expression, was in no hurry to check in new guests. As I waited my turn, I stared bleary-eyed at the digital sign behind the reception desk. A combination of Latin and Cyrillic letters displayed the date, time, and the outside temperature in fast-moving red characters. I made the conversion from Celsius to Fahrenheit in my head. It was slightly below freezing. Despite my heavy coat and snow boots, I felt a distinct chill.

(When I was first contacted about the job in Kyiv, I was excited about the possibility of working in the former Soviet state.) I imagined myself walking through neighborhoods of elegant, pastel-colored buildings, experiencing the culture and seeing the country that had produced the likes of Leon Trotsky, Joseph Conrad, and Nijinsky—but I had my reservations. I didn't speak the language, wasn't trained in the civil law system, and being from sunny California (I worried about the notoriously cold Ukrainian winters.)

I was assured by the home office that the project had expert translators and that my inability to speak Ukrainian or Russian wouldn't pose a problem. As for the difference in legal systems, the local lawyers would help me navigate the nuances of the civil law system, which relies on codified statutes instead of case law, a big deal when you're drafting legislation.

As for the cold weather, I was comforted by the fact that January was the coldest month of the year and that by arriving in February, it would be an easy slide into spring. I convinced myself that if I could manage Kosovo, I could manage Ukraine. So I signed the contract.

When it was finally my turn at the reception desk, Svetlana saw me eyeing the digital sign just behind her—the temperature had dropped two more degrees.

"Don't get used to warm weather," she cautioned in her heavily accented English, "tomorrow it turns cold."

"It's already below freezing," I said cheerlessly.

Svetlana leaned forward on the counter and gave me a heavy-lidded look.

"For most people," she said, "February is a short month—only twenty-eight days. But, for you, I think February will be a very long month."

History of Ukraine

After signing the consulting contract back in January, I realized I needed a better understanding of Ukraine and its people. So I went to a used bookstore near San Jose State University, hoping to find a book that would provide some historical background on the country. A bell clamored as I entered the shop, and the clerk holding a large stack of books asked, "What can I do you for?"

"I'd like a short history of Ukraine," I said cheerfully.

He put the books on the counter and said, "I'll show you what I have."

In the back of the store, shelved with the books on Russia, were two unusually thick paperbacks. He pulled out one with a drawing of two men on horseback on the cover.

"This will tell you everything you want to know," he said. Then he flipped to the back of the book. "It's 890 pages." He reached for the other book. "This one is only 880 pages. Take your pick."

I had a lot of reading to do for the project, and I didn't have time for 900 pages of Ukrainian history. I flipped through the 880-pager; wedged between the last page and the back cover was a bundle of mimeographed pages. The clerk unfolded them, and at the top was the heading "Exam notes: A Short History of Ukraine." He handed them to me and said, "Here you go, no charge."

Even the "Short History of Ukraine" ran twenty-five pages of single-spaced type. It started with Kyivan Rus, the predecessor to modern-day Ukraine, which emerged as a powerful nation in the Middle Ages around the twelfth century. Over the following eight hundred years (mimeograph sheets pages 3–10), the region was invaded, conquered, settled, and reconquered numerous times by various tribes and empires. Even the famed Mongols swept through and took up residence for a while. But by the early twentieth century, Ukraine was firmly under the control of the Soviet Union, and that's when things really got tough.

The mistreatment of Ukrainians by Joseph Stalin, whose rule was marked by repression, purges, show trials, labor camps, and the Gulag, was brutal even by Stalin's ruthless standards. He planned to exploit Ukraine's fertile land to fund infrastructure and other projects in the Soviet Union. To this end, Stalin changed land ownership rights and imposed unrealistic quotas for agricultural production, leading to the "Holodomor" (1931–1933), a famine that may have caused the deaths of upward of seven million Ukrainians.

Over the following decade, conditions under Stalin remained dire, so dire that many Ukrainians welcomed the invasion by the German army at the beginning of World War II. Sadly, Hitler also had exploitive ambitions for Ukraine, and countless Ukrainians were exterminated or expelled from the country to make room for an influx of German settlers. Estimates of Ukrainian civilian losses during this time range between four and seven million.

At the end of the war Moscow resumed control over Ukraine. Stalin declined to participate in the Marshall Plan, which would have helped rebuild postwar Ukraine and modernize its economy. He instituted labor camps and compulsory work schemes instead. After Stalin died in 1953, Nikita Khrushchev, a man born not far from the Ukrainian border, assumed leadership of the Communist Party of the Soviet Union and ushered in a less repressive era.

Ultimately it was a series of unprecedented events, including Moscow's mismanagement of the Chernobyl nuclear power station disaster in 1986, followed by the fall of the Berlin Wall in 1989, which precipitated the unraveling of the Soviet Union, and that led to Ukraine, and thirteen other states, declaring their independence from Russia in 1991.)

Ukraine's parliament, the Verkhovna Rada, adopted a new Constitution in 1996 that provided for democratic elections, a free market economy, and other reforms, each of which required a massive number of new policies and laws.) A number of donors, including the United States, stepped up to provide financial and technical aid but proceeded cautiously to avoid antagonizing Russia. As a consequence, the reform effort was slow going.

Some Do's and Don'ts

The day after my arrival, the project vehicle picked me up at the Theodosius and drove me across town to the office. The driver instructed me to pay attention to the route because the lift was a one-time accommodation. This was a cause for concern. The temperature had plummeted to single digits, and the windchill factor made it feel significantly colder. According to the BBC, a frigid weather system had swept down from the Arctic, and it was likely that the temperature would remain well below zero for the next week or two.

"It's an easy walk," he said. I looked out the window, and a gust of wind kicked up a cloud of ice and snow. I made a mental note to wear an extra pair of tights the next day.

The ride gave me a nice tour of the city. We drove through Maidan Nezalezhnosti (Independence Square), up Khreshchatyk Avenue, past the flashing lights of countless casinos, to a neighborhood of exquisitely maintained buildings.

I reported to Owen, an affable guy in his late fifties who spoke with the thick accent from the Great Lakes area in the United States— Michigan, Wisconsin, or Minnesota.) Owen spent a good part of the morning giving me background information on the project, which involved the establishment of a law center, a new approach for USAID. Instead of bringing in a cadre of Western consultants as had been the case in Kosovo, USAID would be funding a team of local lawyers who would be supported by the occasional international expert (me). He also took the time to lay out the do's and don'ts of living in Kyiv.

"First off, it's Ukraine, not *the* Ukraine. You wouldn't say '*the* Canada' or '*the* France,' would you?"

"I say "*The* United States of America.""

"That's different," he said, but failed to explain why.

"And never whistle indoors," he added with some seriousness. "The Ukrainians believe it will lead to bad luck and lack of wealth. Times are tough enough without tempting fate."

Thinking back to Mr. Yerfest's story, I asked, "Hasn't life in Ukraine always been tough?"

"Well, yes," Owen conceded. "But before, they could blame it on Russia. With independence, there was a great deal of optimism that things would improve, but they've only gotten worse. There's rampant corruption, no justice from the courts, high unemployment, poor health care, significant exploitation of young women, crumbling roads and buildings—the list goes on and on. You'll be approached on the street by ordinary people trying to sell you something to earn a little extra cash," he lamented.

Then as if to drive home his point about Ukraine's poverty, Owen told me the story of his first date with the young Ukrainian woman who would eventually become his wife. She accepted his invitation to dinner only because she was hungry.

The World Bank

Toward the end of the first week, Owen and I went to the office of the

66

World Bank, cosponsor of the law on mortgage, to discuss the division of work and agree on achievable timelines. Originally established in 1944 to provide financing for post-World War II reconstruction efforts, the World Bank reinvented itself as a development agency, providing loans, grants, and advice to governments to promote economic development and alleviate poverty. In Ukraine, the World Bank was focused on creating a modern financial service sector.

Veronica, the World Bank's project manager, a young woman with a thatch of platinum hair, rushed into the conference room and plopped ten or twelve light gray-green project folders on the conference table. Then she took a step back and welcomed what she called the "financial sector reform team." I looked around the table. There were only a handful of consultants, not nearly the number needed to draft and implement the laws and regulations necessary to support to the operation of banks, non-bank lenders, insurance companies, tax collection and other key components of the financial sector. In Kosovo, the financial sector team was at least fifteen or twenty people strong.

Undaunted by the small group, Veronica peppered the various consultants for project updates and possible areas of collaboration. We spoke about the mortgage law, and Owen agreed we could deliver a first draft in five weeks. After the meeting, Owen and I stood on the sidewalk waiting for the project vehicle, and I attempted some small talk. "She has a lot of responsibility for one person."

"She's better than most of the World Bank employees I've met," he said. Then after a long pull on his cigarette added, "The majority of whom are arrogant, annoying, and frequently wrong."

"Plus," Owen turned serious for a moment, "She has Ukraine's best interests at heart, and she's probably the only person in the country who has the connections and muscle to get the law passed. She's our best shot."

Privet Comrade

That night, I called home to check in on my parents. My dad answered, and when he realized it was me calling from Kyiv, he spoke, in a deep sinister voice, *"Privet, Comrade."* (Hi, Comrade.)

I heard my mother in the background, "I'll Comrade you. Give me that phone." She came on the line. "Thank God you called. He's been practicing that for two days."

"So he's doing better?" I asked.

"Good days and bad days," she said. He must have been standing there because she added, "Right, Comrade?" I assured her that I would be back in a few months to help out but added, "I might visit Russia before I come home. I mean, it's just next door."

("Your dad and I would *love* to visit Russia.) Could we tag along? You wouldn't even know we were there. After all, he already speaks the language," she mused. This struck me as a really bad idea. My dad's condition was unpredictable. He'd had a really bad day just before Christmas when he was unable to squeeze orange juice by himself. Taking the long trip to Russia would pose enormous challenges.

"It would be your dad's last big trip," she added, shamelessly working the guilt angle.

"I doubt…" I stopped for a moment to pick my words carefully. I didn't want to hurt her feelings. "… I could manage the three of us in a place like Russia. We would have to take an organized tour to handle the logistics." I was pretty pleased with that response(I'd sidestepped the real issue. I didn't want to take my parents to Russia.)

My mother said she understood, and I didn't think another thing about it.

Mr. Lenin

My first full weekend in Kyiv, the temperature stayed well below zero, but I still wanted to take a walk to get a feel for the city. In a better mood than the night I arrived, Svetlana produced a worn map of the city and recommended that I walk up Khreshchatyk Avenue to the Besarabsky, an indoor market constructed in the early 1900s. The entire walk up and back would be little more than a couple of miles, and I could warm up in the market with a coffee.

"Don't buy the caviar," Svetlana warned me. "My cousin will give you better deal."

I left the hotel just after breakfast and had to hopscotch around large splatters of frozen vomit in front of the small bar next to the hotel. From the looks of things, it must have been quite a Friday night. I crossed Independence Square and made my way up Khreshchatyk, which was less than a mile long but over 100 yards wide. The whole area had been destroyed by retreating troops at the end of World War II and rebuilt in the 1950s and 1960s. I wondered if Mr. Yerfest had laid some of the bricks.

(As Owen predicted, I was frequently stopped by men and women stoop-shouldered against the cold, desperately trying to sell me something—a movie DVD, well-worn children's shoes, plastic key chains, handmade greeting cards, packets of smoked meat, illegal cigarettes— it seemed everyone was willing to endure the biting cold in an effort to earn a few extra kopeks.)

The Besarabsky, with its art-nouveau façade, looked more like a train station than a market. A huge structure with a high vaulted ceiling, it could easily accommodate two American basketball courts. Its size made it difficult to heat, so it was only slightly warmer inside than out. I spent some time marveling at the prime cuts of meat, the beautifully displayed produce, and the gigantic jars of black caviar.

Once I had warmed up some, I exited out the back and crossed the street to the small but well-kept Bessarabska Square. There I was surprised to find a larger-than-life statue of Vladimir I. Lenin, the founder of the Russian Communist Party and architect of the Soviet State.

Despite the cold, I stopped to study the statue. Carved from the same red Karelian stone used for Lenin's Tomb in Moscow, this figure of Lenin was a man in action. Dressed in a three-piece suit, with one arm in front, close to the chest, and the other by his side, the statue successfully conveyed both confidence and strength.

I thought about the monuments that honored our political heroes in the United States. There's Lincoln serenely overlooking the Reflecting Pool at one end of the Capitol Mall, and just across the Tidal Basin, Jefferson stands in his own memorial. They were accomplished men savoring their contributions to the United States, but their figures seemed static compared to this Lenin, which made me feel slightly unpatriotic.

But the big question was—why was a statue of Lenin, an icon of Communist Russia, still standing in this prominent square in downtown Kyiv?

During the Soviet era, statues of Lenin served to remind the Ukrainian people of the Communist Party and its ideology that controlled their lives. But Ukraine had declared its independence from Russia in 1991, over a decade before. It had a new Constitution that provided for a democratic government; it was no longer a communist country. Tbilisi, the capital of Georgia, another former Soviet state, had removed a statue of Lenin from its Freedom Square in August 1991, twelve years before.

This statue of Lenin made me worry that Ukraine might be trying to keep one foot in the Soviet past. Something told me that this would not be the last time I'd see Mr. Lenin's influence during my stay in Kyiv.

The Feline Fest

My contract was short—just over four months—so I decided to stay in a hotel rather than make the effort to find an apartment. Owen warned me that the Security Service of Ukraine, successor to the Ukrainian branch of the Soviet KGB, the highly secretive Soviet-era intelligence agency, was still active. As a Westerner, he advised that no matter where I stayed, I should expect my room to be "bugged" and all my conversations monitored.

The freezing temperature discouraged me from exploring different hotel options, so I extended my stay at the Theodosius. But it wasn't a hardship. The hotel was centrally located and reasonably priced, Svetlana had warmed up considerably, and after two weeks, I finally rated restrained acknowledgment from the jowly security men in the lobby.

There was, however, one rather peculiar aspect of life at the Theodosius that made me hesitate. The old centralized heating system conducted sound as well as heat, and I heard all kinds of things I really didn't want to—a baby crying, business calls back to the home office, and arguments with staff over the slow room service. But on top of this, every Thursday night I was forced to listen to the feline fest.

It usually started about ten thirty, just as I was going to bed. First, I'd hear a faint "mewing," which lasted several minutes. The first time I heard it, the sound was so close that I actually opened my door to see if a kitten was wandering the halls. The "mews" escalated into louder, more intense "meows." It was then that I realized they weren't animal noises—they were human.

The "meows" evolved into a frantic exchange of "hisses" and "growls," punctuated by a weird feral cat noise, best described as a deep-throated yowling. It all culminated in a "climax" that sounded, well, rather painful. After that, things went quiet, but I imagined a long period of tender postcoital pawing and nose nuzzling. As I laid there trying not to listen, I wondered if this was what it was like working with the Security Service of Ukraine, listening to conversations and interactions that weren't meant to be heard.

It was a delicate situation and a difficult thing for me to complain about. So I solicited advice from my friends in the United States for ideas on how to deal with the matter. Collectively, my friends became much too involved. Suggestions came in daily, and some wanted a recording. By far, the best advice was to use the hotel's inter-room phone and bark like a dog. I ended up doing nothing.

TGI Fridays

I worked by myself, and I was fine with that. Ukraine's legal system was so different from what I knew that I needed the time to familiarize myself with the broad principles and drafting style. I plowed through stacks of documents, starting with Ukraine's new Constitution, the old laws from the Soviet area, and then the new laws that might affect the various aspects of efficient mortgage lending. I also reviewed the reports prepared by consultants working in other former Soviet countries who were dealing with the same issues. The Law Center's attorneys were occupied with other projects, or so I was told, which was a bit of a concern considering that some capacity-building was part of my deliverables. I asked Owen about it.

"Well, these guys are new to this private property stuff. They won't be too much help to you on the drafting." This made some sense to me.

"It may also have something to do with the fact that you're an American. Remember that for most of their lives, they've been taught to believe that the American way of life was corrupt and decadent."

Since I didn't have to accommodate the local lawyers' schedules, I settled into a nice work routine. I became a lunch regular at TGI Fridays, an American-inspired restaurant with an upbeat red-and-white color scheme not far from the office. Thinking back, that probably wasn't the best way to shed any American stigma. I sat at the counter and ordered the "special," regardless of what it was. Oksana, a young woman with reasonably fluent English who claimed to be of Tatar descent usually served me from behind the bar.

Regardless of the time or day I visited TGI Fridays, I'd see the same two young men both wearing black jackets, sitting at a window table drinking coffee. After a few visits, I asked Oksana who they were.

She leaned forward and whispered, "They are two men in black jackets." It was the only explanation I was going to get.

Emails from Argentina

While I worked in Kyiv, Roberto was in Argentina waiting to hear about a project in Afghanistan. He was living just outside of Buenos Aires, in a rural area with limited internet. Two or three times a week, he'd walk several miles into town where a sympathetic veterinarian allowed him to use the office internet. I imagined Roberto pecking away at the keyboard with a dog at his feet and a cat sitting on his lap.

His emails, written in the formal English from his elementary school days, were a mix of family information, property improvements, and hopes about the future—both his and ours. He also tried to be helpful. If there was an article in the Argentine newspapers on Ukraine, he'd summarize it in English for me. A couple of tidbits he shared helped me look much more informed about Ukraine than I really was.

As nice as his emails were, I could tell he was growing more and more anxious about the status of his job in Kabul. He needed to go back to work.

The Gym

The weather stayed cold—so cold that it was impossible to spend much time outdoors. My hotel didn't have a gym, but I needed to find a way to exercise. Svetlana phoned her cousin who worked at the Blue and Yellow, a four-star hotel with an indoor swimming pool.

"Is this the caviar cousin?" I asked.

"No," she tsked. "The swimming pool cousin. (They were willing to sell me a "limited, unofficial" membership, provided I paid for it upfront in US dollars.)

The lobby and public areas of the Blue and Yellow gleamed from a recent renovation, but the women's locker room was a disappointment. It consisted of a bank of heavily battered metal lockers and a wobbly wooden bench. At the far end of the room was a huge mirror, with a ledge cluttered with crumpled tissues, several tubes of lipstick, a brush full of blond hairs, and a couple of cans of hair spray. Several pairs of six-inch stiletto heels, decorated with rhinestones, appliqué birds, and silver and gold chains, stood in a line at the base of the mirror.

It took some time to find an empty locker. The first few I opened were full of brightly colored faux fur coats, chenille scarves, and silky shirts. (Then it dawned on me; the locker room was doubling as the changing room for the female escorts who worked in the hotel.)

I undressed and slipped into my swimsuit, but the lockers were too small to accommodate my clunky UGG snow boots. So I placed them next to the stilettos and made my way to the pool.

Except for two doughy boys trying their best to drown each other, I had the pool to myself. When I returned to the locker room, I found two extremely tall, model-esque blonds standing naked in front of the mirror. They had identical chignon hairstyles and perfectly painted faces. The taller of the two was wearing my snow boots.

They froze, briefly, when I entered but quickly returned to their lighthearted Ukrainian chatter. The woman wearing my snow boots looked up toward me and asked, "English?" I nodded.

"I am thinking these boots are..." she turned to her companion for help with the words, "…are not pleasing, yes?" I had to laugh. They were hideous.

"Actually, they're my snow boots," I admitted, pointing to the snow boots and then back at myself for clarity.

When they realized what I was saying, they alternated between laughing and apologizing profusely. As I watched the way they covered their mouths as they giggled, I realized that they were not women; they were young girls—teenagers, really—enjoying a joke.

Anywhere else, their youthful appeal would have landed them jobs that would allow them to keep their clothes on. (But due to Ukraine's economic condition, they made their living by consorting with the fat businessmen who stayed in the hotel. It was heartbreaking.)

I took a shower, and when I returned to the locker room, the young women were gone. I found my snow boots neatly placed next to the rack of glamorous shoes. *girl prostitutes*

Stakeholders' Meetings

By the first week of March, (I had finished reading the mountain of pertinent documents and was ready to meet with the stakeholders—the regulators, banks, insurance companies, notaries, etc.—who could help me identify any legal or policy obstacles that might block the passage of the mortgage law by Ukraine's Parliament.)

I asked about the role of notaries, methods of confirming property rights, and general lending practices. But the conversation always turned to Ukraine's endemic corruption, which was prevalent at every level of society. Bribes were required to secure wedding licenses, register a vehicle, or to get decent medical care, so it was almost certain that bribes would be required at various stages of the mortgage process.)

(The more open stakeholders spoke at length about ongoing scandals involving Ukraine's President, Leonid Kuchma. According to the news reports, there were recordings that implicated Kuchma in the murder and kidnapping of a journalist whose beheaded body was found in a forest outside of Kyiv—a truly difficult scenario to put a positive spin on.

When I was able to redirect the meetings back to mortgage, the general feeling was that it was an essential piece of legislation and that we should push for a modern law. So I continued to feel optimistic.

Taking Over the World

On March 20th I sat on the edge of my bed watching the BBC's broadcast of the predawn invasion of Iraq. Despite the weeks of preinvasion press and protests, I was stunned by bright bomb-lit skies over Baghdad—it was truly "shock and awe." According to then-President George W. Bush, the US-led coalition had a multipronged agenda: disarm Iraq of its weapons of mass destruction, end Saddam Hussein's reign of terrorism, and free the Iraqi people.

Sitting there alone, I viewed the invasion as a primarily American (and coalition) event, something that would be critiqued by non-coalition countries with detachment and probably disdain. But I soon learned that I had miscalculated the global impact of the invasion as the population of Kyiv was in complete panic mode over the possibility that Ukraine was next on the American invasion list.

The grilling started even before I left the Theodosius for work. As I dropped off my room key at the reception desk, Svetlana gently placed her hand over mine and asked, "US come Ukraine?" Her eyes were red and glistening as if she had been crying.

I didn't immediately connect what she was saying to the bombing of Iraq. So I smiled, and in what likely was an appallingly bad accent, wished her "*do-bro-ho ran-ku*" (good morning) and left the hotel.

At work, everyone was in a state of agitation. Yuri, the law center's barrel-chested, highly vocal Russian, spent the morning pacing the length of the big room, bellowing about America's quest for world domination. He spoke at length in Ukrainian (it might have been Russian) but occasionally interjected sentences in English, so I would understand what he was saying.

"The US is taking over the world. They need our resources. Who will stop them?" The idea that the United States would invade Ukraine struck me as highly improbable. I'd spent the last several weekends exploring the city of Kyiv and saw very little in this painfully poor country that would be of interest to the United States. Besides, the Russians were just next door. I was reasonably sure that the new Russian president, a relatively unknown named Vladimir Putin, would object to having the US occupy its neighbor.

Around one o'clock I slipped out of the office for my usual lunch at TGI Fridays. I was looking forward to a break from the escalating theories about America's intentions. Unfortunately, it was more of the same at the restaurant.

"It's happening, isn't it? The US is taking over the world." This was Oksana, my usual waitress, speaking. "All my customers are talking about it. Is it true? Can you tell me?" She, too, was visibly upset. I told her that between Afghanistan and Iraq, I thought the US probably had its hands full. She continued to fret.

On the way home from work, I detoured through the Besarabsky Market, hoping to pick up something for dinner. A poorly dressed man recognized my accent and shouted "Americanski" and made an elaborate show of spitting on my shoe. I was mortified and hurried out of the market without buying anything.

With dwindling meal options, I decided to eat at Anastasia's, a local restaurant known for its varenyky, the Ukrainian version of dumplings or pierogi. The staff didn't speak English, and I thought I'd be safe from accusations about the invasion.

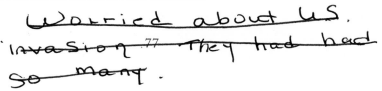

Worried about US. invasion. They had had so many.

77

"So, is it true?" It was the owner, who usually stood in the back of the restaurant barking orders in Ukrainian at the waiters. He caught me by surprise. I didn't realize he spoke English. "America is trying to take over the world?"

Over the last few months, I'd dined in this restaurant at least five times without the slightest nod of recognition. Now he was pumping me for what would be highly classified information—if I had known anything, that is.

After a long, difficult day, I'd had enough. I beckoned him closer and spoke softly—just above a whisper.

"Yes, America is taking over the world. But it's doing it alphabetically—Afghanistan, Iraq..." I counted them on my fingers. "Ukraine and Russia are at the end of the alphabet. So you have nothing to worry about for years. It really depends on how quickly the other countries roll over."

He lingered for a moment, holding the laminated menu against his chest, then slowly walked off.

After a relatively long time, I realized I hadn't been served. I regretted being so flippant. Surely, he wouldn't believe my preposterous theory. I felt bad. I shouldn't have taken my frustrations from this difficult day out on this unsuspecting owner.

Just as I was about to slip out of the restaurant, the owner reappeared with two small glasses and a bottle of yellowish-colored liquid that I suspected was horilka, the notoriously strong Ukrainian vodka.

He filled up both glasses and held one up for a toast.

"You tell good joke. My friends think very funny."

Whatever was in the glass, it burned all the way down my throat. It made the Rakija I had shared with Zivko and Flamur on my way to Kosovo taste like soda pop.

Hitler/Stalin

By April, I regretted not buying one of the long histories of Ukraine in that San Jose bookstore. I wanted to know more about how Ukraine became a country that declared independence but kept a statue of Lenin on prominent display. A country that had championed women's rights but accepted its young women sleeping with foreign businessmen. A country that feared invasion by the United States. I needed insights into these and other contradictions.

There were no English language bookstores in Kyiv, so I scoured secondhand shops for books left behind by other advisors or tourists. In a tiny shop in one of the underground mini-malls that connected to the metro, I found a used copy of *Hitler and Stalin: Parallel Lives* by Alan Bullock, published in 1993. The book outlined the origins, personalities, and legacies of Adolf Hitler and Joseph Stalin, two of history's most evil bullies. But a look at the index revealed a substantial number of pages covering Ukraine. It was a real door stopper, running 1,152 pages of small type, and would take me some time to get through.

I usually read the Hitler/Stalin book when sitting alone at lunch or dinner, and it became a key conversation starter. Strangers saw the dramatic black-and-red cover and approached me to ask questions about the book. It was not unusual for someone to sit down and provide their own take on the two villains. Some told personal stories about friends and loved ones who had suffered at the hands of one or the other. Some would ask, "How's Mr. Stalin today?" The more cynical would inquire, "How many people dead so far?"

The book also led to my meeting Axel, a middle-aged Brit who was married to a young Ukrainian woman. Originally Olga, his wife, had wanted to live in the United Kingdom but changed her mind when, on a visit to Axel's hometown in Essex, a woman called her "another bloody immigrant."

Axel ate lunch at TGI Fridays on the weekends when Olga's

parents visited from Lviv. He introduced himself and, noting my reading selection, asked if I had visited the Great Patriotic War Museum, located just outside Kyiv.

"I'm going as soon as I finish this book," I answered. "Apparently, there are no English explanations to the exhibits, so I'm hoping this book will help me understand what I'm seeing."

"One thing you should know before you visit the museum," Axel spoke carefully as if preparing to deliver bad news. "Russians differentiate between World War II, which involved the Americans and other allies, and the Great Patriotic War, which was limited to the conflict between the Soviet Union and Nazi Germany. The Eastern Front. I know how much you Americans love your war heroes. So if you're expecting to see a lot of smiling 'Yanks' in D-Day photos, you're going to be disappointed."

I felt my eyes narrow involuntarily.

"Surely, they mention the Lend-Lease program." I was referring to the US government program under which the United States supplied materials to the anti-fascist coalition of countries during World War II.

"Well, that's why I'm mentioning it." Axel was almost apologetic. "The Russians tend to downplay the role of the Americans in the defeat of the Nazis."

"Tell me," I asked with a bit of attitude, "how do you downplay the delivery of 14,000 airplanes, 400,000 jeeps, 12,700 tanks, and 15 million pairs of boots?" This was like ingrate Anna and her salted butter—but a hundred times worse.

Axel raised his hands and said, "Don't kill the messenger."

Now I really wanted to see what was in that museum.

help draft new democratic laws

Foreclosure and Eviction

Revising Ukraine's draft mortgage law was tough, extremely technical work—much harder than what I had done in Kosovo. Only with the 1996 adoption of the new constitution did Ukraine recognize the concept of private property. Before that, people only had the right to use their residence, not own it. Consequently, the mortgage law raised countless policy issues that had to be carefully thought through and discussed.

By mid-April, the draft law was in good shape, but there were two areas—foreclosure and eviction—that proved problematic. Briefly, *foreclosure* is the legal process by which a lender takes ownership of a home or real property after the borrower fails to make payments or otherwise defaults. *Eviction* involves the removal of occupants from a property and taking possession. The longer it takes to enforce a loan, the less likely lenders are willing to lend. So swift foreclosure and eviction processes are critically important to creating a robust mortgage market.

In the United States, the bank and lending lobbies have ensured that foreclosure and eviction are relatively quick processes. Some states have done away with requiring court orders due to the time and expense involved in that process. During my time working with the mortgage lender in California, I had concerns about the streamlined approach to foreclosure and eviction. The purchase of real property is one of the biggest investments a family or business will make. An unforgiving foreclosure process can have extremely harsh consequences.

More often than not, it's your "average Joe" who has every intention of repaying his mortgage but hits one of life's unavoidable speed bumps—a lost job, family illness, accident, or death of a spouse—and things get difficult. Those were the borrowers I pitied and tried to cut some slack. In Ukraine, I worried that a hardline approach to foreclosure would lead to homelessness and financial ruin for those who were desperate for money and new to the concept of a mortgage.

As it turned out, Ukraine wouldn't be adopting the American rules on foreclosure. Its new constitution guaranteed a "right to housing," interpreted to mean that families could not be evicted unless they had an alternative place to live. Additional limitations were placed on the eviction of families with children. One of the local attorneys informed me that these provisions were holdovers from the Soviet-era social protection safety nets. They didn't align with free market principles, but I privately supported the approach—at least in the short-term.

Back in February when I stood in front of the statue of Lenin in Bessarabska Square, I had a feeling that I would see the influence of Mr. Lenin elsewhere in Ukraine. And here he was in the new constitution and new legislation.

The Flea Markets

Spring finally arrived the first week of May, and I was able to spend my weekends walking around Kyiv exploring its churches, large squares, shady plazas, and other sites of interest. The Mariinsky Palace, a landmark for baroque-style architecture, was an easy walk from the hotel but was never open due to "permanent reconstruction." But I settled for lunches in the beautiful gardens.

I'd walk down the Andriyivsky Descent that connected the Higher city (old Kyiv) and the Lower city (Podil district) and examine various Ukrainian souvenirs, including colorful wooden Easter eggs, embroidered peasant blouses, and old Soviet artwork.

Along the traffic-filled streets, men and women established makeshift shops by spreading small pieces of cloth on the sidewalks. These flea markets sold everything and anything that might bring in some cash. There were decks of cards from airlines that no longer existed, lighting fixtures without glass, chipped kitchen canisters, and countless wire potato mashers. The sellers beckoned me to buy, and I always tried, but most times I couldn't find anything that I could use or even give away.

One afternoon, I walked by a woman who seemed destitute, so I took some time to look over the items she had for sale. Next to an old-fashioned eggbeater, I found a small packet of costume jewelry. Through the clear wrapping, I could see a pair of cheap gold-tone earrings, probably from the fifties or sixties, that were both rectangular but didn't quite match, and an unattractive cat-shaped brooch with a bent ear. I figured one of the young girls at the hotel might enjoy them, so I paid more than what she asked by refusing to accept the change. She was overwhelmingly grateful.

Back at the hotel, Svetlana was on duty and welcomed me with her usual half-smile. I pulled the plastic pouch out of my pocket and shook the contents out on the reception desk counter. The earrings and the cat pin tumbled out.

Svetlana snapped up the brooch and held it tight against her chest, and at the same time, emitted the feral cat noise that I recognized from the Thursday night "feline fests." Finally, part of the cat mystery was solved. After that, I cast a suspicious eye toward the two jowly men who sat in the lobby.

Final Draft

(After almost three months of research, working to balance the rights of lenders and borrowers, and pushing for free market concepts against the Ukrainian preference to retain pieces of the Soviet safety net, the draft mortgage law was ready for World Bank review) I was pleased with the product. The draft law was simple and clear, and could be easily translated into Ukrainian, but there was a list of open policy issues that required additional discussion.

Owen arranged a meeting with Veronica at the World Bank offices.

We sat in chairs in front of her desk, like kids sent to the principal's office. She scanned the long list of open issues, taking time to refer to the explanatory notes. As we waited I looked around the office. It was crammed with large gray-green files labeled "tax reform," "deposit insurance," and "pension project," to name a few. It was an overwhelming amount of work, and so few resources.

"This is good," Veronica announced. "I understand the issues and have to take these matters to the decision-makers. If we need your help to redraft, I will call on you."

And with those words, my part in the drafting process was over. It had been an interesting three months, notable for a variety of unexpected twists and turns. I felt a pang of post-project uselessness. I would miss being involved in the drafting of the mortgage law.

The next day, I entered TGI Fridays with a swagger of accomplishment. Axel sat in his usual seat at the counter and greeted me with a silent toast from his wine glass. It was early afternoon, but I had a feeling that Axel had been drinking for a while. I explained that the mortgage law had been delivered to the World Bank.

"So, soon I will wake up in a country with the perfect mortgage law, am I right?" he asked.

"It's not perfect. Not by a long shot. But it's definitely a step in the right direction." I said a little defensively.

"Any concerns that the very poor people of Ukraine will mortgage their property or sell it in desperation and have no place to live?" he slurred.

"Well, that's a risk in any mortgage arrangement anywhere in the world."

"Yes, but in the United States, you've had over two hundred years of capitalism. There's a better understanding of the risks involved in putting your home up as collateral for a loan."

I wanted to say, "Don't be so sure about that." I had seen borrowers eagerly signing the mortgage documents in my sub-prime days. They gleefully signed in anticipation of that family cruise to the Caribbean or that fully loaded Chevrolet Suburban. They showed no interest in the bold type that warned them that they could lose their homes for non-payment.

"I do worry about that," I said solemnly.

"And what about those families who will be powerless to protect their property from the criminals in this country because the judiciary is ineffective? The people who will be chased out of their homes by men in black jackets wielding bats. Does your "step-in-the-right-direction" law address that?"

He was right. It was impossible to put all the pieces of the free market economy in place at the same time. It was inevitable that some people would get hurt in the process.

The World's Policeman

At the end of April, Roberto emailed that his company had finally won a contract in Afghanistan, and he would be flying to Kabul via Frankfurt. I was thrilled. I hadn't seen him in four months, not since we parted in December with a long kiss at the airport in Pristina. I encouraged him to apply for a Ukrainian visa, but there wasn't enough time. So I booked a cheap flight to Frankfurt.

My flight arrived a couple of hours before Roberto's, so I waited for him in the terminal. As the passengers from his flight streamed through the arrival gate, I saw the top of his yellow-blond hair. I struggled to hold back the tears.

He had put on some weight, and the extra pounds made him look younger, healthier, and more handsome. When he got close enough, he dramatically dropped his bag and placed his hands on either side of my face.

"We are in an airport. People are expected to kiss in airports. It is…what is the word…mandatory." And we did. We shared a long, inaugural kiss, the thrill of which ran down to my toes and bounced back again. And after a few more, Roberto said, "Those are your January kisses. You have four more months coming." It felt good to be adored.

We ate dinner in the hotel restaurant, and it was almost as if we had never been separated. When he wasn't kissing my fingertips, he was asking about people and things that were important to me—my parents, Kate, Piro, and of course, the work in Ukraine. It was almost as magical as the evening we first met in Kosovo.

I talked about the painful history of Ukraine and the beauty of Kyiv. I recounted the days after the bombing of Baghdad and mused about how the Ukrainians were panicked over a possible invasion by the United States. I also raised the issue that no weapons of mass destruction, the main premise for invading Iraq, had been found. So what had it all been for?

Roberto didn't hesitate. "Regime change. The US went in to get rid of Saddam Hussein, and if you ask me, it was long overdue."

This took me aback. I was surprised that Roberto would support the invasion based on what seemed to be false premises.

"In Argentina," he explained, "when the Junta was in power, we suffered the same kind of state-sponsored terrorism. There were death squads and at least 30,000 people disappeared. They took a student in my college class, and we never saw him again. So I know how it feels to hope the United States will come to the rescue."

"But why the United States?" I asked. "Why does the US have to send our sons and daughters to fight in these places? Why can't some other country take on the expense and death toll?"

He reached up and gave my hand a tender squeeze. "Because that's who you are. You're the world's policeman. After World War II, the US insisted on taking the role. Besides, what other country can do

86

it? You won't see Russia in Iraq—well, at least not officially. And it's not a role for the United Nations."

I had flown all the way from Kyiv for this dinner, and this really wasn't the discussion I intended to have on our first night together. I wanted to hear how much he missed me. But this conversation set the tone for the next two days. We revisited and rehashed the US invasion of Iraq for the next 48 hours. It was not the romantic weekend I had envisioned.

The Magician's Assistant

(On my return to Ukraine, I called my parents to check in and tell them I was back in Kyiv.)

"I found a tour." My mother interrupted me. She sounded good—almost chipper.

"Great. Tour for what?" This was a good sign. They were traveling again.

"For Russia. Remember you said that if I found an organized tour, we could go to Russia with you."

"Um, did I really say that?" I remembered a much different conversation. ·

"Yes, and we've already paid a nonrefundable deposit. The organizers are sending you the forms directly." Taking my elderly parents on a trip to Russia was pretty much the last thing I wanted to do. But I was stuck. It would be my dad's last big trip.

(I paid the deposit and started the process of obtaining a visa, which required a visit to the Russian Embassy in Kyiv) an impressive three-story building with an imposing façade of decorative columns. I held up my passport, and the disinterested security guard waved me through the gate.

The embassy's entry hall was cavernous but almost completely devoid of furniture. There were a few empty bookshelves, a stack of broken chairs, and near the entrance, a small wooden desk manned by a bespectacled man with no hair. He used an ancient-looking phone to ring the visa office, which was close enough that I could hear both sides of the conversation while standing at his desk.

A tall, well-dressed woman with a head of golden curls emerged from one of the offices down the hall. She was all smiles and sweeping arm gestures in the manner of a magician's assistant. She seemed overly friendly, especially considering I was in the Russian Embassy. She brought a one-page visa application but held on to it until I demonstrated that I had sufficient cash to cover the fee. She collected my information, money, and passport and instructed me to wait while she prepared my visa.

When she returned, she held my visa between her thumb and index finger and asked me to check the spelling of my name. Everything seemed to be in order, so she closed my passport, handed it to me, and insisted I immediately tuck it away for safekeeping. I left the embassy thinking that the visa application process was surprisingly easy.

Corruption Savants

(With my work on the mortgage law complete, I focused on preparing training sessions for the local lawyers) I was looking forward to this part of the project. I didn't know the local attorneys well, but I could tell they were a good team. They were young and full of good-natured mischief. If they shared a joke in Ukrainian, someone always translated and explained why it was funny to Ukrainians.

In the training sessions I started with the basics: business organizations, securities (debt and equity), bank lending, bankruptcy, and dispute resolution. They were quick to grasp the legal concepts underpinning a free market economy but were unwilling to accept what I had to say wholesale. Instead, they asked intuitive questions and challenged some points as being completely unsuitable for Ukraine.

There was a heated debate over business name registration. Someone argued that requiring unique business names was unrealistic. Everyone wanted to name their business after their little girl, and since there were so few female names used in Ukraine, uniqueness was not possible. There were ten shops with some form of the name "Olga" in the surrounding blocks alone.

There was a similar row over commercial litigation. I noted that large corporations worried about a "home court advantage" or being unfairly treated by small-town judges. So I asked, "If there were a case between a poor local resident and a large corporation, who do you think would win?" The response was quick and unequivocal, "Whoever pays the biggest bribe."

On the topic of secured transactions, a complicated system that facilitates the use of movable property as collateral for credit, they listed the various ways that criminals could misuse the regime to their advantage—and each example was spot on. I realized I was working with "corruption savants."

Over time, the local lawyers started to warm up to me. They wanted to know what I thought of Ukraine and what the world thought of Ukraine. I provided some optimistic answers tied to the possibility of joining the European Union and what that might mean for the standard of living of the Ukrainians and the opportunities for its young population, meaning them. I followed up by asking them what they thought about Ukraine's future.

Their responses were cautious but insightful. Everyone had a story about the euphoria they felt back in 1991, when the government declared its independence, but there was a sadness in their eyes. Well over ten years on, the progress was disappointingly slow. But they were sure things would improve. Things had to.

(Later that day, one of the attorneys swung by my desk and confided that is was difficult for Ukrainians to feel truly independent in light of Russia's frequent statements about Ukraine always being part of Russia. As he put it, "It's very much like having a gigantic bear peeking over the fence. Sooner or later he will get hungry.")

The War Museum

I'd finally finished the Hilter/Stalin book and was ready to visit the Great Patriotic War Museum. I set aside an entire Saturday, so I could take in the full experience. I walked from the center of town and entered the vast museum complex through the "Alley of the Hero Cities," a tunnel paneled with depictions of soldiers engaged in various battle scenes. A recording of up-tempo songs by a male chorus propelled me forward to the main plaza. The plaza is dominated by the immense Motherland Monument—a sixty-two-meter-high, titanium female figure holding a shield and a sword, which commemorates the Soviet Union's victory over Nazi Germany. There were rumors that the Japanese wanted to buy it for the value of the metal.

I bought a ticket at the front window and walked five steps to the front door where another woman tore it in half. The ticket taker spoke rapidly, presumably a list of rules and limitations. I put up my hand to indicate I didn't speak Ukrainian, but she closed her eyes and completed her spiel. When she realized I was an English speaker, she mumbled something under her breath and guided me through the door with a bit of a push.

About midway through one of the first galleries, on the reverse side of a poorly lighted panel, I found a small plaque—no more than eight by eleven inches—dedicated to the Lend-Lease program between the United States and its allies, including Russia. It had a black-and-white photo of one of the massive transportation ships and a paragraph or two of Cyrillic text. (It was the only mention of the United States that I saw in the entire museum.)

To me, this was more than "downplaying" the US support to the Soviet Union. In my mind, relegating the Lend-Lease program to a small plaque on a dark wall was nothing less than revisionist history. I can't explain it, but I felt the slight personally.

Annoyed, I continued my tour of the museum. There were thousands of objects on display, each representing a different aspect of the war. I spent a long time in front of the large photos of the massive destruction caused by the Battles of Stalingrad and Kursk—tanks on fire, blood-splattered faces, broken bodies, hunger, and desperation. There were uniforms, war documents, embroidered handkerchiefs, canteen kits, sweetheart souvenirs, and family photos that brought home the human sacrifice of the conflict.

(It was a long, gut-wrenching afternoon. I examined a series of charts and was able to deduce that they reflected the immense loss of life due to combat, starvation, exposure, disease, and massacres) The numbers were in the millions. My education on World War II had primarily focused on the European and Pacific theaters (I was unaware of how much the Russians had suffered during and after the war) I was embarrassed by my initial annoyance over the abbreviated recognition given to the American contribution to the Russian–German conflict through the Lend-Lease.

Social Studies Book

The Hitler/Stalin book was a terrific resource, but it was unlikely that I'd ever read it again. So I decided to return it to the Metro shop where I had originally purchased it. With any luck, another expat would benefit from reading the book as I had. The woman behind the counter could not understand that I didn't want to sell it; I just wanted to give the book back. So we agreed on an exchange, and I went to the English language section to find another book. There were only three books in English—the King James Bible, a Danielle Steel romance, and a fifth-grade US social studies book.

I pulled the social studies book off the shelf and checked the date. It had been printed in the 1960s, back when I was starting elementary school. I leafed through the colorful, heavily illustrated pages. The first section was dedicated to "Our Near Neighbors" and covered Canada and Mexico in eight pages. The Canadian pages were embellished with cartoony drawings of the Canadian flag, a smiling moose, and a bottle of maple syrup. The pages on Mexico showed the Mexican flag, a piñata, and a sombrero.

The next section—a full ten pages—covered the United Kingdom and European countries and had photos of Big Ben, a pair of wooden shoes, a couple dancing the flamenco, and the leaning Tower of Pisa. Collectively, the Scandinavian countries received three pages.

I flipped to the back of the book to find the Soviet Union. The write-up was less than half a page, and there were no whimsical, enhancing pictures. Just like the small Lend-Lease plaque in the Great Patriotic War Museum, we, too, had trimmed the history and the prominence of our rival.

The Elephant in the Room

My last weekend in Kyiv, I made a final visit to the Pechersk Lavra, the large World Heritage Site that dates back to 1051. On previous visits, I had explored the museums and churches, including the spooky cave church that I toured by candlelight. This time I was looking for something in particular—the depiction of an elephant on one of the church walls. I wandered around the side apses and naves of one of the main churches until I found the elephant in a secular fresco near a back staircase.

According to the translator at the law center, the Ukrainian artist who painted the elephant had never seen an elephant in person. And as there were no photographs back then, he had to rely on a description provided by a third party. It was immediately clear that a lot was lost in the process.

Instead of the massive bulk and power of an elephant's head, shoulders, and legs, the elephant looked more like a dog hovering over its dinner bowl. Its eyes looked forward as a human would, rather than being placed on either side of the head looking out. The ears were almost comical. Rather than the large ears that can lay flat against the elephant's head, these were cupped and scalloped around the edges, as if they had been finished with pinking shears.

(As I stood there, it struck me how this sweet but inaccurate rendition of an elephant illustrated the risks of trying to recreate something as complicated as a free market economy or a democracy if you haven't seen it in action) I just prayed that on future examination, my work in Ukraine on the mortgage law wouldn't be subject to the same ridicule as this little elephant.

Visa Problems

My contract ended the last week of May with little fanfare. I flew to Frankfurt to meet my parents, who were flying in from California. We would all fly to St. Petersburg on the same flight. But as I checked in, the clerk noted a problem with my visa. My name and other information were correct, but the date of entry was wrong, and I would not be allowed to board the flight to St. Petersburg. I thought back to my visit to the Russian Embassy and the blond woman—the magician's assistant—who had been so overly friendly. I realized she had carefully covered the date of entry with her thumb. Sneaky. I should have expected a trick at the end.

A new visa required an application to the Russian Embassy, which was still in Bonn, the city that served as the capital of West Germany. So I put my elderly, jet-lagged, thoroughly confused parents on the plane to Russia while I took a bus to the train station.

I arrived in Bonn late afternoon. The embassy was packed with extremely aggressive clerks from numerous German tour operators who held stacks of passports. It was a matter of elbowing myself up to the small window and forcing the person working behind a screen to take hold of my passport. I was about to give up hope when my passport was snatched from my hand, and I was instructed to return the next day.

I found a cheap hotel room near the embassy and ate dinner in the lounge, where I met a couple from Vermont. They, too, were in Bonn to obtain new Russian visas. The ones they obtained in the United States also had the wrong entry date on the visa. We all agreed it was quite a coincidence.

That night I checked my email at the hotel. There was a message from Owen. (The Law on Mortgage had passed the Verkhovna Rada the first week of June. Veronica had done it.)

Tour of Russia

While I loved my parents dearly, accompanying them on a twelve-day tour of Russia, most of which was on a riverboat, was not my idea of an ideal vacation. But there I was, trudging up the gangway, smiling as best I could, while they waved at me from one of the upper decks.

The activities director, a handsome young Russian who used a lot of American slang, helped me with my luggage.

"This will blow your mind," he said. "Our ship was designed and manufactured in East Germany before the fall of communism."

I looked at the ugly, short, squat vessel and said, "I could have guessed."

After the initial hugs and kisses, my mother took me aside and made it clear that she needed a break, and I had to take care of my dad. She'd get him dressed in the morning, but after breakfast, he was all mine. I was responsible for involving him in activities, keeping his glasses clean, and making sure his fly was zipped.

The tour started in St. Petersburg, traveled down the Volga, stopping at World Heritage Sites in Yaroslavl and Kizhi, and ended in Moscow. People on a once-in-a-lifetime vacation have little interest in getting to know an old man with Alzheimer's or his attendant daughter. So we made the most of what the ship had to offer. We were first in line for any shore excursions. We worked the daily quiz, participated in sing-alongs, and attended "Meet the Professor" talks on the history of Russia.

The Professor nights were held in the large upstairs lounge where chairs were arranged into two sections as if in preparation for a small wedding. There were always empty seats.

The first talk was about the Tsars, and my dad sat in stony silence. The second talk was on the Cold War, and he turned to me and said, "Well, that was interesting."

The final talk was on the Great Patriotic War, and the professor spent a good deal of time discussing both the size and brutality of the battles of Stalingrad and Kursk. At the end of her talk, she acknowledged several World War II veterans on the tour and asked if anyone had a personal story to tell with a Russian theme. To my dismay, my dad, who had difficulty stringing together his dinner order, raised his hand. I heard a groan from the back of the room, and two couples stood up to leave.

"Dad," I put my hand on his arm and gently pushed it down. "Why don't you tell me the story over a drink in the back bar?"

"No," he was rather agitated. "I want to tell the group." And he stood up.

"I served as a sergeant with General Patton's Third Army in Germany, and I want to tell you how I learned that World War II was over." The two couples who were about to leave sat back down to listen.

In the beginning, his storytelling was painfully start and stop, but he eventually found a rhythm. The combination of being on a ship, interacting with new people, and engaging in daily activities brought back pieces of my father that I hadn't seen for years.

"My unit was patrolling a remote area in the German countryside, and we came upon a detachment of German soldiers. The commander approached me, and in perfect English, asked to see the highest-ranking officer. I knew enough German to understand that they had run out of gas. I realized that if Berlin could no longer supply its infantry, the war was at an end."

An enormous tear rolled down my face.

"I appreciate the story," the speaker interjected, trying to cut my dad off, "but we're looking for stories with Russian themes."

"Let him finish," a man called from the back of the room. My dad turned around and thanked him.

"The Germans wanted to surrender to us, the American army, because they were terrified of how they would be treated if the Russians captured them. I heard the German commander say, 'The Americans place a higher value on life than the Russians.' That's my Russian theme."

That story, and my dad's telling of it, made him a bit of a celebrity on the cruise. Several passengers came by to shake his hand and pat him on the back. Even my mother agreed to sit with us at meals again. I thought back to Axel's comment about Americans loving our war heroes—we even love the old ones, and thankfully, even the ones with failing brains.

CHAPTER 3

Dhaka, Bangladesh

2004

I Wanted the Job

"Do you know what you're getting into? Is it even safe?" My mother held a few slick fax pages in her hand, which I presumed was the consulting contract I was expecting. I was getting used to this exchange—we had it every time I took on a new project.

In early 2004, an Australian firm contacted me about a short-term assignment in Dhaka, Bangladesh. It was an ongoing project funded by the Asian Development Bank, or the ADB, the institution that promotes social and economic development in Asia. They needed an attorney to finalize a law that promoted the use of movable property (equipment, machinery, vehicles, etc.) as collateral for credit, a system known as "secured transactions." I knew it would be a challenge, but I wanted the job.

"Taking this job in Bangladesh is a good career move," I said. I was grasping at straws. "It will allow me to expand my subject matter expertise and give me South Asia experience." My mother narrowed her eyes, so I spoke faster. "It'll be an advantage if I apply for jobs in India, Nepal, or say Bhutan."

"Boo-tan." My mother responded sarcastically. "Is that really a country?"

97

I didn't mention that I had a personal reason for wanting the job. Roberto was still in Kabul working on a hush-hush project for the US Embassy. In the global scheme of things, Dhaka and Kabul were in the same neighborhood, just fifteen hundred miles apart. It was a long shot, but I hoped we could meet up in New Delhi, which was conveniently located just a short plane ride between the two.

But my mother had a point. I didn't know that much about Bangladesh. The little I knew came from the insert that accompanied the live album set, "The Concert for Bangladesh," released in 1971. George Harrison, the former Beatles guitarist, had organized the concert and the album to raise awareness and funds for Bangladesh after its violent separation from Pakistan.

I didn't remember any of the songs or the musical celebrities who contributed their time. What stayed with me was the cover image of a malnourished child sitting naked behind an empty food bowl—an actual child wasting away because of international politics.

I searched the internet, but there wasn't much practical information about Bangladesh. So I made a trip to the nearest Barnes & Noble bookstore and consulted the most recent Lonely Planet guide. I flipped through the introductory pages on history and poverty, but took some time reading the six pages dedicated to infectious and insect-borne diseases—everything from diarrhea to hepatitis to Japanese B encephalitis. Reassuringly, the section on travel hazards was comparatively short, limited to a couple of paragraphs on pickpockets and irritating crowds.

I didn't consider that the guide was released in 2000, a full year before the 9/11 attacks against the United States. It didn't mention the ensuing increase in Islamic extremism in Muslim countries around the globe, including Bangladesh. I would learn about that the hard way in a remote village, a six-hour boat ride away from Dhaka.

My voice still breaks whenever I tell the story of how the events unfolded that day and how I came to feel the sickening fear that stays with you long after a dangerous situation is over. It was a strange case of the wrong place, wrong time, and wrong nationality.

Arrival in Dhaka

Dhaka is literally on the other side of the world from California, so there was some discussion about which way I would travel around the globe. But by mid-March, my travel plans were finalized and I would transit through Heathrow. My flight to London was uneventful, but the connecting flight to Bangladesh was troubling. Instead of the convenient British Airways flight that left Heathrow at a reasonable hour and flew directly to Dhaka, I was booked on Biman Air, the national airline of Bangladesh, which left Heathrow at midnight and had a five-hour layover in Dubai.

The overhead bins were full, so I tried to stow my computer bag under my seat. I found a large loose object that turned out to be my life vest. Disturbingly, the word "reject" was stenciled across the bag in big blue letters. As for the flight itself, recent traveler reviews on the internet say it all: Biman flights were *"cramped and overcrowded,"* *"the crew could be more polite,"* and the ultimate understatement, *"service is extremely poor."*

In Dubai, we picked up a group of pilgrims still in a state of euphoria from the Hajj, the annual Islamic pilgrimage to Mecca—a reminder that Bangladesh was over ninety percent Muslim. Some still wore their Ihram clothing—two pieces of unstitched white cloth and a pair of sandals. Others sported red, henna-dyed beards.

I tried to nap on the Dubai to Dhaka leg but was awakened by two Bangladeshi youngsters, a boy and girl, trying to rub the light color off my arm. The woman across the aisle shook her head and admonished them to stop, explaining in a loud voice, "She was born that way. It does not come off." As if it was a defect. On their way back to their

99

seats, the young girl turned around and stuck her tongue out at me as if I was somehow at fault.

The guest house in Dhaka forgot to send a car to pick me up at the airport, so I accepted a ride with Amos and Sarah, a couple of Christian missionaries who arrived on the same flight. I wanted to ask Amos about the challenges of teaching the Gospel in a Muslim country, but as we exited the airport parking lot (I completely tuned out. It was my first glimpse of Dhaka and its notorious poverty. It was worse than I could have possibly imagined.)

Both sides of the road were littered with rag remnants, broken bits of plastic, empty cartons, pieces of splintered wood, and every kind of trash imaginable. Children in filthy T-shirts and little else stood by the roadside staring at the passing traffic. Small groups of thin, bony women wearing thread-bare saris sat cross-legged in the dust, unsheltered, engaged in the hard, hazardous work of chipping bricks into smaller pieces. This scene replayed mile after mile along the road into town—and then it got worse.

We crossed a bridge spanning one of the many waterways that flow through Dhaka to the Bay of Bengal. A group of impoverished women and children in ragged clothes stood on the dark, litter-strewn shores. Some of the structures didn't even rise to the level of shacks.

("These people are Dalits.") Amos answered my question before I asked it. ("They are the 'untouchables' who do the 'unclean' jobs in the city, such as street sweeping, scavenging, and burying the dead. They inherited the position from their parents—and will likely pass the same job along to their children. Despite attempts to abolish the caste system, it continues in many South Asian countries.")

I thought back to my mother's comment and realized she was right. I had no idea what I was getting myself into.

Development Factors

Experts on poverty and its causes identify a number of factors to help explain why some countries are less developed than others. The short-list includes political instability, corruption, natural disasters, and over-population. In 2004, Bangladesh suffered from these and a number of other contributing factors and, as a result, was ranked one of the poorest countries in the world.

As for political instability, Bangladesh has the distinction of being the only country to declare independence twice within a period of fifty years. It first separated from India in 1947 and then violently from Pakistan in 1971. The separation from Pakistan led to the bloody nine-month "War of Independence," which, along with other causes, contributed to an unprecedented famine.

Twenty years of successive military coups and political assassinations plagued the newly independent country. A democratic government was only reestablished in 1991 after a military dictator was forced to resign. Since then, two powerful families have battled for political domination.

High levels of corruption caused by decades of political turmoil also work to keep Bangladesh poor. As a result, "rent-seeking" (the collection of bribes), inappropriate use of public funds, and other forms of corruption became embedded in the Bangladesh government and the private sector.

The country's problems are compounded by its climate. Bangladesh is bisected by the Tropic of Cancer, the northern boundary of the tropics. It is routinely hit by typhoons, monsoons, and cyclones, causing extensive flooding and weather-related damage. Due to its extremely hot summers (above 100°F) and warm winters, Bangladesh is a veritable petri dish for diseases. Tuberculosis and leprosy are still prevalent.

Finally, as one of the most densely populated countries in the world, Bangladesh must cope with the variety of problems caused by too many people. (Overpopulation places a strain on access to food, shelter, education, and health care. It also gives rise to unemployment due to insufficient jobs and business opportunities.)

But despite these and other negative factors, there were small indications that Bangladesh was making progress. (Both urban and rural poverty numbers were declining, and there was cautious optimism for the country's future.)

Dhaka Project Staff

(The woman at the Australian firm that hired me spoke at length about the strong project team.) Raoul, the ADB project manager in Manila ("a nice guy, but a bit of a micromanager," she confessed), would be in frequent contact through phone calls and emails. This appealed to me because Raoul was highly regarded as a credit expert. I was looking forward to working with him.

(In Dhaka, I'd report to Nigel, the team leader, who had served as a member of the British Parliament.) (He was well-connected, I was told, and would be able to open a lot of doors.) On the technical side, an expert had submitted a preliminary report and would arrive within a month or so to finalize recommendations regarding the design and location of the public registry, a key component of the secured transactions system.

(As the project's missing piece, I was responsible for reviewing the Bangladeshi laws governing credit, meeting with various stakeholders to confirm their appetite for reform, and revising a draft law prepared by a previous consultant. (All my findings had to be reflected in a detailed end-of-mission report.)

(In addition to the international consultants, the project had a local advisor, Ellie, a Bangladeshi attorney.) She surprised me by coming to the guesthouse during her off-hours to introduce herself. An experienced lawyer with a commercial law background, I soon learned she was both good at her job and well respected by the legal community. She probably could have handled the project on her own.

Ellie was a portrait of calm self-assurance. Her wardrobe was made up of gloriously beautiful saris. She wore her dark hair in a neat bun, covered by a length of sari fabric that further accentuated her mystique.

She had a good sense of humor and was kind enough to advise me on what a female advisor should know about navigating Dhaka. Avoiding being groped by the lecherous Bangladeshi men was high on her list. She counseled that I was never to get into an elevator alone with a man—the stairs were usually the safer option. If I encountered a man, whether in the elevator or on the stairs, I should stand to one side, place my arm over my chest, and turn toward the wall.

First Morning Commute

On my first morning, Nigel picked me up in a private taxi for the ride across town to the project office. Nigel was extremely good-looking in a square, establishment way. Despite the heat and humidity, he wore a blazer with a turtleneck underneath. We left early to avoid the worst of the morning traffic, but the road was already heavily congested. Large colorful trucks decorated with uplifting messages of faith and the driver's hometowns roared down the roads, spewing exhaust and zigzagging dangerously. A fleet of green, three-wheeled vehicles, known as "CNGs" (for "Compressed Natural Gas") and noisy motorcycles raced alongside. On the edge of the road a fleet of pedicabs—a combination rickshaw and bicycle—tried to keep up with the traffic flow.

As we drew closer to the commercial area, merchants, pedestrians, and beggars entered the mix—many balanced huge baskets of tools, fruit, clothing, and other items on their heads.

"Those baskets must be so heavy," I said. "They should use carts."

"The baskets are a way of avoiding the 'cart tax,'" Nigel explained in his upper-class British accent. Seeing my confused look, he continued. "The police stop vendors with carts and extract bribes. So to avoid being stopped, vendors carry those huge baskets. I've been told the number one injury in Bangladesh is a crushed vertebra."

As we drove along, Nigel talked about the country's unpredictable security situation.

"While Bangladesh has traditionally been a tolerant country," he explained, "after the 9/11 attacks in the United States, Islamic extremism is on the rise. Bangladesh has seen increased terrorist activity in recent years, including attacks on activists, religious minorities, and," he paused to emphasize his point, "foreigners."

"Which means I have to be careful," I said, mostly to prove I was listening.

"Which means you have to be careful," he repeated. "If you don't want to end up a headline, you must always be aware of your surroundings."

"Got it," I said. But I didn't quite believe him. Everyone I'd met had been so friendly, so welcoming.

We stopped at a traffic light, and the pedicabs slowly wove their way up the line of waiting vehicles. My presence in the taxi's back seat was met with surprise and, in some cases, shock by other drivers. A couple of them circled around to get a second and third look at me. Our driver turned his head slightly and said, "They are men from the village. They have no manners." Then he warned me to check that my door was locked.

While I surveyed the drab, run-down neighborhood from the taxi, Nigel went over the project's goals and expectations. As I listened, a set of warehouse doors burst open, and a spectacular river of vibrant colors streamed out. Pinks, blues, reds, greens, and yellows swarmed into the street (These were the brightly colored saris and salwar kameez (tunic and pants ensemble) of the female garment workers leaving their factory jobs at the end of their shift.)

(At the time, the textile industry in Bangladesh employed upwards of three million workers, of whom eighty-five percent were women.) That day's shift spilled out onto the sidewalks and flooded the street, weaving their way among the vehicles. Young, beautiful, and wrapped in the fluidity of the fabric, it was impossible not to make a comparison to a kaleidoscope of butterflies.

Hundreds, maybe thousands of these women flowed into the street. So many that when the light changed, we were unable to move forward. The driver turned around and explained, "These women are the future of Bangladesh. They deserve this small courtesy."

The Spice Market

(The project office was on the third floor of a dirty office building) The two small elevators were always full to capacity, so on Ellie's advice, I took the stairs. If I met male traffic coming the other way, I crossed my arms across my chest or turned toward the wall to avoid inappropriate touching.

For the first few days, I sat by myself, reviewing the stack of laws that governed credit (Bangladesh had been part of India at the time of the Raj and inherited a legal framework enacted by the British.) (Consequently, some of the laws were over a hundred years old and failed to capture the modern approach to finance. To bring the legal framework up-to-date, as many as a dozen laws would need to be revised. It would be a tremendous amount of work)

(My project shared the office space with a team working to establish an Anti-Corruption Commission. Mark, the team leader, introduced himself and offered to escort me across the street to see the indoor market. But as part of the deal, he made me promise that I would never visit the market by myself. He was adamant about this—it was for my own safety.

In stark contrast to the heat and dust of the street, the market was cool, calm, organized, and relatively dust-free. The majority of stalls sold colorful spices from Southeast Asia: huge sacks of cumin, cinnamon, and cardamom. Mounds of garlic, ginger, dried chilis, and peppers were also on display. I felt an incredible urge to dig my hands into those large bags and watch the vibrant particles sieve through my fingers.

I'd seen photos of markets like these in glossy coffee-table books, but being there in person, enveloped by the intense aromas, and listening to the eager vendors, made it a scintillating experience.

I took a step back and bumped into a group of people I didn't realize were behind me. Mark gave me a gentle nudge with his elbow.

"This is why you can't risk going to the spice market alone. As a Western woman in Bangladesh, you'll always draw a crowd, and crowds in Bangladesh are unpredictable."

I Wanted to Stay

By the end of the third week, the project was in disarray. Raoul, the ADB project manager in Manila, had accepted a high-profile evaluation assignment in Afghanistan. He would not have the time to provide guidance to my project. Nigel had resigned as team leader—without telling me—and was already heading up another project. And if that weren't enough, the other technical advisor notified our mutual firm that she would not be returning to Bangladesh.

If I'd been more experienced, I might have sized up the situation and taken the next plane out of Dhaka, but I wanted to stay. I initially took the job in hopes of meeting up with Roberto, but now it was more than that. The work was interesting and might possibly help

Bangladesh achieve its economic goals. But more than that, Dhaka was exotic. The colorfully painted trucks and rickshaws, the women and girls in saris, the unusual food, and the gritty, traffic-filled streets entranced me, and I wanted to experience more of it.

The Hartal

The first week in May, one of the two major political parties announced a four-day hartal, an enforced strike that involved the shutdown of shops and other workplaces. Mahatma Gandhi popularized hartals in India in the 1920s and 1930s as nonviolent protests against the British. But in Bangladesh, they were used to protest a wide range of issues and could quickly turn violent.

As a Westerner, I was cautioned to avoid all demonstrations or political gatherings and was urged to spend the entire four-day hartal in the safety of my guesthouse. I had a lot of reading and drafting to do but still made a last-minute visit to one of Dhaka's large video stores to stock up on illegal DVDs.

Dhaka was awash in bootlegged movies. Illegal copies of new releases were widely available with nicely replicated cover art. Many had been surreptitiously filmed in a movie theater, and it was not usual to see the silhouette of a patron making a visit to the toilet or snack bar appear on the screen. That was all part of the experience.

I made my selection—a few classic Bollywood movies recommended by Ellie—and over the weekend became a Bollywood fan. I learned the names and histories of Bachchan, SRK, and the other Bollywood stars. I quickly took sides in the various ongoing feuds between actors.

When I went downstairs for lunch, the staff who must have overheard the distinctive music coming from my room, asked me if I had a favorite movie and chatted about the plots, which were basically all the same—boy meets girl, boy can't have girl, boy gets girl. But it was nice to make a connection with the guesthouse staff, and for the rest of my stay, we exchanged bits of gossip about our Bollywood favorites.

Stakeholder Meetings

(Once I'd finished reading the pertinent laws and regulations and could speak with some authority on Bangladesh's legal framework governing credit, Ellie and I were ready to meet with the business community. We needed to introduce the modern credit concepts and gauge the appetite for reform. Ellie helped me prepare a list of stakeholders and set an aggressive schedule of meetings that included bankers, lenders, lawyers, politicians, advocates, and representatives of other donor projects.

Usually, Ellie and I traveled to meetings together—she had a private car and driver—but occasionally I'd go on my own. The guesthouse was good at finding a reliable taxi driver who didn't mind transporting a Western woman, which was an issue for the more conservative Islamic drivers. While I felt perfectly comfortable waiting outside to be picked up, the guesthouse manager insisted I wait in the lounge.

"It's for your own protection," he'd say. I appreciated his kindness.

A particularly chatty driver, with an Islamic black-and-gold tasseled medallion hanging from the rearview mirror, asked me where I was from, what I was doing in Bangladesh, and how long I was staying in his country. I gave a brief overview of the project, its purpose, and how it would help small businesses.)

He moved on to more personal questions and asked if I was married and had children. I made the mistake of telling the truth: no husband, no children. He let out a howl, banged his hand on the steering wheel, and yelled, "Allah, why me?" Apparently, as a single woman without children, I was bad luck.

Of course, Ellie knew how to handle the situation.

"You should always claim to be a widow with a son," she explained in her lilting English. "But if you prefer to say you are married, you must be prepared to explain why your husband is not with you. It's best if you say that he's out of town or that you'll be meeting him later. They will feel more comfortable if you can assure them that you are attached to a man." I had complete faith in Ellie, but as a Western woman, this was extremely hard to take.

Economic Lab Rats

In the meetings, Ellie and I made a good team—East meets West. She would introduce the project, and I'd explain the technical aspects of the reform (While most of the meetings were routine, the one with the bankers' association stood out for a number of reasons.)

First off, we were late. Despite allowing considerable time for the traffic and parking, we were held up and then had trouble finding the right offices in the building's back annex. I'm not saying I ran, but I definitely walked at a brisk pace. Ellie trailed behind.

"Are you all right?" I asked when I was really saying, "Will you hurry up?"

"Jamie, I cannot run in a sari," she said, puffing a little more than the exertion warranted. "A sari is like origami in fabric. It holds its shape only because of some expertly executed pleats and fabric tucks. Sometimes I cheat by using a safety pin, but it can quickly unravel with too much movement. I do not run."

("You never run?" I asked with genuine interest.)

"No, I never run," she responded with just a hint of indignation. I apologized and slowed down, and we walked the rest of the way to the meeting.

I blamed our late arrival on the heavy traffic, an excuse that was readily accepted. Ellie took the lead and introduced the project, explaining that it was part of a bigger effort to improve the country's business and credit environments to create sustainable jobs and alleviate poverty.

Before I could start my overview, a young compliance officer interrupted with questions about other countries and their respective experiences with the reform. I explained that some version of the law was in effect in all of the fifty US states, in Canada, and more recently, Australia. In the US alone, an estimated \$350 billion worth of credit had been extended under this system.

"Ah, but those are Western countries," he noted. "Are you sure this system will work in Bangladesh? Or are we just your economic lab rats?"

I had to take a moment and think. While there was no apparent reason that the system wouldn't work in Bangladesh, I couldn't say with certainty that it would. No one could. But I pressed on with the explanation of how it would likely improve the credit environment.

Big Cats

As I grew more comfortable with life in Dhaka, I decided I could safely take a CNG vehicle from the project office back to the guesthouse. While CNGs looked like a whole lot of fun, I knew I had to be careful.

The passenger seat was made out of metal, but the sides of the CNG were translucent vinyl, which could be rolled down during inclement weather. The absence of real windows or doors makes the passenger an easy prey for the opportunistic robber, so it's best to stow personal effects on the ledge behind the seat. You are also easily targeted by the wide variety of impoverished groups—beggars, destitute mothers, etc.—who plead for handouts.

At the first stoplight, a decrepit man with severe skin problems approached me. His nose was badly disfigured, half of it seemed to be missing, and he had large lumps on his face and earlobes. His shirt collar was open, and I could see discolored patches of skin on his chest. He raised his hand for change, and it was stubby and claw-like. The driver barked at him, and the man moved to the next cab.

"He has leprosy," the driver explained. "You should not give him money because the government has facilities to help people in his condition." I shrugged, not knowing how best to respond.

Back at the guesthouse, I phoned home, and my dad answered. I told him about my encounter with the leper who approached me in the CNG.

"Really, in the city of Dhaka?" he sounded surprised.

"Yes. Just roaming around the street," I confirmed. "He seemed nice enough, but the driver shooed him away."

"But I thought they were extinct in that part of the world," he added.

His comment confused me and I asked, "Dad, what are you talking about?"

"Leopards. Big cats. What are you talking about?"

"Lepers. People with terrible skin disease." And despite his advancing dementia, we enjoyed a good long laugh over the misunderstanding.

Women's Advocacy Group

The project report was finally starting to come together. I'd summarized all the existing laws that would be affected by the reform and how they needed to be amended. I also had enough information to write up the section on stakeholder support. There was, however, a piece that I had been putting off—gender.

Gender focuses on how laws, power structures, and social norms treat men and women differently. Failure to consider gender in a reform analysis runs the risk of missing an opportunity to improve the lives of women or worse, putting them at a new disadvantage. The development agencies profess to prioritize gender as a crosscutting issue, but in 2004 it always seemed to take a back seat to the broader area of economic development.

Ellie was a strong proponent for gender equality in Bangladesh and was able to get me an invitation to a daylong conference hosted by a women's advocacy group. The agenda was long and diverse, covering various issues that affected the lives of Bangladeshi women and girls: equality under the law, violence against women, education, and access to credit.

The first speaker, Aahana, wore a bright floral sari and talked about the unequal protection women receive under Bangladesh's legal framework. The constitution ensured equal rights for all citizens but included a carve-out for certain "personal matters." Consequently, Islamic law and custom, which consistently favored the rights of men over women, governed key life events such as inheritance, marriage, and divorce.

As an example of this inequality, Aahana noted it was legal in Bangladesh for a husband to commit his wife to an insane asylum for asking for a divorce. Some of those women were trapped in those places for years due to a lack of legal recourse.

The next speaker, a young woman wearing Western-style clothes, raised concerns over the working conditions of women in the garment industry. This led to a lively discussion on the importance of these working women and the empowerment of all women in Bangladesh. But one woman questioned whether the women working in factories were paying too high a price for their financial independence.

"It will only be a matter of time," she said, "before one of these poorly maintained factories is gutted by a fire or other calamity, and it will be our women and girls who die. That is not progress for women." Everyone agreed that more had to be done to protect the women who worked in the factories.

The last item on the agenda was access to credit and the work of

Muhammad Yunus, who pioneered microcredit and microfinance. In the 1970s, Yunus began giving small loans to women in rural areas to buy seeds, chickens, and other income-generating items. It was an innovative way of giving women financial independence, and it also brought unexpected social consequences. The ability to contribute financially to the family gave women a voice in the household, which was previously unimaginable in conservative Bangladesh. Further, children were eating better, and more girls were going to school.

A few things struck me about the conference. These women were organized. They were fully aware of the wide range of challenges facing the women and girls of Bangladesh and collectively saw themselves as catalysts for change. They appreciated that the situation of the women in the factories, the future of Bangladesh, could be leveraged to improve the conditions for all women. And most importantly, they were fully committed to taking action. I'd have to find a way to reflect all this in the report.

The Final Presentation

Under the consulting contract, Ellie and I were required to make a formal presentation to stakeholders, an all-day affair that required a detailed PowerPoint presentation explaining the project, the proposed reforms, the technical aspects, and the need for training and public outreach. We also had to include so-called "success stories" from other countries to demonstrate the real-life benefits of the reforms.

I prepared a fifty-page PowerPoint that Ellie reviewed. In addition to clarifying a number of points, she changed the color scheme from my go-to red, white, and blue to the more appropriate green and red, reflecting the colors of the Bangladeshi flag.

On the day of the presentation, Ellie arrived in a glorious, vibrant sari, and I stood next to her in my less glamorous uniform:

an ankle-length skirt, T-shirt, and long-sleeved cotton cardigan. We tag-teamed the presentation; Ellie would speak, and I'd add detail, and she'd do the same for me. We were delighted that participants asked questions and wanted copies of the presentation.

In the afternoon, a television crew arrived to film the event. That evening our presentation took up a short segment on the news, and Ellie and I became mini-celebrities. The clerks at the video store recognized me, as did the guesthouse staff. The woman at the pharmacy yelled to her husband, "Abhoy, this woman here with the bad case of diarrhea? She was on the news last week. Remember?"

The next week Ellie and I met to discuss the final report, which needed to include an assessment of the level of stakeholder support. Looking through our notes, it was clear that the private sector fully supported the reform. But there was a rumor that not everyone was on board. Certain members of parliament were opposed to the reform because they believed, erroneously, that the new regime would publicize their past defaults on personal loans.

And since a key component of the reform was a new law, the lack of parliamentary support meant there could be no reform. In her calm, comforting way, Ellie said, "We will have to be satisfied with planting seeds. Hopefully, things will be different in the future."

The River Cruise

At the end of May, just a couple of weeks before I was scheduled to leave Dhaka, I received an email from a travel agency regarding an overnight river cruise. It was the inaugural voyage of a recently refurbished passenger boat, and according to the email, I would see the "vibrancy of Bangladesh's rivers, floating markets, experience life in a typical village and eat an authentic Bangla meal." It sounded great.

On the morning of the tour, two affable young men picked me

up at the guesthouse in a large white van. They recognized me from my television appearance and immediately asked if I was married. Following Ellie's advice, I said, "I'm a widow with a son." They smiled and nodded approvingly.

I was joining a group of twenty French tourists who were finishing a tour of South Asian countries. Bangladesh was their last stop before flying back to Paris. They were already on board the riverboat when I arrived at the dock, preparing for the long trip by rubbing each other down with La Roche-Posay sunscreen. The older of the two guides went below deck and started the engine, and a thick cloud of black exhaust enveloped the passengers.

The weather was perfect—not too hot—and once we were underway, a cool breeze fanned us. We waved at passengers on nearby multi-level ferries, and they took our photo in return. After crossing a confluence of waterways, we puttered close to the shore, and we were granted a peek into the life of Bangladesh's less-fortunate. Laborers carried stacks of bricks, sometimes five and six high, on their heads. Women thrashed clothes on rocks. Young boys, with perfect smiles, bobbed joyfully in the water with the aid of buoyant aluminum pots.

As we traveled away from Dhaka, Bangladesh's famous natural beauty became more apparent. We passed mangrove-covered beaches, flocks of birds in flight, and on a couple of occasions, Bangladesh's picturesque floating markets selling a variety of fish, fruit, and handicrafts. The French tourists took hundreds of photos of the smiling vendors.

After six hours on the water we docked at the small, nameless village where we would spend the night. Because of the time-consuming photo taking at the floating market, we arrived late, and it was getting dark. The tour guides were anxious to get us to our accommodations, which required us to walk through the village.

The arrival of a group of Western tourists was an event, and the entire village turned out and crowded both sides of the narrow pathway, forcing us to walk two-by-two in a long column. I was one of the last passengers off the boat, so I brought up the rear. Everyone was tired from the heat and the long journey, so we trudged along in silence.

Someone from the village called out, "Where are you from?"

I heard a strong, heavily accented male voice respond, "We are French." And then a woman quickly added, "But we have one American."

There was immediate movement on both sides of the path. I could hear the young men from the village as they worked their way down the line of tourists asking the question over and over, "Are you the American? Are you?" They were definitely coming for me.

Then I heard another accented voice. "She is in the back."

What were they thinking?

The two young tour guides realized what was happening and dropped back to flank me, but I doubted how much they could do. They were soft city kids, no match for the powerfully built men from the village.

I had thought that by taking a tour I'd be safe, so I hadn't taken any of the recommended precautions. I hadn't bothered to register with the US Embassy in Dhaka. I hadn't told anyone, not even the guest-house, where I was going—and to be honest, I had no idea where I was. All I knew was that I was a six-hour boat ride away from Dhaka, in a rural village with no cell reception. We were on a finger of land surrounded by water, so there was nowhere to run. I was terrified by how things might play out.

When the young villagers reached the rear of the line, they pushed the guides aside and grabbed hold of me by my shirt and backpack. I felt a sting on the side of my neck—a scratch from one of the men's long nails. My heart hammered in my chest, and my right leg shook.

Oblivious to it all, the French tourists walked on, leaving me and the tour guides behind, surrounded by the growing mob.

I needed a miracle—some amazing quirk of fate to get me out of this awful situation.

Then a lone male voice came out of the fading light, "Where did you go to school?"

Everyone froze.

The mob surrounding me parted slightly to give me a view of a village man, probably in his mid-thirties, sitting in a low beach chair next to the path. He wore shorts, a baseball cap, and a T-shirt that didn't quite cover his large belly. He looked at me, and then at different people in the crowd, then back at me. It took me some time to find my voice.

"Berkeley," I was able to choke out. "I went to Berkeley in California." All heads swiveled toward me and then back to the man in the chair. It was as if the entire village was watching a very slow tennis match.

He nodded.

"I spent a couple of semesters in the agricultural program at Nebraska." Again, all heads turned toward me as if waiting for a response and then back to the man in the chair. "Those people were really good to me—made me feel welcome."

Then after what seemed like an extremely long time, he said, "Leave her alone."

To my complete surprise and relief, they did. The two thugs released their grip on my backpack and gave me a gratuitous shove that caused me to stumble forward. I drew a long, shaky breath and readjusted my shirt, which had been stretched out of shape. The tour guides scrambled to their feet, stood on either side of me and escorted me over a small bridge to the sleeping accommodation.

"What happened back there? Why did they grab me?" I asked the guides, still shaking.

"Bangladesh has always been a tolerant country," the older one answered. "But with the recent invasions of Afghanistan and Iraq, some people have become very angry. We are so very sorry."

Rooms were quickly assigned, and I was given a suite on the top floor. As an extra security precaution, I was locked in my room until dinnertime.

I remember the authentic Bangla meal being a disappointment— just a few bowls of rice, fish curry, and lentils. One of the French men came to my end of the table. "You almost caused us a lot of trouble today." If he was flirting with me, he was going about it the wrong way.

"Oh, no." I tried not to show my anger. "You almost caused *me* a lot of trouble today."

He sniffed and returned to the rest of the group. When the meal was over, I was escorted back to my room and locked in for the rest of the night.

After breakfast, the French group toured the central market and spent the rest of the time buying locally made handicrafts. I was secreted back to the boat, where I waited with a large man who had been paid to protect me.

I couldn't help but think back to all the gentle warnings I'd received over the past several weeks. Nigel, the team leader, had cautioned me to always be aware of my surroundings. Mark, the anti-corruption advisor, had warned that as a Western woman in Bangladesh, I would always draw a crowd. And the guesthouse manager had insisted that I wait for the taxi in the lobby rather than on the street. Despite all this, I never thought anything would happen to me.

I kept to myself on the trip back to Dhaka. The ride gave me time to revisit the events of the previous day. But for the kindness of someone in Lincoln or Omaha who'd hosted the agricultural exchange student from Bangladesh who defused a difficult situation, my day might have turned out much differently.

Roberto's Suspension

The guides drove me back to the guesthouse where I phoned Roberto, still furious about the obliviousness of the French tourists. But just as I was getting to the good part, he cut me off.

"I've been suspended from my job," he blurted.

"What?" I was a little annoyed that he wouldn't let me finish my harrowing story.

"I accidentally insulted the wife of an important Afghan partner, and I've been suspended," he continued. "The thing is, I wasn't trying to insult the wife. I was insulting the partner."

As Roberto explained it, despite repeated instruction, the Afghan partner was unable to assemble a HESCO basket, a particular type of security wall made out of mesh and rock. Frustrated, Roberto said, "Bring your wife next time. I bet she could figure it out." Afghanistan is a culture that prizes female virtue, and it's extremely risky to make any kind of comment about a man's wife. It was Roberto's second project in Afghanistan. He should have known better. "If I had said, 'Bring your cat next time,'" he complained, "it wouldn't have been a problem."

"So does that mean you'll be able to meet me in New Delhi?" I asked, trying not to sound too excited.

"That's what I'm trying to tell you. Tomorrow morning I'm going to the Indian Embassy to apply for my visa. I can be in New Delhi by Friday."

No Bodies on the Street

The next day, I attended my last meeting in Dhaka. It was with a Bangladeshi executive of a well-known accounting firm with offices in all the world's major cities. The firm provided services to a wide range of businesses, many of which would benefit from the proposed reform, so I was interested in hearing what he had to say.

The accountant, a large man with Coke-bottle glasses that magnified his eyes, greeted me enthusiastically. Stylishly dressed in dark windowpane-patterned trousers, a light blue dress shirt, and a pair of suspenders richly embroidered with the logo of the New York Mets, he could have easily walked out of a Manhattan office building.

He spent a good ten minutes extolling the virtues of Bangladesh and its unlimited potential. He spoke about the country's perfect location on the Ganges-Brahmaputra Delta, the world's longest uninterrupted beach at Cox's Bazaar, and the increases in personal income across the board.

He was relaxed and friendly, and I thought he would be open to answering a difficult question that had nagged me since I first arrived.

"Sir, let me ask a question," I started. "Before coming to Dhaka, I read several reports on Bangladesh, and the numbers were a bit dismal. But over the past few weeks, I've spoken with taxi drivers, business people, lawyers, and women's advocates, and everyone is so optimistic about Bangladesh's future. How do you...?"

"Remain so positive?" He asked my question for me.

He stood up and beckoned me to the window. "Look out there. What do you see?" I saw a block of ugly concrete structures built without regard to safety codes, the usual snarl of traffic, street vendors, beggars, dirt and pollution, and plenty of stray dogs.

"Since 1991, when democracy was reestablished in our country, we have come a very long way. People have food to eat, and almost everyone has something to wear. I can't remember the last time I saw a dead body on the street. Every country has problems, but we are steadily solving ours. Regardless of what the statistics say, Bangladesh is moving forward."

I went back to the guesthouse and pulled up the most recent reports on Bangladesh on the internet. The important financial, trade, and social numbers were, in fact, inching in the right direction, albeit at a very slow rate.) Granted, a lack of dead bodies on the street is a low bar. But the private sector was optimistic, and the women understood their power in improving their situation. Bangladesh was on the threshold of something exciting. I, too, had been converted and rewrote the final report to be more positive

As I boarded the plane to New Delhi, I thought how one day I'd like to return to Bangladesh to see if the progress continued. But if there's an open seat on an overnight river cruise with a group of French tourists, you can count me out.

CHAPTER 4

Moscow, The Russian Federation

2004

Asia Is in Russia

"No lunch for you today?" Sergei, the Russian team lead, peered around the bulky computer monitor but continued typing.

"You can freeze wolves out there," I responded theatrically. I used colorful Russian sayings whenever possible. Sergei chuckled appreciatively.

It was the second week of December 2004, and the days in Moscow were short, less than seven hours long, and cold—really cold. The temperature hovered in the low teens, and I'd already learned a painful lesson about the icy pavements. I was still tender and bruised from a tumble down a flight of Metro stairs earlier in the week.

"The potato ladies will be missing you," he added with a bit of a smirk. The potato ladies operated a lunch cart down the street from the office and offered a fairly diverse menu. But with my nonexistent Russian, I settled for a baked potato every day. I'd point to the crude drawing on the menu, and they'd slide a steaming foil-encased potato across the counter. The price varied wildly depending on which lady was working, something I found extremely irritating.

Instead of braving the cold, I stayed at my desk and worked on a printout of the *New York Times* crossword puzzle. Ten down, six letters,

"Asian Capital" was giving me trouble. I noted the options: Manama (Bahrain), Astana (Kazakhstan), Taipei (Taiwan), and possibly Moscow.

I wasn't sure whether Moscow belonged on the list. Although more than seventy-seven percent of the Russian territory is located in Asia, most of Russia's population lives on the European continent. Which begged the question—was Moscow an Asian capital or a European one?

I hesitated to ask Sergei. We had been through a lot over the last five months, honest mistakes on both sides, but we had managed to work through them. With only two weeks left on the project, we were on the home stretch. I thought we had something close to a friendship, but I'd never admit that to Sergei. It might be construed as a weakness. But I decided to risk it.

"Sergei, is Russia in Asia?" I held up the crossword puzzle so he'd understand why I was asking.

He stood up, placed his hands on his hips, and thought for a moment. Then I saw the gleam in his eye.

"No, Jamie, Russia is not in Asia." He was trying to hold back a smile. "Asia is in Russia."

Visiting the Home Office

After leaving Dhaka, I met up with Roberto in New Delhi. We spent two weeks touring the "Golden Triangle" of India's famous tourist sights—Delhi, Agra, and Jaipur. The guidebook promised that the spirituality of India would "transform" me, but disappointingly, I returned to California pretty much the same person. Roberto flew back to Kabul. His suspension was over, and he went back to work.

Back in San Jose, I learned that I wouldn't get paid for my four months in Bangladesh. The Australian firm that had hired me declared bankruptcy, and the Asian Development Bank wasn't inclined to make good on my request for payment. But it wasn't a complete disaster. My

paid consultant

How funded these development World Bank

time in Dhaka had given me the secured transactions experience I wanted on my resume. In less than a month, a Maryland-based firm hired me for a project in Moscow funded by the World Bank. I would serve six months as the team leader and manage a small crew made up of international and local consultants.

I hesitated when I saw the "team lead" title on my contract because I had never overseen a project before. I mentioned my lack of management experience to the young woman in Maryland, and she responded, "You can write reports and get them delivered on time, can't you?"

On paper, the project requirements were fairly straightforward. As the team leader, I was responsible for liaising with two Russian ministries and overseeing the work of several technical advisors. The deliverables included a draft law on secured transactions similar to what I worked on in Bangladesh, as well as a registry report, a training and public outreach plan, and two separate study tours (for Russian officials) to countries with modern secured transaction systems. Biweekly updates on our activities and findings had to be filed with two relevant ministries in both English and Russian. It all seemed manageable enough.

So I was somewhat surprised when my firm took the unusual—and rather expensive—step of flying me to Maryland for a two-day pre-deployment meeting. I spent the first morning meeting the home office staff, filling out tax forms, and learning the firm's administrative policies and procedures. The remaining time—a full day and a half—was spent reviewing the minutiae of the project contract.

The time in DC was all about making sure my firm got paid. There were industry rumors that the Russian ministries, admittedly new to the development scene, were using flimsy and sometimes manufactured excuses to avoid paying consulting fees. A New York firm had been stiffed for using the wrong font size for its project reports. A firm in DC received only partial payment for a report that was two days late. It

(Russians not only pay consultant fee)

development scene

was my responsibility, I was told, to not only meet but whenever possible exceed each contract provision, no matter how small or seemingly insignificant. Still, there were a lot of unknowns and ways for the project to go sideways.

The biggest unknown was our local implementer, the Russian Regional Press Group, or RRP for short, a high-profile media company with purported connections to the Kremlin. They would be providing transportation, translation, and other logistical support. Technically they were our partner, but I was quietly advised to treat them with caution and assume that their loyalties lay elsewhere.

While those days in Maryland assured me that I had a strong, supportive home office team, I wanted to speak with someone who had first-hand knowledge of Russia. I called a colleague who had worked in Moscow in the early 1990s during the big push to privatize state-owned assets. I met him for a drink at the Old Ebbitt Grill across from the US Treasury in Washington, DC, and asked him about working with the Russians. I got much more than I expected.

"They're Russians, Jamie. They will lie and lie—even when they have no reason to lie, they will lie. It's their culture. They are master manipulators. Remember what Ronald Reagan said about the Russians, 'Trust but verify'? Don't waste your time on trusting. Go straight to verification."

Armed with that advice, I boarded a plane to Moscow.

History of Russia

I flew British Airways out of Dulles and transited through London so I'd arrive in Moscow on August 1st, the contract start date. I was bumped up to business class on the London to Moscow flight and enjoyed the luxury of a small glass of champagne while I watched the economy passengers make their way toward the back of the plane.

It may have been the champagne, but I wasn't suffering from the anxiety I usually felt when starting a project. Despite the harsh words about Russians by my colleague at the Old Ebbitt, I felt unusually prepared for the job. This was my second visit to Moscow, and I'd learned a lot from the Professor Nights on the cruise. Plus, I'd read the Hitler/Stalin book in Ukraine—all 1,152 pages. So I had a fairly good grasp of recent Russian history.

The last passenger to board was a rather scruffy forty-something wearing black-rimmed glasses and a corduroy sports coat. He plopped down beside me, jammed a computer case under his seat, and introduced himself. Igor, a lecturer at a London university on Soviet and Communist Studies, was traveling to Moscow to conduct research for a book he was writing.

He eyed me up and down and said, "Let me guess. You're a geologist going to Moscow on behalf of a large oil company."

"Nope," I returned. "I'm a lawyer working on a credit reform project." The sides of his mouth curled down slightly as if to say, "just as bad."

After takeoff, Igor leaned on the armrest and said, "The secret to getting things done in Moscow is to know the history and, more importantly, to think like a Russian. So how are you on the history?"

"Pretty good, I think." I was trying to be modest.

"Okay. Tell me what you know. Just the highlights."

"Let's see, there was the three hundred years of Romanov rule, which ended in 1917 with the Russian Revolution. The Bolsheviks, led by Vladimir Lenin, seized power and eventually established the Communist Party and the Soviet Union. After Lenin's death, Stalin came to power." I paused briefly. Igor was sipping champagne and motioned for me to continue.

"World War II, known as the Great Patriotic War in Russia, took a terrible toll on the country. After World War II the USSR emerged as a superpower and entered the Cold War with the United

States) Then came Sputnik, the Bay of Pigs." I was rushing. ("Then in 1986, Perestroika–Glasnost served as roadmaps to economic and political reform. (In 1991, the USSR collapsed and now it's the Russian Federation." Okay, I might have been showing off a bit.)

"Close enough," he responded. "But can you think like a Russian?"

This was uncharted territory for me, so I gave him my "I have no idea" grimace.

"Let's play 'good guy, bad guy.' It's a game I play with my students in London. You give me the names of two Russian leaders, and we'll discuss whether he was a good guy or a bad guy for the country. Go ahead, give me two names."

"Joseph Stalin and Mikhail Gorbachev," I said.

"Disappointingly obvious," he responded. "Okay. Joseph Stalin. In your opinion, was he a good guy or a bad guy for Russia?" He was leaning into me. I could smell stale tobacco on his breath.

"Bad guy. Definitely a bad guy," I said emphatically. (Stalin terrorized his own people for thirty years, causing the death and suffering of millions.")

"Bzzt." He made the sound of a buzzer, indicating the wrong answer. ("The purges, labor camps, and the Gulag were bad for sure, but Stalin was in charge during World War II. You cannot discount the national pride attached to the Soviet victory over Nazi Germany.)

"And that makes him a good guy?" I asked incredulously.

"Portraits of Stalin are reappearing across Russia," he added. "Now, what about Gorbachev? Good guy or bad guy?"

I was more cautious with my response. "Gorbachev was a good guy?" I answered tentatively. "He instituted the Perestroika–Glasnost initiatives, which, as I said before, were roadmaps for restructuring the Soviet political and economic system)—"

"Bzzt." He didn't let me finish. ("Initiatives that backfired spectacularly and led to the collapse of the Soviet Union.) He is known as the man who single-handedly lost an empire. Gorbachev is no hero to the Russian people.")

I plumped up a miniature pillow, tucked it in the crook of my neck, but I didn't get any sleep. Using examples of my own choosing, Igor made me question my preparedness for working in Moscow. That familiar anxiety returned—once again, I realized that I didn't know what I was getting myself into.

My First Week

(My hotel was located about a mile from the Kremlin—close to the action but not too expensive—a favorite of short-term consultants. I arrived too late in the evening for the restaurant service, so I went to the small bar area for dinner. The bar was full of geologists and energy experts, all talking over each other about hydrocarbon exploration and potential finds.)

A blond American couple, long-limbed and athletic-looking even in middle age, sat at a corner table with a toddler. The child had a slightly Asian appearance and was dressed in about five-hundred-dollars worth of Ralph Lauren children's wear—a long-sleeved Polo shirt, a pair of shiny brown corduroys, and a tiny puffy vest. I thought it was a bit late for a child so young, but he sat quietly on the woman's lap, hunched slightly forward, wholly engrossed in the man who was reading *Goodnight Moon* in a soft, soothing voice.

That first week on the job was relatively uneventful. RRP's black SUV ferried me back and forth from my hotel to their gleaming offices outside town. The driver claimed to speak "little English," something my friend in DC warned me about. An elite operation such as RRP would never put me in a vehicle with a driver who couldn't listen in on my phone conversations. Not a chance. In fact, he fully understood when I politely asked him to turn down the techno-pop blaring from the radio.

The RRP employees on the project—Vlad, Alex, Sergei, and Dimitry—were the best and brightest of that first generation to come of age after the unraveling of the Soviet Union, almost fifteen years earlier. They were young and well educated, with strong English skills, and exceptionally careful in their dealings with me. At first, I worked in a common room full of employees who spoke in Russian on the phone while updating spreadsheets. But a few days in, I was moved to a separate room, and for the next six months, I sat across the table from Sergei, who kept a close eye on me.

I was assigned a translator named Sophia, a young woman in her early twenties, with a rash of dark freckles across her nose. Her English skills were good, but she needed coaching on the difficult terms and definitions that were specific to the secured transactions law. We worked through the concepts and then a long list of legal terms, and just when I felt she was getting the nuances of the law, she advised me that she was leaving RRP for a better-paying job. I would have to go through the same exercise the following week with her replacement.

I took Sophia out to lunch on her last day of work and asked the usual questions about her family, education, and plans for the future.

"I'm engaged," she said glowingly. "My fiancé is a very clever man. If the police stop us, he knows how much to bribe them. It's a very useful skill here in this country."

Roberto's Arrival

Roberto flew from Kabul to Moscow at the end of my first week. I had mixed feelings about his arrival and his plan to stay with me in Moscow. My per diem wasn't much, so if we wanted to stay near the center of town, we had to share a very small hotel room. But any reservations I had about Roberto joining me in Moscow disappeared when I saw him walk through immigration at Sheremetyevo airport. He looked different—stronger, more confident.

We went back to the hotel, and I lay invitingly on the bed. Roberto lay down next to me, put his arms around my waist, leaned in close, and whispered, "Can we go see Red Square?"

His suggestion snapped me out of my reunion bliss, but I completely understood. I'd visited Red Square back in 2003 as a tourist with my parents, and it is an amazing sight. For one thing, it's huge. At 800,000 square feet, Red Square is equivalent in size to fourteen American football fields. For another, it stands at the very heart of Moscow. To the west is the Kremlin, the official residence of the president of Russia. To the south lies St. Basil's Cathedral and its colorful domes.

I first saw Red Square as a kid when one of Russia's annual Victory Parades, the Soviet Union's annual commemoration of the capitulation of Nazi Germany in 1945, was televised. As the procession of countless troops, tanks, and missiles streamed by on our black-and-white TV, I must have looked concerned because my dad nudged me with his elbow and said, "Don't worry, kid. It's all show."

Roberto stood in the middle of Red Square in awe. "It's not just big," he said. "It's strangely powerful." My mother was similarly affected by Red Square. When we visited just a couple of years before, I remember her slowly turning around, saying, "I can't believe I'm in Russia. I just cannot believe it." Thinking back, I had a premonition that I'd be returning to Moscow. I just didn't know it would be so soon.

The Babies

At breakfast the following day, a different American couple sat with a blond-haired toddler at a table near the buffet. Roberto stopped to chat with them for quite a long time, then sat down across from me with a heaping plate of eggs and undercooked bacon.

"That's probably the fifth youngster I've seen this week," I said. "Is he being brought in to meet his grandparents?"

"They are not bringing him in. They're taking him out," Roberto whispered. "That couple has been trying to adopt that kid for the last two years, and they finally received legal authorization to take him to the United States. According to the parents, there are an estimated 600,000 orphans in Russia, and about 7,000 are adopted every year by American couples. So he's a pretty lucky kid."

Over the ensuing months, Roberto and I followed the rotation of American couples enrolled in the Russian adoption process. The little adoptees came in every shape and size, reflecting the vastness of Russia itself. We cooed over children with blond hair and blue eyes, probably from the Finnish-Baltic region in the north, children with darker Eastern Eurasian features from the south, and every combination of DNA in between.

Roberto congratulated each set of parents and found something special to say about their child, even the ones with noticeable divots in their heads and those who drooled nonstop. He'd comment on the child's bright eyes or heartbreaker smile. It was a tender part of Roberto that I hadn't seen before.

Commuting by Metro

Roberto convinced me that we'd have much more freedom to explore Moscow if I passed on the rides in the RRP vehicle and took the Metro to work. Once we mastered the Cyrillic alphabet and could recognize the names of the stations, the system was easy to use. Much is made of the design and opulence of the Moscow Metro stations—the marble walls, sparkling chandeliers, Art Deco murals, and colorful mosaics—but the true beauty of the Metro system is its operational efficiency.

About seven million passengers use the Metro every day, at a cost

of about fifteen cents a ride. During the busiest hours those exceptionally long trains—some just a few feet shorter than the height of the
Washington Monument—were in and out of the station in less than
a minute. A large red digital clock at one end of the platform confirmed it. Those passengers who failed to demonstrate sufficient alacrity
received a sharp verbal rebuke, and the occasional push, from one of the
uniformed Metro guards.

In addition to being quick and efficient, the Metro gave me
insights into Moscow that I would have missed behind the tinted windows of RRP's SUV. I wouldn't have witnessed the man who brought
his own chair, complaining loudly that he could never find a seat. I'd
have missed the inebriated teenagers on the Koltsevaya line (ring line)
who rode around and around for hours because they had no place to
go. And it was impossible to forget the elderly blond twins who dazzled
in matching coats of iridescent sealskin.

But it wasn't just humans. The Metro had canine passengers as
well. Almost daily I saw dogs wait patiently on a station platform, enter a
car, then ride a few stops before exiting. According to the hotel's concierge,
these dogs understood how to use the Metro and rode it into the city each
morning to scrounge for food. They'd take the same train back again in
the evening to the safety of the suburbs—just like any other commuter.

The Legal Advisor

The project legal advisor, Jay Baker, a plump Floridian with limited
patience, arrived in Moscow in late August. During my briefings in
Maryland I was warned about Jay. With the increased popularity in the
secured transactions field, Jay had turned into a bit of a prima donna,
complete with outsized demands and full-blown temper tantrums.
Someone suggested that I might be the person to straighten Jay out,
but behavioral therapy was not part of my contract.

133

As part of the project design team, Jay had awarded himself two large chunks of work. In addition to drafting the legislation, he was scheduled to return to Russia the following year for a long-term training and public outreach contract. This would involve several months of traveling across Russia educating the local officials and lenders on the secured transactions system. I encouraged him to keep a journal; it would be an amazing story.

He was fully aware that his work was critical to fulfilling the contract and getting our firm paid, and he used that as leverage to set his own schedule.

"Don't take it personally," he smirked, "but I won't be taking any direction from you." I mean, how could anyone take that personally? That said, his demand for independence wasn't completely unwelcome. I had enough on my plate. To keep up with the schedule and ensure final payment, I'd have a half-day between finishing one report and starting another.

With Jay in-country, I scheduled an introductory meeting with the project's various participants, including Jay, the RRP team, the local attorneys who would be working with Jay, and me. We spent a good amount of time discussing drafting sessions, delivery dates, and possible meetings with the private sector. Olga, a rail-thin female attorney who held her cigarette between her thumb and index finger, had some questions about the public registry of security interests, a key component of the secured transactions system.

In heavily-accented English, she said, "I am of the opinion that this public registry" (she paused to take a long draw on her cigarette) "may be problematic for the Russian Federation and the Russian people."

"Why do you think that?" This was Jay, already bored.

"The public registry of security interests, as I understand it, provides information about the borrower's assets. Yes, I am right?" She looked to both of us for confirmation. "Russia has very, very clever criminals. I fear our smart criminals will use this public registry to find assets worth stealing." The point had some merit.

Jay abruptly raised his hand, a sign that he would be fielding the question. "The US has had these registries for over fifty years." His face was unbearably smug. "If what you suggest were possible, our criminals would have figured out how to take advantage of the registry a long time ago. I hope you're not insinuating that Russian criminals are better than American criminals."

Everyone in the room, except Jay, shot furtive glances at each other. I think most people would agree that Russia has the best criminals in the world. It's not even close. Jay made us look naive and unprepared.

Mr. Nyet

Once Jay had a few days to settle, I scheduled a meeting with our counterparts at the Ministry of Finance and the Ministry of Commerce. Our delegation included Jay and me, a couple of RRP officials, and our new translator, Irina, a young woman who desperately wanted to make a good first impression.

After a delay at the entrance—the names on the approval sheet were in Russian (Cyrillic) and our passports were in English—a uniformed clerk led us down a high-ceilinged corridor to a large room that once must have been stunning. The walls were faded but showed hints of a rich blue with contrasting trim, embellished with a series of stylish cornices near the ceiling. The five of us took seats at the extraordinarily long, wooden table that could have easily accommodated twenty or more attendees.

When the representatives from the ministries arrived, we all stood up. There ensued an awkward few moments with everyone trying to shake everyone else's hand. Tatiana, my primary contact at the Ministry of Finance, introduced herself. Tall, slim, and stylishly dressed, she was a stand out. She could easily rub elbows with players at the world leader conferences in Davos and Aspen.

(The real decision-maker, however, was Tatiana's boss, a large man who bore an unfortunate likeness to Leonid Brezhnev, the Soviet politician who served as General Secretary of the Communist Party until his death in 1982) He had the same imposing physique, dark wavy hair, craggy lines defining his face, and wildly unkempt eyebrows. Tatiana took the lead and introduced each member of the Russian team. Each name was long and difficult for the Western ear. I didn't catch any of them but smiled and nodded while pretending to write them down.

The Russians opened with a twenty-minute welcome, and after translation, we were already thirty minutes into our one-hour meeting. I was later advised that this was the Russian way of keeping things short. In the interest of getting all the information we needed, I rushed through our introductions and gave a quick overview of the project. Before allowing an opportunity to respond, I moved on to the list of meetings we needed to draft the law and make other recommendations. I read them aloud, and after each suggestion, waited for translation and response.

"Workshops with the Bankers' Association." I looked up optimistically. Tatiana's boss waited for the translation and responded, "Nyet."

Irina translated his response. "Our illustrious colleague from the Ministry of Finance has just answered. He has said, 'No.'"

I continued down the list.

"Meetings with the retailers offering credit on consumer products." I looked across the table at our colleagues.

"Nyet."

Again, Irina translated. "Our illustrious colleague from the Ministry of Finance has just answered. He has said, 'No.'" I remained undaunted.

"Presentations to Ministry staff and other government agencies." I looked across the table for some support.

"Nyet."

Before Irina could start again, I leaned forward and held my hand up in her direction. Then, as politely as I could manage, I said, "Thanks, Irina. I don't think we need translation on this."

I continued down the list, and he shot down each suggestion with a firm "Nyet." And that's how he earned his nickname. After that, we just referred to him as "Mr. Nyet." It was much easier than using his real name.

The takeaway from that meeting was simple enough. The Russians would control the process. They wouldn't even take our word regarding what meetings we needed. It was possible that they were only testing the reform waters and were not actually ready to move forward.

The Great City of Moscow

Roberto and I took advantage of everything Moscow had to offer. He'd meet me after work and we'd walk along the Moscow River, drink beer in Pushkin Square, or find a restaurant where we could eat outside in the warm evenings.

We were out of the hotel early on the weekends, and if the weather was good, we'd find something to do outside. We'd ride the Metro out a few stops and take the long walk back to the city through a pristine wood of birch trees. We became regulars at the Park of Fallen Heroes, where we learned the names of the erstwhile Soviet leaders. We frequented the shops on Arbat Street, had favorite dancers in Gorky Park, and followed the map to the graves of Russia's dead politicians and celebrities in Novodevichy Cemetery.

Sometimes we'd just sit against the warm wall of the Kremlin and watch wedding parties come and go. Every weekend dozens of couples observed the old wedding traditions from the Soviet era, which included visiting Red Square and the Tomb of the Unknown Soldier just around the corner. While there was the occasional limousine, these wedding parties usually arrived in noisy, exhaust-spewing Ladas. After parking in the lot behind St. Basil's, they'd drink a bottle or two of cheap champagne and then set off on their Red Square pilgrimage.

When the weather turned, we'd be the first in line for the museums and other indoor attractions. We visited the Treasury and its collection of Fabergé eggs; the Diamond Fund to see the diamond-encrusted jewelry and crowns worn by members of the royal family; and the Pushkin State Museum of Fine Art to see rare paintings by famous artists. If the opportunity presented itself, we'd slip in with the large tour groups and listen to the English-speaking guides talk about Moscow and the history of Russia.

A couple of times we waited in line to see Lenin's mummified body on display in the sleek marble mausoleum just outside the Kremlin wall. Lenin's body is kept in a pristine state, under precise temperature and lighting conditions in a glass sarcophagus. Guards take their roles very seriously and are quick to rebuke visitors who chat or put their hands in their pockets.

Cold War Memories

On our long walks, Roberto asked me questions about growing up during the Cold War. Having been raised in Buenos Aires, he had no sense of how it had affected our day-to-day lives. I explained the "duck and cover" drills in school, where we'd practiced hiding under our school desks as a defense against a nuclear attack. Roberto enjoyed ridiculing the preposterousness of surviving a nuclear bomb by crouching under a wooden desk.

I also explained the tension that surrounded the 1972 World Chess Championship between challenger Bobby Fischer, an eccentric twenty-nine-year-old American, and defending champion Boris Spassky of the

Soviet Union. It was played at the height of the Cold War and seen as a true superpower matchup in Reykjavik, Iceland. It was "us" against "them."

It may be hard to believe, but there was real drama in that match. After making a number of last-minute demands, Fischer arrived in Iceland just a few hours before he would forfeit. Fischer lost the first two games, and Sister Catherine, my high school geometry teacher and mentor of our Chess Club, had us pray for Fischer before each class. Fischer came roaring back to become the 11th World Chess Champion on September 3, 1972.

"In a way," I explained, "the match was an embodiment of how we saw ourselves and the Russians. Fisher had done it on his own—a self-made chess genius—full of moxie and self-determination. That was America. Spassky, on the other hand, had the resources of the Soviet Union, a huge advantage." It was the same type of perceived disparity that allowed us to rationalize losses at the Olympics and other events.

That Ride Across Moscow

The due date for the first set of reports, a key deliverable under the contract that would set the tone for the remaining five months, was scheduled for the last Friday in August. I arrived at the office early and read a "gentle reminder" email from my firm. The fifty-page reports had to be delivered to two separate ministries by "close of business," which we agreed was five in the afternoon. I was ready, more than ready. I had the translation department's firm promise that the Russian version of the report would hit my desk midmorning. After that, it would be a matter of making copies, packaging, and then dropping them off at the pertinent ministries.

Sergei noted that Moscow's Friday afternoon traffic was notoriously bad and recommended that I leave the RRP offices no later than three o'clock. I found the driver, "Little English" Mikhail, and we left the offices at two thirty, which gave me a full two and a half hours to get across town and make drop-offs at the two ministries. I sat in the front seat next to Mikhail, with a map of downtown Moscow on my lap. I wanted to track our progress.

An hour and a half after leaving the project offices, we were nowhere near where we needed to be. Moscow is an ancient city and has a radial ring plan typical of many of Russia's older cities. Unfortunately, what worked in the twelfth century when horses and oxcarts used the roads was less effective now that the roads were full of SUVs. The closer to the center, the denser the traffic became. To make matters worse, Russian drivers felt no compunction to abide by the traffic rules. A three-car accident further added to the congestion.

And things only got worse. A major road was closed for repair, and the detour road was congested due to cars illegally parked on the sidewalk. The police were conducting document checks, and it took some time for Mikhail to find the proper papers. I received texts from Sergei asking if I'd made the deliveries. I ignored them.

"I don't think we make it this afternoon." Mikhail was giving me his personal assessment of the situation.

I closed my eyes and thought for a moment. The whole project would be put in jeopardy if we missed this first delivery. We had to find a way to make it. So I went for the jugular and played the *superpower* card.

"I bet an American driver could make it on time." Mikhail sat motionless for a moment, giving me a hard stare, and I stared just as hard right back. He smirked, looked out the side window, and then back at me. He knew exactly what I was doing. He slid on a pair of sunglasses, made a show of locking the doors, and then he hit the gas.

That ride across Moscow was hair-raising. Mikhail jockeyed for position with the equally ruthless SUV drivers. He drove up on the curb a couple of times and flew through a traffic light that had already turned red. A cacophony of horns and squealing brakes followed. At one point, I hid my eyes behind my hands and shrieked, which caused Mikhail to laugh out loud and slap his knee. He was enjoying himself.

Once we arrived at the Ministry of Commerce, gaining entry and finding the right offices presented additional challenges. Not all the signs were in English, and I struggled with my limited knowledge of the Cyrillic alphabet. The elevator was out of service at the Ministry of Finance, so I charged up the stairs two at a time. I made the final drop-off out of breath with just a couple of minutes to spare. I climbed back into the vehicle, and Mikhail and I shared a high five.

"Ha. American driver. Ha. Russian driver best." I caught Mikhail looking at himself in the rearview mirror.

I sat back in my seat. "Wow, that was truly awful."

"In winter, it gets worse." There was a hint of pity in his voice.

I had to find a different way to make the deliveries.

Long-term Visas

Both Roberto and I entered Russia on thirty-day tourist visas that could not be renewed or extended. So that last weekend in August we had to leave the country to secure new ones. The Ministry arranged for the Russian Embassy in Finland to issue me a long-term visa, which would allow me to stay until the end of the year. Roberto joined me, hoping he could secure a long-term visa as well.

The stern woman behind the visa counter in Helsinki was not interested in us or in our story. She took possession of our passports and after a quick look, returned them separately with preprinted visa application forms tucked between the pages. Roberto, an Argentine, was given a card of about three-by-five inches that required only the most basic information: name, address, age, and national identification number.

As a US citizen, I was issued an eight-page form that required the better part of my life history. In addition to the usual personal information—full name, previous names, date of birth, and home address—I was required to provide a complete employment and educational history going back to elementary school. If I had been arrested, they wanted a description of the crime and a copy of the police record. They also wanted the names, birthdates, addresses, and occupations of my eighty-year-old parents, and details about my reasons for visiting Russia, including the names of all hotels, means of payment, and institutions I planned to visit. Finally, I had to attach a list of each country I had visited over the past ten years, with specific dates and addresses. It would be difficult to skip any of the travel information. They could cross-reference the information I provided against the stamps in my passport.

Roberto completed his form quickly and submitted it to the clerk. I dragged a heavy chair over to the large wooden table and started filling in my form. Roberto wandered around the small room, humming softly, as a means of emphasizing our disparate treatment by the embassy. When I looked up, he would shake his hand, demonstrating hand fatigue. It was a long process, but at the end of it, I was assured my visa would be approved, and I was instructed to return the next day.

At dinner, we chatted with a couple at the next table that happened to be US diplomats visiting from Norway. After an appetizer of reindeer meatballs (and the obvious "Rudolph" jokes), I gave them a brief rundown of my visa application experience. They laughed and explained that I had only my own government to blame.

In the late 1990s, the US experienced an influx of Russian nationals, many with criminal records. To get the background information necessary to identify the bad guys, the US Department of State developed a Russian-specific visa application—an eight-page questionnaire with attachments. The Russian government simply appropriated the US "Russian-specific" application, translated it, and used it for visa applicants from the United States.

Beslan School Hostage Crisis

We returned to Moscow with visas in hand on the morning of August 31st, the same day a female suicide bomber blew herself up outside Rizhskaya Metro station. It was the latest in a series of terrorist attacks linked to Chechen rebels. A similar bombing had occurred in February, killing at least thirty-nine people and wounding more than a hundred and thirty. This latest blast left ten people dead and fifty wounded, but only because the bomb had detonated prematurely at the Metro entrance.

This sad news about the Metro bombing was wholly eclipsed by what happened the following day. On September 1st, armed Chechen rebels took more than a thousand hostages—mostly children—at a school in Beslan, North Ossetia, a Russian-controlled area in the North Caucasus region. Masked men and women carrying weapons and wearing bomb belts burst into Beslan's School Number One and opened fire in the courtyard where a beginning-of-the-school-year ceremony was underway.

The hostages were shepherded into their school sports hall and seated beneath basketball hoops strung with explosives. The hostage-takers demanded recognition of the independence of Chechnya and Russian withdrawal from their region.

At dinner Roberto and I discussed the crisis. I explained how the United States had been paralyzed by two hostage-type situations in the early 1990s involving religious and military groups. First, there was Ruby Ridge in 1992, which led to a violent eleven-day standoff involving the family of Randy Weaver in Boundary County, Idaho. Then the following year another situation developed at the compound that belonged to the religious sect Branch Davidians in Waco, Texas.

"Jamie," Roberto gripped my hand across the table, "the Beslan situation won't be counted in days." He paused to see if anyone was listening. "It will be counted in bodies. Putin has publicly stated that he will not deal with terrorists, and he means it. I think Putin's exact

words were, 'Russia does not negotiate with terrorists. Russia elimi-
nates them.' You can't get much clearer than that."

Roberto was right. On the third day of the standoff, Russian security forces stormed the school with flamethrowers, grenade launchers,
and other heavy weapons. The explosions caused an inferno resulting
in the collapse of the roof of the gymnasium where the hostages were
held. An estimated 334 people were killed, including 186 children.
More than 700 people were wounded.

I thought back to the "Meet the Professor" nights on the Volga
river cruise I took with my parents the year before. Specifically, my
father's story about realizing World War II was over when Berlin could
no longer supply its troops in the field. It was the comment of the sur-
rendering German officer that stuck with me, "The Americans place a
higher value on life than the Russians."

I believe that the public outcry from the deaths of 334 people,
mostly children, would have been deafening in the United States. Those
responsible would have lost their jobs; long careers would have ended.
But whether it was because we didn't speak the language or didn't
have access to the right publications, we didn't hear a similar outcry
in Moscow.

Registry Advisor

Theo, the registry advisor, arrived in mid-September. He hailed from
a humble Midwestern state and brought a practical, commonsense
approach to the reform process. I liked him immediately.

I knew about the public registries and how they operated from my
experience at a part-time job in law school. I earned extra money by
conducting registry searches for a large law firm in town. But back then,
the registry was paper-based, which meant the information was kept
manually on cards, making the search process tedious and uncertain.

With the introduction of the internet, these modern registries were digitized and the same information was publicly accessible online.

Theo had to prepare recommendations regarding the registry's capacity and design requirements, along with a ranking of the various agencies that might serve as the registry's host. He needed data on proposed lending programs and future loan volumes, as well as an understanding of the operational mandates of candidate agencies and their respective interest in taking on the registry function. Obtaining this information required face-to-face meetings with various government agencies, private sector entities, and the larger lenders—all of which required the approval of Mr. Nyet.

Theo and I prepared a detailed list of potential stakeholder meetings. Taking a lesson from my first meeting with the Ministry of Finance, we supported each request with an explanation of why the meeting was critical to Theo's responsibilities and the success of the project. We were fairly confident that the whole list would be approved.

We were wrong.

At the meeting with the Ministry, we weren't given a chance to explain our requests. Mr. Nyet approved only seven out of the twenty-five entities listed. My extremely polite and extraordinarily deferential pushback to Mr. Nyet's editing was useless. Basically he was vetoing any ministry, agency, or private sector entity that might claim a legitimate interest in taking over the reform effort.

The New Courier

I addressed the document delivery issue by recruiting Roberto to make subsequent deliveries by Metro. It was a good, practical solution. The Metro was much more reliable in light of the end-of-the-week traffic, and I had every faith that Roberto was resourceful enough to find another way to the ministries if one of the lines was down.

But using Roberto raised a different concern. Roberto tended to over-involve himself. With his much-improved English, he was more outgoing, and he was constantly engaging someone in conversation. It's a wonderful trait and one of the reasons I loved him, but I didn't want the Russians to know I was using my boyfriend to deliver the reports. So before his first delivery, I gave him a list of instructions—do not speak, just drop off the packages and leave as quickly as possible.

Thankfully, the delivery went without a hitch. As instructed, he phoned me after each drop-off.

"Did you speak to them, Roberto?"

"No. I promise." He probably had his fingers crossed behind his back.

Meetings with Stakeholders

With the help of RRP, we scheduled meetings with the limited list of stakeholders approved by Mr. Nyet. Without exception, the meetings were held at the stakeholder's office, which allowed more people to attend. In Bangladesh, similar meetings involved two or three officials, at most. In Moscow, it was not unusual for us to walk into a room of twenty people.

With Irina translating, we gave an overview of the secured transactions system. I could always see the exact moment when the system's benefits became clear to the attendees. There was a significant change in facial expression. You could almost see their brains thinking through whether, in the long run, it would be a good or bad thing for the industry. There were always a lot of questions.

"The registry, as I understand it, provides a lot of information about the borrower and the borrower's assets," one of the CEOs commented. "And if it's public, anyone can access this information."

This was the same issue raised by Olga, the female attorney working with Jay. I indicated to Theo that I would field the question.

146

"Are you worried that Russia's clever criminals will use this public registry to find assets worth stealing?"

"No. Not criminals. I am worried that our clever government will find assets and make me pay more taxes." Everyone in the room laughed.

"The American Sputnik"

At the entrance to one of the Metro stations, I saw a flyer for Van Cliburn's 70th Birthday Concert, scheduled for the end of September. I asked Roberto to buy tickets.

"Who is he?" Roberto was unenthusiastic. Over the past several weeks, I'd dragged him to some unusual events. There was the Ukrainian Culture Night, where the crowd nearly crushed us, and the Bolshoi Ballet, which, thinking back, he didn't say much about.

"Van Cliburn? The 'American Sputnik'?" I questioned enthusiastically. Roberto was unmoved.

I explained that Cliburn had achieved worldwide recognition at the tender age of twenty-three, when he won the inaugural International Tchaikovsky Competition in Moscow in 1958, at the height of the Cold War.

"He plays the piano?"

"Yes, but it's more than that." I explained that Cliburn was a national treasure who played a big part in my childhood. He appeared on my favorite television programs—*The Ed Sullivan Show, The Mike Douglas Show,* and even *Mister Roger's Neighborhood.* But it wasn't just Americans who loved him; Russians had fallen in love with him as well. I promised it would be a magical night.

Roberto reluctantly bought tickets, and on the day of the performance, I asked him to bring a bouquet of flowers to present to Cliburn at the end of the show. It's customary in Russia, the United States, and elsewhere to present flowers to the artist to show appreciation for their work. Roberto arrived with an extravagant bouquet of red roses, wrapped in a protective plastic sheet and tied with a sumptuous red ribbon.

"There are only nine flowers," he explained. "When I told the florist the bouquet was for Van Cliburn, she explained that a bouquet of an even numbers of flowers is considered unlucky in Russia." We shrugged in unison, and he stowed the bouquet under his seat until the end of the concert.

(Compared to the opulence of the Bolshoi and other theaters, the concert hall was austere.) The auditorium walls were painted a dull color and lacked the elegant adornments that I had grown accustomed to in other buildings. But high up on the walls, near the ceiling line, were a series of portraits of Russia's great composers. Using our basic Cyrillic, we slowly translated the names—Stravinsky, Tchaikovsky, Mussorgsky, Rimsky-Korsakov, and so on. The woman next to Roberto leaned in and whispered, "We Russians have an unequaled cultural history."

Cliburn appeared on stage to thunderous applause and some cheers. Before taking his seat at the piano, he thanked everyone for coming to his 70th birthday celebration. He dedicated the concert to the memories of the victims of the Beslan School tragedy. The applause was more cautious this time.

A friend once accused Cliburn of sensationalism, complaining that he rushed the difficult classical pieces to impress the audience. I don't have that kind of expertise; I thought the concert was wonderful. Even with two encores, the evening was over much too quickly.

As Cliburn took his bows, the Babushkas, the elderly women credited with keeping the Soviet Union operating, came down from their balcony seats to present modest floral tributes to Cliburn. One was a single carnation wrapped in bright paper. Another was a wilted rose with a sprig of green. Some of these women might have attended the concert almost fifty years earlier when Cliburn won the Tchaikovsky

Competition. Cliburn accepted these tributes with the graciousness that played a big part in his worldwide appeal.

Roberto and I looked at each other and had the same thought. Our bouquet was too showy, and it seemed selfish to steal that moment from fans that had loved him for fifty years. We left the bouquet under the seat, hoping that whoever cleaned the hall that night would enjoy the roses.

The Temper Tantrum

Jay typically worked in the afternoons and evenings to accommodate the schedules of the local attorneys who had regular day jobs. I kept tabs on him through emails and phone calls and made sure that he submitted his updates on time. One morning, the office team was quietly working when Jay unexpectedly burst into the office, took a seat at one of the empty desks, and proceeded to make an unnecessary amount of noise unpacking his computer. The message was loud and clear—he was in a bad mood.

I turned around and mouthed, "You okay?" His lips were tightly pressed together, but he nodded.

After a few minutes of internet work, Jay snapped his computer shut and launched into a tirade about the sorry state of Moscow and the Russian people. Given all his complaints, his outburst must have been a long time coming.

"This city is a total dump." He spoke not just to me but the entire room. At first, I thought he was kidding. How could anyone not love Moscow? The culture, the museums, the history—what's not to like? But he was just getting started.

"The whole city smells like a public toilet." I didn't turn around. Instead, I kept my eyes on Sergei to see his reaction. Sergei's expression didn't change. I only detected a slight hardening of his eyes.

"And you can't walk down the street because cars are blocking the pavement." Well, he had a point there. Illegal parking was rampant. But I doubted Jay did much walking.

"It's overcrowded, and the people here are sick, really sick. Have you seen the long lines outside the pharmacies?" In fact, there was a pharmacy next door to our hotel, and there was always a long line outside.

"What were we worried about all those years during the Cold War?" I probably should have stopped him, but I didn't want to risk a bigger blowup in the office.

"You know, I really hate this place." And with that, he shoved his computer back in his bag and stormed out of the office without saying goodbye.

Sergei was staring at me from across the table. "First, our criminals are not good enough for Jay, and now it's our greatest city."

Just as I was about to make excuses, Vlad, one of the high-ranking RRP officials, entered the room. It was so soon after Jay's departure that I suspected the office was monitored. Vlad and Sergei spoke at length in Russian. I watched Sergei reenact what happened. He mimicked Jay in a low gravelly voice and pretended to shove an imaginary computer into a bag.

After Vlad left the room, I gave Sergei some time to cool off. I watched him take a sip of tea from his Yuri Gagarin Space Flight commemorative mug. I had a Neil Armstrong Moon Landing mug at home and regretted not bringing it. The Russians weren't the only ones up there in space.

Finally, I asked Sergei, "What did Vlad say?"

"He said, 'If Mr. Jay is not happy in Moscow, Mr. Jay should not be in Moscow.'" This was really bad. If Jay was forced to leave, we wouldn't complete our deliverables, and my firm wouldn't get paid—and that would reflect badly on me.

"Well, maybe you can hold off taking any action until Jay finishes the draft law." I raised my eyebrows in attempt to enhance my suggestion. "Get the most out of him before sending him home."

Sergei smiled. "Only a few months in Moscow, and you already think like Russian." Igor, the lecturer on the flight from London, would be so proud of me.

"But I told Vlad that we should not make an elephant out of a fly." And then he nodded as if that saying meant something to me.

It took me a minute to process the words—*"should not make an elephant out of a fly."* Maybe it was the stress and embarrassment I felt over Jay's peculiar behavior, but I started to laugh, and I couldn't stop.

I looked across the desk at Sergei. Usually expressionless and impossible to read, he was clearly perplexed. I leaned back in my chair, put my hands over my face, and laughed harder. I finally had to take a few minutes in the ladies' room to collect myself.

"I'm guessing 'don't make an elephant out of a fly' means the same as 'don't make a mountain out of a molehill,' which is what we say in the US." I was back at my desk, doing my best to demonstrate that I had regained control.

"Yes," he said in a stern voice, "I'm thinking it's the same thing and no less ridiculous." I took a large sip of coffee, hoping to maintain my composure.

"It's a common Russian saying." Then he paused, and I saw that familiar gleam in his eye. "I'm not hanging noodles on your ears." (The Russian version of "I'm not pulling your leg.") He knew what he was doing, and I started laughing all over again and had to leave the office early to avoid embarrassing myself further.

Mr. Ethan Hunt

The drama with Jay had some benefits. It loosened up the office a bit; Sergei and I, along with the other Russians, began to chat a little more.

151

The next week, Sergei asked, "May I ask you about another American man who behaves badly?" I nodded, and Sergei continued, "I would like to know what you think about Mr. Ethan Hunt."

"Ethan Hunt?" I didn't know who he was.

"Mr. Ethan Hunt is the Impossible Mission Force agent played by Mr. Tom Cruise in the *Mission Impossible* films. I have a question about the *Ghost Protocol* movie." I hadn't seen the movie, but Sergei explained the situation. In the film, Hunt carried out an undercover operation in Moscow to expose a terrorist bombing of the Kremlin and an attack on the International Monetary Fund. According to Sergei, Hunt looks up an address in the public telephone directory hanging in a phone booth in Moscow. When he finds the address he wants, Hunt tears out the page and goes about his impossible mission.

"This behavior was offensive, am I correct?" Sergei asked. At this point, the translator and other staff had gathered around. Everyone agreed that it was wrong to tear the page out of the phone book and that Hunt had behaved badly.

Even though I didn't know Ethan Hunt, I felt compelled to defend him. "Well, he had a lot going on, right? I mean having to save the Kremlin and all." Sergei tilted his head. I was on thin ice. "Maybe he didn't have a pen and paper handy?" I added.

"No. It is an inadequate excuse." Sergei was very serious about this breach of etiquette. "He has ruined the directory for other users."

"It was inappropriate." I conceded the point.

"As a related matter," he turned as he spoke to the other Russians in the room as if to prepare them for my answer, ("Moscow does not have personal phone directories. It is against our culture to have our personal information made publicly available.)

Now, this last point was extremely interesting. The fact that the Russians didn't have a public phone directory brought clarity to the concerns being voiced about the public registry. It was then that

I realized it was highly unlikely that the secured transactions reform would go forward anytime soon.

My Arrest

The first week in October, Roberto flew back to Buenos Aires to take care of some family business. Two days before his departure, we went over the list of items that he was responsible for (maintaining the residence permits, deliveries to the ministries, etc.) to make sure that nothing would fall through the cracks.

While he was gone, I kept up my long weekend walks. One Saturday, I took the Metro out and walked through Gorky Park, across Red Square, and then up Tverskaya Street toward the hotel. Just past Pushkin Square, I was stopped by two police officers checking for residence permits. Despite the cool temperatures, they were still wearing summer uniforms and the iconic large "dinner-plate" hats.

I wasn't concerned. I always carried my passport so I could show my residence permit if stopped, and Roberto had assured me he would renew my residence permit before he left. I handed over my passport, admittedly with a bit of attitude. The officer flipped through the pages, found the permit page, and announced, "Two days expired. You are under arrest. You go to Moscow jail." Then he grabbed the sleeve of my winter coat and started pulling me down the street.

This was bad. Really bad.

"Wait. Wait. Wait." I was instantly humbled and contrite. "Let's go to my hotel. It's just up a block or so." I thought the concierge could help me with this problem.

The officer's eyes grew wide. He tipped back his hat and yelled, "Go to your hotel?" He clearly misunderstood my intent. "Demetri, this lady wants to take me to her hotel."

"For the residence permit," I clarified. "Just for the residence permit. Nothing else."

"Too late. You are expired. You go to jail," he said.

"I work with RRP." I was hoping to take advantage of the rumors that RRP had strong ties to the Kremlin. But the police officer was unimpressed.

"Please, let me call someone," I begged.

"Okay, you call." He was impatient but willing to work with me.

I called Irina, the project translator, and explained my predicament. I could hear in her voice that she was frightened for me. I thought back to my first week when my original translator had a boyfriend who knew how to calculate bribes. Where was she when I needed her?

"Jamie, whatever happens, you cannot go to Moscow jail," she said. Then added, "I'm not sure how to say this, but some people do not come back from Moscow jail. Do you understand what I am saying?"

I handed the phone to the officer, and after a brief discussion, he handed it back to me.

"Jamie, I couldn't talk him out of arresting you. Please, call Alex. He's snowboarding in the mountains. The police might listen to a man."

It's a testament to Alex's good character that he took my call when he was on the slopes. I handed the phone to the officer, and after a substantial amount of back and forth, a deal was struck. Alex told me how much I needed to pay, and before hanging up, he wished me a "good rest of the weekend," as if nothing was out of the ordinary.

"Now, you pay money or go to jail. You choose." I was a little slow on the uptake. In my defense, I was new to paying bribes. I thought there'd be more covertness, a little more skulduggery, but the transaction took place right there on Tverskaya Street, in full public view.

In the end, it was rather disappointing. I dug into the pocket of my big winter coat and pulled out a wad of small bills. As I counted off the rubles, he counted along, loudly, in Russian, trying to hurry me along. I placed the bills in the palm of his hand. He quickly recounted the bills and handed back an extra. Then he tipped his big dinner-plate hat, smiled pleasantly and said, "Spasibo," thanking me, and walked off.

I ran back to the hotel about ten dollars poorer.

Roberto's Birthday

Roberto returned to Moscow in late October, just in time for his birthday on November 1st. I had to work that day, but the head of RRP's translation department helped me arrange a private tour of the Red October chocolate factory, which at that time was headquartered in central Moscow. Red October was famous for producing the Alenka chocolates with their iconic image of a young girl in a headscarf. The factory sent Roberto home with ten boxes of chocolate, which he wouldn't share.

For his birthday dinner, I'd made reservations at one of the nicer restaurants near Pushkin Square. The restaurant was breathtakingly beautiful. It had light pastel walls accented with pristine white trim and rich tasseled drapes. The tables were elegantly set with white tablecloths, glowing candles, and gilt cutlery.

We started with caviar—prepared the Russian way with crème fraiche, lemon wedges, hard-boiled eggs, mini potatoes—and blinis, the traditional Russian pancakes. As we enjoyed our appetizer, Roberto leaned forward and said, "Something's burning." We simultaneously looked back toward the kitchen and saw dark smoke seeping under the door.

Our highly agitated waiter ran over and announced what we already suspected: there was a fire in the kitchen. We needed to leave the restaurant quickly—*just as soon as we paid the bill.* And despite the black smoke billowing out of the kitchen, Roberto insisted on negotiating. In the end, they agreed to deduct the entrees, but we owed them for the wine and caviar, even though we didn't have time to finish them. We'd been in Moscow long enough to take it in our stride. I paid what we owed, and we left the restaurant.

Final Reports

Arrangements for the second study tour were finalized, and the team of officials departed Moscow in early December. The group would visit New York and Sacramento where they dearly hoped to meet then-Governor Arnold Schwarzenegger. As savvy as Russians are, I was terrified they'd be mugged in New York City. I coached Tatiana against falling for any of the classic New York City scams: pickpockets working as teams, unmarked and unmetered cabs, and the three-card monte card scam that is impossible to win.

"Jamie, we are Russian. We will be fine." And they were.

In their absence, I worked on finalizing the reports and preparing the last submission. The training and public outreach plan was severely flawed and had to be rewritten. For one thing, it failed to address how the Russian Federation disseminated information, a critical underlying issue of the plan. After all, thousands of officials, businesses, and end users would be affected by the new system and would have questions about how it worked.

On her return from the United States, I called Tatiana for some more information. With quite a bit of pride, she explained that although the Soviet Union had been dissolved, the system for distributing information was still in place. It was possible to send information to each and every town and village across the whole of the Russian Federation within 48 hours.

I stood up and looked at the large map that hung on the office wall. The beige color, which denoted the Russian territory, the largest country in the world by almost double, extended nearly halfway around the Northern Hemisphere. There must have been hundreds of thousands, maybe a million, small towns and villages. The transmission of information is taken for granted today in the cyber era. But to be able to disseminate information on that scale before the advent of the internet was indeed truly remarkable.

The Last Document Delivery

Roberto made the last delivery of documents in the last week of December without incident. The following Monday, I came into work to find a message from Tatiana with the heading, "Your delivery man." This was going to be bad.

The email read, "I want to ask about the cheerful messenger who delivers the packages of documents. It's always a pleasure to see him, but we don't know anything about him except that he takes three sugars in his tea. Where is he from? He joined us for a piece of holiday cake last week, but he wouldn't tell us anything about himself."

I printed out the email and took it back to the hotel for Roberto to read. I watched his face as he read it.

"That's so nice," he smiled. He was clearly touched that the Ministry staff thought so kindly of him, but then remembered he was under strict instructions not to engage the Russians.

"I'm so embarrassed. I know what you told me." I was surprised; he was suffering over this. "But they are such nice people. They always offered me tea or coffee. So when they asked if I wanted to join them for cake, I couldn't refuse."

That was Roberto, over-involving himself.

With that final delivery, my part of the project was over. After my street arrest for an expired residence permit, I would not risk being in Russia without a valid visa, and mine would expire at the end of the week. As we walked through the lobby one last time, Roberto stopped to congratulate new parents and coo over a couple of babies.

It was snowing hard, and a somber "Little English" Mikhail arrived at the hotel to drive us to the airport. Roberto explained that we only wanted to go to the rail station and would take public transit out to the airport. Mikhail's mood improved dramatically, and he reenacted our wild ride across Moscow to make that first document delivery back in August. We both laughed. After six months, I was ready to go. Roberto and I landed in London in time to celebrate New Year's Eve.

Payment Approved

In February, I returned to San Jose. I was filling out applications for new jobs when I received a call from the firm in Maryland. The news was mixed. The good news was that the Ministry of Finance had certified completion of the project requirements, and my firm had been paid in full. But the vast training program was canceled. I was already familiar with the pertinent sentence that was read to me over the phone. "If Mr. Jay does not like Moscow, Mr. Jay should not be in Moscow."

CHAPTER 5

Kabul, Afghanistan

2005

How I Got There

On September 11, 2001, Islamic extremists hijacked four planes and carried out suicide attacks against Washington, DC, and New York City targets. The images of the two Boeing 767s plowing into the twin towers of New York's World Trade Center were broadcast worldwide. These attacks, which became known as "9/11," killed nearly three thousand people, most of whom were just starting their workday. US intelligence agencies identified Osama bin Laden, head of the Islamic terrorist group al-Qaeda, as the mastermind and believed he was hiding in Afghanistan.

President George W. Bush gave the Taliban, the radical Islamists who ruled Afghanistan, a short time to extradite bin Laden to face prosecution in the United States. When the Taliban refused, Bush rallied a coalition of countries to join the hunt for bin Laden, and on October 7, 2001, the Taliban-controlled areas of Afghanistan were hit by air strikes.

Most of the Taliban and al-Qaeda officials, including bin Laden, escaped to neighboring Pakistan, leaving a leadership vacuum in Afghanistan. While the hunt for bin Laden would continue, the international community agreed that a more secure Afghanistan was in the world's best interests. More than a billion dollars was pledged to address the country's poor infrastructure, weak governance, and stalled economy. Over the next several years, this base amount more than doubled annually; by 2005, Kabul was swarming with hundreds of international advisors working on highly lucrative contracts.

The first few weeks of 2005, Roberto and I traveled around Europe. At the end of January, his firm summoned him back to Kabul to prepare a bid for an anticipated USAID project—something to do with school and health clinic repair. Around that time, a well-known British firm was soliciting an attorney to work in the Afghan Ministry of Commerce. I sent them my resume, and after a lengthy hiring process, I joined Roberto in Kabul in the spring of 2005.

Wazir Akbar Khan

That first weekend in Kabul confirmed that, once again, I didn't fully appreciate what I was getting myself into when I accepted the job.

My firm had several ongoing projects, with advisors embedded in the Ministry of Finance, Ministry of Tourism, and the Afghan Parliament. To limit the time and risk of traveling around the city, it operated guesthouses close to each of the relevant ministries. The guesthouse for the Ministry of Commerce was being renovated, so I was assigned to a house in Wazir Akbar Khan, a wealthy, relatively safe neighborhood not far from the US Embassy. This turned out to be rather serendipitous, because Roberto's compound was close by—just on the other side of the heavily secured block where the World Bank was located.

I was thrilled the first time I stepped through the security door of Roberto's compound. Beyond the small but well-kept garden with a postage-stamp-sized lawn and a line of neatly pruned rose bushes, sat a relatively modern house, probably built in the 1970s, made of glass and

160

polished wood. It must have been a showpiece at one time, but even in its current, unloved condition, it would be a nice place to spend time.

"I love it!" I exclaimed. Roberto stood next to me as I admired the house.

"It's really nice inside," he said. "It has two large sitting rooms, four beautiful bedrooms, a couple of bathrooms, and a fairly modern kitchen. And there's a larger garden and a brick barbeque in the back." I turned to him and smiled adoringly.

"I'm so glad I'm here," I cooed. "Are you going to give me a tour?"

"Well," he paused, "I don't actually live in that house. It's reserved for the company officers. I felt my eyes narrow.

"You mean those guys who are always in Dubai?" I asked.

"Yeah. They don't let anyone else use the house. I live over here," Roberto motioned to his right. I peered around him, and only then did I notice an enormous shipping container sitting next to a massive yellow generator. I looked at the container, then back at the beautiful house, and frowned.

"It's not so bad," he said with his usual optimism.

He opened the container door, and I was hit full in the face by a blast of stale air that left a plastic taste in my mouth. He snapped on the air-conditioning unit, which shuddered to life, while I silently surveyed the tiny room. There was a makeshift desk, one chair, a steel clothes cabinet, and a bed too small for two people. It was horrible.

That Flash of Ankle

The next day, Roberto suggested we visit the open-air market near the Kabul River. He assured me it was completely safe and would give me a better understanding of modern-day Afghanistan.

I dressed in a long-sleeved shirt and an ankle-length skirt, my "uniform" from Bangladesh, another Muslim country. I also covered my head with a brightly colored scarf.)Even if my outfit missed the fashion mark, I hoped the Afghans would appreciate that I was trying to respect their culture.)

We stepped through the security door about 10 a.m., and the street was already congested with cars, trucks, and buses of every size and description jockeying for position. When I commented on the excessive horn honking, Roberto explained, "The Afghans like to drive with one hand on the wheel and the other on the horn."

As we approached the first intersection, I heard a deep male voice shouting a short distance away. I turned to see an elderly gray-haired man forcing the upper half of his body out the narrow window of a small passenger van. His right hand was balled in a fist, and his face was contorted in rage. While I couldn't be completely sure, he seemed to be shouting at me.

Roberto drew close and gently grasped my upper arm.

"What a nice man. He's saying, 'Welcome to Afghanistan.'" I looked again, and it was pretty clear that the man was saying something very different.

Not two minutes later, a large truck with a group of workers riding in the back stopped at a light just a few feet away. With the same aggressive passion as the man in the van, they too shouted in our direction. Thankfully, the traffic light changed, and the truck moved on.

Still by my side, Roberto offered, "Nice guys. Afghans are world-famous for their hospitality."

Finally, a woman about my age, dressed in a long, conservative jacket, walked up and pointed to the six-inch slit in the back of my long skirt. Apparently, each time I took a step, I revealed a flash of ankle. That glimpse of skin was the source of all the anger. While my outfit had been acceptable in Dhaka, it was immodest by Afghan standards. The elderly woman lifted her skirt a few inches to reveal a pair of ruffled pantaloons, something you might see in Scarlett O'Hara's wardrobe. If I was to wear a skirt, even a long one, I needed the proper undergarments.

"I think I've had enough culture for one day," I said, my way of hinting that I wanted to return to the safety of the compound. But Roberto insisted we continue on to the market. I was glad we did.

The market was an acre or more of small shops and stalls, packed with people, noises, and exotic aromas. It hinted at what Kabul must have been like back in ancient times when the country sat at the cross-roads of the various trade routes known as the Silk Road. Back then, Afghanistan's cities hosted the Chinese caravans carrying silks and other merchandise from the east, and European caravans carrying wools, gold, and silver from the west.

A row of money changers, men of every age and dress, sat at the entrance of the market. Each conducted business from a low table piled high with bundles of bills, called "Afghanis," neatly bound with thick rubber bands. Roberto pulled me aside so we could watch them count the stacks of loose Afghanis by flipping through the bills with mechanical precision.

"These guys are always here," Roberto whispered in my ear. "I'm not sure if they operate legally, but they give you the best rate if you need to change dollars into Afghanis."

We walked down the main aisle of the market, and we were warmly welcomed. The vendors didn't care that I flashed a bit of ankle; they beckoned me to their stalls. The finer wares from the Silk Road days were gone, but there were plenty of other things to buy—colorful birds in cages stacked five and six high, fresh fruits, woven baskets, paper kites, car parts, cooking oil, poultry (alive and dead), school supplies, bolts of cloth, aluminum pots, cheap imported shoes, and so much more. There was even a stall that offered to repair your broken china.

We stopped to try aushak, a type of homemade ravioli in a white sauce, and were seated at a white plastic table with a large boot print on one corner. A Western couple snacking in the market was unusual, and shoppers stopped to take our photo. Best of all, parents encouraged their shy daughters to come up and shake my hand. As we sat there, Roberto whispered in my ear, "Always remember that these are the people you're working to help, not that 'asshat' who shouted at you from the van."

Too Close for Comfort

The following morning we were awakened by the frightening high-pitched whistle of a rocket in flight. The sound was unmistakable. I recognized it from all those World War II movies I watched Saturday mornings as a kid. In the movies, the whistle is always followed by a loud KA-BOOM! And considering we were in a container, basically a gigantic sardine tin, it was a cause for concern.

Roberto grasped my hand and gave it a hard squeeze.

("It's the insurgents trying to hit the US Embassy. Their aim is bad, and they frequently overshoot the target." There was no place to take cover, so Roberto and I lay side-by-side staring at the ceiling.)

"If this turns out to be a real problem," Roberto was referring to the possibility that the rocket might obliterate the container and us, "I want you to know I really love you."

"Thanks, I know. I love you too." It was a very emotional moment, and my response was clumsy. But I couldn't think of anything better to say.

(In the end, the rocket landed a few blocks away, leaving a small but not insignificant hole in a vacant lot.)

That afternoon I came back to find Roberto and several of his workers piling sandbags on the container's roof. I shaded my eyes and called up in his general direction.

"Will those sandbags be enough to protect us?"

He stood up and called back, "No, but the authorities should be

able to identify body parts." I laughed until I realized he was serious. It
had been a tough couple of days.

The Ministry of Commerce

The Ministry of Commerce building was located out on Darulaman
Road, a thirty- to forty-minute ride from Wazir Akbar Khan, depending on traffic. Each day Jaleel, a young Afghan with a closely cropped
beard, ferried me to the Ministry but varied the route, a security measure to avoid setting a pattern that might make us an easy target.

No matter what route we took, I always enjoyed the ride to work.
Kabul teemed with activity. Burqa-wearing mothers holding toddlers
on their hips. Vendors wearing pakol caps, selling plastic jugs of gas
from the back of trucks. Young men crammed on a single motorcycle,
sometimes four deep. And the very old men squatting in doorways and
chatting over cups of tea. The city was recovering from the war, which
made me feel optimistic about Afghanistan's future.

The recently appointed Minister of Commerce, Hedayat Amin
Arsala, was an Afghan with an impeccable reputation. Educated in the
United States, he left a prestigious job at the World Bank to participate
in the resistance against the Soviet occupation of Afghanistan. After
serving as vice president under Afghan President Hamid Karzai from
2002–2004, he was appointed Minister for Commerce, but also continued to serve as a senior advisor to the president.

For security reasons, the Minister's office was tucked away at the
end of a long, hard-to-find corridor and protected by several armed
guards and a metal detector. Because his policies directly affected the
operations of most Afghan businesses, the corridor was always congested with individuals hoping to influence the Minister on a particular
policy or matter.

The visitors sat cross-legged on the floor, chatting quietly, occasionally standing to greet a new arrival. Their clothing brought back the magic of centuries past—large billowy pants, knee-length tunics, vests, and suit jackets. Many wore the traditional Afghan-style turban, made of material carefully wrapped around a cap, tied to allow a long piece of material to trail down the back. Those that didn't have full beards had a respectable amount of stubble.

These men looked very similar to those who had yelled and shaken their fists at me during my first weekend in Kabul. So when I needed to pass by, I shuffled awkwardly to avoid exposing any more ankle than necessary.

Hakiki

The Minister made frequent trips back to the States to see his family, so on most issues I dealt with Hakiki, the Minister's right-hand man. Hakiki had a cheerful disposition, strong English skills, and an appreciation of Western humor. He was short and round, and what little hair was left on his head was salt-and-pepper gray. He wore glasses with thick lenses that failed to hide a droopy eye. I think even Hakiki would admit that he wasn't particularly good-looking, which generated a great deal of crass speculation about what else Hakiki might have going for him. Under Shari'a (the Islamic Code), Afghan men may take multiple wives, and Hakiki had recently bagged his limit by taking his fourth.

Someone cautioned me that Hakiki had a reputation for being "crafty." I will only say that on a couple of occasions he insisted that I conduct a rush review of documents, purportedly for the Ministry, only to get to the last page and find Hakiki's personal business name and address. That was Hakiki.

Kabul Project Staff

My project had three other international advisors, all of whom were British. Edward, the team leader, was a doughy thirty-something who had spent some time in the military. Recently married, Edward tended to focus on the less technical aspects of project management—how the tea was made, the luncheon menu, and the proximity of his office to that of the Minister's.

Elizabeth was an institutional organization advisor. She was a good ten years older than I, and her preference for enormous sunglasses made her look like an aging film star. She told endless stories about how she'd overcome adversity through the steely strength of her character. Bill worked in the foreign trade area. I never fully understood what he did, but he worked quietly, collecting information and writing a report.

The local staff comprised Amooz, the head translator, two female junior translators, a tea lady named Miriam, and a roster of drivers. Amooz handled all the verbal translations, and he was an absolute pleasure to work with. He was conscientious and frequently asked insightful questions to better understand the subject matter. One time he asked, "What is the exact meaning of 'yada, yada, yada'?"

"You mean like, *Seinfeld* 'yada, yada, yada'?" I asked.

"I'm not sure. It's just that a consultant said this 'yada, yada, yada' many times in yesterday's meeting."

I tried to explain it was a substitute for words that were too tedious to say. I found myself tangled up in a long explanation and finally ended with, "and yada, yada, yada," which Amooz seemed to understand.

The female translators sat in the office for long hours translating documents from English into Dari and Pashto, the two main local languages. From where I sat, their work looked terribly dull.

Miriam, the elderly tea lady, spent her days making tea to Edward's high standards and tidying the desks of the expats. She spoke no English but made a point of greeting me every morning in Dari.

Miriam was more recognizable to me from the back than the front, because each day at noon, she unfolded her prayer rug in front of my desk and prayed in the direction of Mecca, Islam's holiest city. It was a series of movements that required balance and agility. Just watching her stand up and kneel made my bad knee ache.

But we weren't the only project in the Ministry. The World Trade Organization had a project working to improve Afghanistan's trade regime, but they worked in a different part of the building, and I never saw them. There was also an economist named Kathleen, funded by USAID. Kathleen was petite, highly professional, and generous with her knowledge. The Minister had complete faith in her, and she was allotted a prized office on the long corridor near his office.

Box of Laws

Under the contract, I was required to review the then current commercial and financial laws and prepare a list of legal reform recommendations designed to improve Afghanistan's overall business and investment environment. I spent my days reading through the stack of laws amassed by the project or left behind by other consultants. It was tedious work. Afghanistan's legal framework had developed over a long period of time and reflected a patchwork of several different legal traditions. My job was like peeling an onion—lots of layers that could reduce a consultant to tears.

For example, the Civil Code, the backbone of Afghanistan's legal framework, was enacted in 1977 but was heavily influenced by the Egyptian Code, which was based on the Napoleonic Code of 1804. Consequently, the bulk of the Civil Code was essentially two hundred years old. But there was an additional twist. It had been tailored to reflect certain provisions of Shari'a, particularly as it pertained to family matters, including marriage and divorce.

168

I admit to spending too much time reading the Civil Code provisions on marriage and divorce, especially since they probably wouldn't be included in my report. But they gave me a fascinating peek into Islamic law. One provision prohibited the remarriage of a divorced woman if she swore. Of course, I spent a couple of hours sending an English version of the provision to my divorced female friends, who all responded with some version of, "F*ck it, I'm screwed."

I made steady progress on my review, and about halfway through the stack, a consultant I'd never met before burst into my office and unceremoniously dropped a large cardboard box on my desk.

"I fly out tomorrow, and I didn't know what to do with these." He was already halfway out the door.

I peered over the edge of the box and then back at the consultant, "What are they?"

"They're copies of the commercial laws that are being prepared by other projects. Some might not be up-to-date, but you can contact the various projects to get current versions." There must have been fifteen different laws in the box.

"Are these projects working with the Ministry?" I asked.

"No. They're mostly non-government organizations that saw a need and decided to draft a law."

I stood up and dug through the stack of documents. There was a copy of an environmental law drafted by the United Nations, a draft law on competition prepared by an American law firm, three different versions of a law on foreign investment, and eight or ten others.

"I'll get these delivered to the right person," I said, trying to be a team player.

"Sounds good." Just before he had fully closed my office door, he poked his head back in and said, "Just so you know, Hakiki thinks you're the right person to handle these laws." He shut the door before I could respond.

I lugged the box of draft laws to Edward's office across the hall. He saw working on these laws as a way to assist the Ministry and look good in front of our donor, the Department for International Development, the United Kingdom's version of USAID. I was excited to think I might be back in the legislative drafting business.

Roberto's Project

While I toiled away at the Ministry, Roberto spent his days making calculations for the school and health clinic repair project. As he explained it, USAID invited him to a meeting of construction contractors, and as he entered the conference room, he took a look at a set of blueprints on the table and said, "That roof is going to cause you problems."

The USAID engineer sitting at the end of the table barked back, "We know. That's why you're here. Sit down."

The roof design, which affected an estimated eighty schools and clinics, failed to take into consideration the extra weight of snow accumulation. So there was a major risk that the roofs would collapse with the first snowfall. With winter only a few months away, there was some urgency to get the structures repaired so they could be safely used through the cold months. At that time, there was no agreement on how to facilitate the repairs, or more importantly, who would bear the costs.

Roberto liked to muse about the differences between the British and the American cultures. "Your London firm welcomed you with an email, something along the lines of, 'We are pleased to have you on our team.' When I met with USAID, I was told to 'sit down and shut up.'"

The London Bombings

While there were signs that Afghanistan's security situation was deteriorating, the first terrorist bombing that occurred after my arrival took place not in Kabul but in London. On July 7, 2005, London suffered a series of coordinated suicide attacks targeting morning commuters traveling on the city's public transport system. The attacks killed fifty-two people and injured another seven hundred. As our firm's home office was in London, everyone in the project house was gripped by the news.

That evening I came back to the project house and found a group of consultants watching the rescue coverage from earlier in the day. The visuals from London were gut-wrenching. A mangled double-decker bus looked as if it had been pried open with a can opener.

I went upstairs to change my clothes, and when I returned, the room was empty except for a smartly dressed woman I didn't know.

"It's a sad day," I offered. Someone said this to me the morning after the 9/11 attacks, and I'd drawn some comfort from it.

The woman turned toward me and, in a British accent, said, "You can't imagine how awful this feels." Then she turned back to the television.

I didn't want to upset her further, but I felt I had to say something. "I think, as an American, I understand how devastating this must be for you."

She turned around a second time and positioned herself to face me full on. "It's different for the British. The Americans have been asking for it—"

I held up my hand and cut her off in mid-sentence. "You need to be very careful about what you say next." I was surprised by the emotion in my voice.

This was not the first time someone suggested that the United States "deserved" the tragedy of the 9/11 attacks. Just a couple of months back, a Dutch woman cornered me by the toilets in an airplane so she could tell me, "The rest of the world hates your country. Of course you're going to be bombed." But I wasn't going to tolerate it in my own house. No sir.

She took a deep breath and said, "It's just different for us." And without further explanation, she turned back toward the television, ending the discussion.

I was so angry that I left the project house, stomped my way through the heavily guarded World Bank block, and along the streets of Wazir Akbar Khan to Roberto's compound. He was filling out a spreadsheet when I pounded on the container door. I recounted the woman's comments as I paced around the container. Roberto was supportive at first, but as soon as I had calmed down, he said, "I know it hurts to hear this, but the United States has a lot of enemies. There's a perception that Americans are pretentious, overly privileged, and hypocritical."

"Not tonight," I fumed. "I can't hear this tonight." Instead of talking it out we both went to bed angry. I would have made him sleep on the couch—if we had had one, that is.

The Lunch Protest

Our workday in the Ministry started around eight o'clock, and we broke for lunch around noon. The expats were driven to a newly established guesthouse for an elaborate, three-course lunch served by the household staff. The local staff remained at the Ministry and ate modest local fare ladled out of an industrial-sized container. The stark contrast between the lunch arrangements for expats and those for the local staff smacked of a new era of colonization, and Elizabeth and I didn't want any part of it.

So we staged an "eat-in" and refused to join the expat luncheon caravan to the guesthouse until the local staff received better treatment. The two of us stayed in my office and ate the same lunch prepared for the local staff—a piece of flatbread and a clump of gray meat in a watery broth. The bread was wonderfully crispy and fresh, but the meat was tasteless, fatty, and vile. But we were making a point.

I had just taken a small bite when Elizabeth asked Haadee, one of the female translators, about the meat. She tried to be tactful.

"Is this a type of lamb?" Elizabeth asked in her proper British accent.

"Oh no, it is camel meat," Haadee answered cheerfully.

I leaned out the window and let my mouthful of partially chewed meat drop to the shrubbery below. I kept my head out the window in an attempt to hide the fact that I was laughing. Elizabeth saw all this and caught the giggles. She turned to Haadee and explained that we weren't laughing about eating camel meat, which we were, but that we were enjoying being in Afghanistan, which we were not at that particular moment.

But the protest had some effect. Edward allowed the local staff to eat a higher quality lunch at the guesthouse, but they had to eat in the garden to preserve the difference between the expats and local staff.

Religious Studies

The lunch protest made me a favorite with the local staff. Amooz particularly appreciated the gesture. So when the other consultants were out of the office, he'd take the opportunity to practice his conversational English—a sign of a good translator. He'd stand in the middle of the large office, dressed in one of the impeccably tailored suits made by his uncle, and explain something about Afghan history or custom.

For example, one week he detailed the strict parameters for beard-keeping, a religious requirement under the Taliban that carried possible prison sentences for those who dared to trim the prickly growth under the neck.

"Excuse me, Miss Jamie?" I looked up, glad for a break from the law I was reviewing. "Did you know that a woman named Miriam is very important in the Islamic religion?" It was time for another lesson.

"Really?" I put my pen down and gave him my full attention. "I'm listening. Tell me, why is Miriam important in the Islamic religion?"

"In our religion," Amooz continued, "a woman named Miriam gave birth to a child without…" he paused to find the right words, "… without having relations with a man." He gave me a sheepish look. "Do you understand what I am saying?"

To the surprise of many, Islam and Christianity incorporate some of the same doctrines, including the virgin birth. The Biblical and Islamic accounts differ significantly, but the basic narrative is the same.

"Was Miriam's baby named Jesus?" I asked.

"Ha!" He slapped his hands together in a display of delight. "See how much you know about Islam?"

Born in Kabul and raised in the isolation of the Taliban era, Amooz had no idea that Jesus played the starring role in Christianity.

Roberto, the Engineer

There was a wild expat social scene in Kabul, or so I was told. Without the use of a car, Roberto and I were limited in what we could do and where we could go. Most evenings we ate at a small Italian restaurant a couple of blocks from Roberto's compound, but occasionally we'd make a trip across town to the Chinese restaurant. Decorated with the familiar tasseled lanterns, it was no secret that the restaurant served as a poor cover for a brothel. We'd sit with Dan, an American engineer, who peppered Roberto with questions about how to source materials and deal with an Afghan construction team.

These dinners gave me my first glimpse of Roberto, the engineer. Gone was the warm, engaging man with whom I shared a container. He was a tough businessman and boss. In response to Dan's questions about hiring a strong team from a pool of untested workers, Roberto advised, "At the start of the week, have your local guy bring in ten or fifteen workers. Three of those guys will be really smart. If they had the chance to attend school, they would have been brain surgeons or rocket scientists. At the end of the week, pay everyone, thank them for their time, and bring the three smart guys back. Do the same thing the following week with another new team of ten or so. At the end of two weeks, you'll have at least six quick learners."

Another time Dan raised a more delicate problem.

"We have a zero-tolerance policy for theft," he started.

"And something is going missing," Roberto interrupted. "And you don't want to investigate because you don't want to find that your good guys are stealing from the site."

"Exactly," Dan confirmed.

"I'm guessing tape measures." Roberto sat back confidently.

"How did you know?" Dan asked in amazement.

"We had the same problem when we built the tunnel over at the US Embassy," Roberto explained. "For the Afghans, a tape measure shows they are doing skilled work. They want to impress their families. And while they can sneak a tape measure out, they can't bring it back in because they are searched every morning for weapons."

"How did you solve the problem?" Dan asked.

"We bought a tape measure for each worker, even if he didn't need it. It was understood that everyone was responsible for their own. They'd hang them on their belts as a bit of a status symbol. It was the last time one went missing. Problem solved."

Foreign Direct Investment

When the Minister returned to Kabul, Edward and I spoke with him about his legislative agenda. He was unequivocal in his response. He wanted to prioritize the Law on Foreign Direct Investment, which made a lot of sense. Foreign direct investment, where foreign businesses invest in domestic companies, can play a critical role in a country's development. It brings long-term solutions such as infrastructure, jobs, and innovation. Key to encouraging foreign investment, especially in an emerging market, is a well-drafted law that gives potential investors assurances on how they will be treated on important issues such as taxation, litigation, eminent domain, and other business areas.

There was already a draft Law on Foreign Direct Investment—in fact, there were three of them. A different group had drafted each one, taking a different approach without any effort at coordination. Minister Arsala supported the version drafted by consultants hired by USAID, and he wanted to submit it to the Afghan Parliament as soon as practicable. There were a number of open policy issues, and the Minister asked me to reach out to the tax guys for guidance.

Since foreign direct investment wasn't my area of expertise, I contacted the original drafters who were back at their regular jobs in the United States. They took the time to explain how they first came to Kabul during the dicey days after the invasion to meet with the Minister and get his blessing to move forward. They held workshops to explain the purpose and need for the law and prepared a draft for stakeholder review and consideration. They returned to Kabul to hold additional workshops to consider comments from the private sector and finalize the draft. It's how all legislation should be drafted. I was looking forward to playing a small part in moving the law forward.

The Bike Ride

In the evenings and on weekends, Roberto and I would take walks around the neighborhood, but I grew desperate for some real exercise. Roberto came up with the idea of borrowing a couple of bikes from the housekeeper. We would take a ride on a Friday morning, the sacred day of worship for Muslims, when the streets of Kabul would be post-apoc-alyptically empty.)

Looking back, it was probably a bad idea. Despite a hiatus in bombings inside the Kabul city limits (there was always the threat of an opportunistic kidnapping (A Western woman on a bicycle would not go over well with the conservative Taliban) As a separate matter, I'm a terrible bike rider. I always have been. The two times I rode a bike as an adult ended in spectacular wipeouts. But Roberto was so enthusiastic about the bike ride he was impossible to resist.

Around six o'clock on the morning of the ride, Roberto and I cautiously eased our bikes out of the security gate. A gray mist hung low, adding to the eerie emptiness of the street. I wore a salwar kameez, a modest pant and tunic outfit that I bought in Bangladesh, and a headscarf. Being out in the abandoned streets at that early hour felt dangerous and exciting.

We rode down the empty street toward the market area, also deserted on a Friday. Silently pedaling along was absolutely glorious. There wasn't a bus, car, person, or even a dog; we were free to take up the whole road. Feeling more and more confident about my balance, I pushed on ahead, and my scarf blew down around my shoulders. Roberto rode up next to me and whispered, "I love you for doing this."

We rode up to the Kabul River, which was a real disappointment. It was a stark concrete culvert strewn with garbage and stagnant pools of water being explored by a few mangy dogs. I turned around to point something out to Roberto, but he was gone—vanished!

I put on the brakes, which screamed from lack of use. I looked in every direction, but no Roberto. I slowly circled around and then peddled back the way we had come. As I grew more concerned, I pedaled faster. I hit a rock, lost control of the bike, and fell to the pavement. My right arm stung immediately, and my knee took a hard bump. I stood up and brushed the gravel out of the scrape on my arm. But still no Roberto.

Panic took hold of me. The housekeeper didn't speak English, Roberto's bosses were in Dubai, and it would be very hard to explain to my project managers why I was out bike riding in Kabul. I was reluctant to call out for fear of calling attention to myself. If the Taliban had taken Roberto, yelling would do no good. I picked up my bike and limped alongside the river when out of the corner of my eye, I saw movement and froze. It was a beaming Roberto appearing from one of the side streets.

"Where were you, Roberto?" I was exasperated to the point of tears and, at the same time, annoyed that he would leave me alone. He was completely oblivious to the upset he had caused me.

He saw the state I was in and tried to comfort me by rubbing my arm. "You know," he paused briefly, "you need to be more adventurous."

It was exactly the wrong thing to say to me.

"Oh really?" I was instantly furious. "I'm a Western woman riding a bicycle in downtown Kabul at seven in the morning. How much more adventurous could I possibly be?" There may have been an expletive in that sentence.

There was no point in talking. I simply pointed my bike toward the disgusting garbage-strewn Kabul River and let it roll down the steep bank. I stomped back to the compound by myself, leaving Roberto to retrieve the bike from the filthy water and muck.

Back at the container, I cleaned up my bloody elbow and knee and examined the rips in my salwar kameez. When Roberto returned, I was lying on the bed pretending to read a book, and he came and lay down next to me.

"I'm sorry," he said. "It was wrong of me to leave you alone like that. We agreed to ride together."

"I was worried about you. Can't you understand that? We're in Kabul, after all."

After a few make-up kisses, I offered to help him return the bikes to the housekeeper. He replied, "Oh, let's hang on to them. Maybe we can take another ride next week."

I loved Roberto dearly, but there was no chance that I'd let him talk me into another bike ride around Kabul.

Trip to Bamiyan

Tourism can play a significant role in a country's economic development. It creates a huge number of jobs for cooks, drivers, cleaners, tour guides, and lower-skilled workers. It can also bring in significant foreign revenue. James, the advisor embedded with the Ministry of Tourism, was responsible for creating a campaign promoting Afghanistan as a new trendy vacation destination. His goal was to convince the world's more adventurous travelers to skip Nepal and visit Afghanistan.

James had a monumental task.

For one thing, he didn't have much to work with. The Babur's Gardens, the Kabul Museum, and the Kabul Zoo—Kabul's top visitor sites—were all in varying states of disrepair. Undaunted, James focused on promoting beautiful Bamiyan, the lush green valley stretching through central Afghanistan located 140 miles northwest of Kabul.

Bamiyan had been a major stop along the Silk Road, and at one time it was the home of the world's two largest standing Buddhas. In December 2001, the Taliban blew them up because they considered them idols, the worship of which was a grave sin under Islam. The Buddhas were gone, but it was still possible to climb up the ancient stairways and view fifth- and sixth-century wall paintings.

As part of his promotional campaign, James wanted to film a video of "Western tourists" enjoying a day in the peaceful valley. He put out a call for volunteers who were willing to fly up to Bamiyan in an old Russian helicopter. Roberto and I were the first to sign up.

179

Following James's strict instructions, everyone dressed in tourist attire. Roberto borrowed a hideous Hawaiian shirt from his boss's closet that was several sizes too big for him, and I wore a pair of jeans and a long-sleeved T-shirt. James stood behind the videographer, reminding us to smile. You have every reason to be happy. You're in Afghanistan.

We boarded the old Russian helicopter and strapped ourselves in. There were no doors to close, so it was literally a hair-raising ride and so noisy that it was impossible to talk without shouting.

While most of the group rushed to the site where the Buddhas once stood, Roberto and I took a long walk so we could view the massive rock from across the valley. In addition to the two enormous empty niches where the Buddhas had stood, Roberto pointed out that the rock was riddled with smaller holes and crevasses. As we walked closer, we realized they were caves—hundreds of caves—and despite the lack of doors, electricity, flush toilets, or other facilities, each cave was occupied by a family. caves

As we walked silently in front of the cave openings, we saw the meager possessions of those families: a handmade hearth, a few cooking utensils, some blankets, and dirty plastic toys. Even Roberto, who had an amazing talent for finding the positive side of things, could find nothing to say about the conditions of the cave dwellers.

"This is not a scene that will bring tourists to Afghanistan," Roberto whispered.

The Workshop

I continued to prepare my project report but also worked on finalizing the Law on Foreign Direct Investment. In late August, I was invited to a legislative workshop on the future of Afghanistan's legal framework. It seemed like a good opportunity to meet the other lawyers and talk about forming a commercial law group to help avoid conflicting laws and duplication of work. As an added bonus, the workshop was to be held at the old InterContinental Hotel, which despite no longer being part of the luxury hotel chain, still had a highly regarded restaurant.

The meeting was already in progress when I arrived and a speaker, who was dressed in a bespoke suit, was concluding his presentation.

"Concerning the situation here in Afghanistan," the speaker said, "rather than trying to update and harmonize the existing laws, the better approach is to repeal laws and let the markets solve the country's economic problems." *repeal laws*

Several hands shot up in the air, and he called on a man in the front row.

"Afghanistan needs a legal framework that encourages business activity, trade, and economic growth," the man stated. "Or is the expectation that it will live off of foreign aid forever?"

A man on the other side of the room responded without being called upon. In a loud booming voice, he said, "Afghanistan is striving for a free market economy. Foreign investors need to be able to operate freely without being hampered by unnecessary red tape. So at this point, I agree with the speaker. The better approach is to hold off enacting any new laws."

The man in the front row took up the challenge, "If Afghanistan is going to avoid becoming a failed state, money must come from somewhere other than aid. Surely, we can all agree on that. So in the short term, you have two choices, drugs or foreign direct investment. To encourage foreign investment, you must have a legal framework that protects the interests of the investors. That will require modern laws. End of story."

The man with the booming voice responded. "The type of investor who will take on the risk of investing in war-torn Afghanistan will have no interest in dealing with a corrupt bureaucracy."

It was an interesting debate, but it bothered me that it was taking place at a workshop between consultants and not with the Minister. I briefly thought about mentioning the Minister's plan to move forward with USAID's version of the Foreign Direct Investment Law, but worried I'd be kicking a political hornet's nest and decided to keep quiet.

That night, Roberto and I ate dinner at our favorite Italian restaurant. I gave him a summary of the workshop and the debate over the strategies of Afghanistan's legal framework.

"What are you going to do?" he asked. "About the law, I mean."

"Me? Nothing." I snapped the last breadstick and gave half to Roberto. "The Minister wants to send the law to the Parliament. As a lawyer, I have an obligation to support my client. The fact that I'm in Afghanistan doesn't change that."

Change of Plan

The next morning Edward, the team lead who I rarely saw, came into my office and shut the door behind him.

"The project will no longer be supporting the Law on Foreign Direct Investment," he announced. I could tell he was nervous. First, his hands were in his pockets, then on his hips, then back in his pockets again.

"Wait. *What?*" I wasn't sure I heard him correctly.

"The project is taking the position that this version of the law is inappropriate for Afghanistan's current needs and won't be supporting it," he said. Effectively, our project (read Edward) was going against the specific instructions of the Minister. There are words for this kind of behavior—"duplicity" and "subversion" are two that came to mind.

"Okaaaay," I said, in that exaggerated way that really means, *I think this is really stupid.* "But aren't we undermining the Minister—the Minister we're here to support? Won't this damage our relationship with Arsala?" But Edward had made up his mind and instructed me to hand off the draft to Hakiki. (And just like that, we were out of the foreign direct investment business. Well—almost.)

When Hakiki swung by my office with a copy of the UN's environmental law, I handed him the foreign direct investment file. He held the manila folder close to his chest and gave me a hard look as I explained that the project was no longer supporting the law.

"Okaaaay," he said in the exact same way I said it to Edward. Then he added, ("Last time I checked, you work for the Minister. Find out where this is coming from. Make some calls.)

Always up for a bit of detective work, I contacted Abed at the Investment Support Agency, an office with a group of young Afghans who always seemed to be flying off to Singapore or Geneva for additional training. I was pleased with the way the phone conversation went: "Yes, of course, we support whatever the Minister wants to do."

But ten minutes later, Abed phoned back with a completely different position. As he explained it, he had "misspoken." (The Investment Support Agency would not be supporting the Law on Foreign Direct Investment as it was "inappropriate for the needs of the country.") Curiously, he had used the exact same language that Edward had used just the day before. (Someone had gotten to Abed and helped him to change his mind, which raised the question, who or what had that kind of influence?)

I explained the situation to Roberto, who commented, "Edward is British, right?" I nodded. "He's full of that old British hubris, isn't he? Imagine coming to another country and going against the wishes of the Minister. Unbelievable."

(But thinking it over, I knew there was only one entity with enough muscle to get Abed to change his position on the law) (The entity that paid his salary and financed all his foreign trips—the US government.) I confirmed my suspicions with a couple more calls to people who made me promise not to mention their names. So I scheduled a meeting with USAID.

The New Golden Rule

(Hakiki and I hoped that a face-to-face with USAID would resolve any issues the US government had with the draft law.) He thought it would be a good idea to bring along three young Afghans who would be implementing the law—if it passed, that is. After making it through the complicated embassy security (our laptops and phones were confiscated), our delegation from the Ministry was escorted to one of USAID's shabby conference rooms.

While we waited, the young Afghan men spoke quietly to Hakiki in Dari. Out of courtesy to me, Hakiki explained that they wanted to understand how he could manage four wives at the same time. I'd wondered the same thing myself. The young men hung on Hakiki's every word and periodically nodded. When Hakiki finished, everyone sighed as if learning the secret to life.

We met with Patrick, a cocksure, short-term USAID staffer who had worked as a juvenile public defender in Philadelphia, or maybe it was Pittsburgh, before signing up for Afghanistan. He had no experience with trade or foreign investment laws. To get our discussion on the right foot, (I gave a brief overview of how the law was drafted and reminded him that USAID had funded the work) I added that Minister Arsala supported the draft.

Patrick tipped back in his chair and folded his arms across his chest. "Who is this Arsala guy anyway, and why does he think he can call the shots on this law?" The eyes of the Afghans, loyal to Minister Arsala, a man so well respected, flared with anger.

"Well, it's Hedayat Amin Arsala, actually." I couldn't believe I had to explain basic governance to this guy. "He's the Minister of

Commerce, but you might remember the name from when he served as vice president under President Karzai." Patrick waved his hand in a dismissive "the name means nothing to me" gesture.

I continued. "The Ministry of Commerce is in charge of foreign investment, among other things, and has responsibility for this law."

Patrick leaned forward and clasped his hands almost primly on the table and asked, "Do you know what the Golden Rule is?"

As youngsters, we learn the "Golden Rule" is "Do unto others as you would have them do unto you." But somehow, I knew that whatever Patrick said next would be an embarrassment to me and to the US government's efforts in Afghanistan.

"Enlighten us," I said dully.

"The Golden Rule," he paused for dramatic effect, "the Golden Rule—is he who has the gold makes the rules." Then he laughed, an ugly foghorn-sounding laugh.

It was hard to think of anything more inappropriate to say in front of Afghan colleagues. In that one quip, Patrick had done away with any pretense that USAID was supporting the democratic process, at least with respect to a law it didn't like.

Of course, Hakiki, with his appreciation of Western humor, thought this new Golden Rule was hilarious. And with his close relationship with the Minister, and the Minister's association with President Karzai, it was highly likely that Patrick's imbecilic Golden Rule would be repeated at Karzai's dinner table that night.

I reached into my backpack and pulled out my copy of the draft law. I thought Patrick and I could review each article and identify the provisions that were objectionable to him and the embassy.

"You've read the law, right?" I asked offhandedly. But Patrick's demeanor changed, and he looked a little sheepish.

"Well, no, actually," he said. "I haven't read the draft. But I have a pretty good idea what's in it." This was preposterous. How do you negotiate with a guy who hasn't even read what he was objecting to? There was no point in prolonging the meeting. I jammed the document into my backpack.

Hakiki and I walked to the main road, already full of afternoon traffic, to wait for the Ministry's vehicle. I tried to distance myself from Patrick and the Golden Rule.

"That was infuriating," I said. "What happens next?"

Hakiki shrugged. "The Minister will send the draft law over to the Parliament for consideration." Then looking over at me with a mischievous grin, "As far as I know, no one in that big building," he motioned toward the embassy, "is a voting member of Parliament. So it will be a test of this new Golden Rule. Maybe he who has the gold doesn't make the rules."

Roberto's compound was just a couple of blocks away, and with the afternoon traffic picking up, I didn't want Hakiki to have to go against the traffic to get me home.

"I can walk from here," I said. "Or do you think I'll be risking kidnapping?"

Hakiki was checking his phone, presumably for a message from his driver. He looked up at me, bemused. "No one gets kidnapped during rush hour." He gestured to the bumper-to-bumper traffic. "How would they get you out of the city?"

So when the light changed, I crossed the street and headed toward Roberto's compound. Within moments a car pulled up beside me. The male passenger rolled down his window, leaned his head out, and yelled in my direction. No doubt something about the slit in my skirt.

After the frustration of the meeting, my patience was at an end. I stopped and yelled, "Give it a rest, okay?"

The man was taken aback, surprised that I spoke. He opened his mouth, but no words came out. Instead, he rolled up the window and the vehicle sped off, leaving me in a cloud of exhaust fumes.

I Needed a New Job

The next morning, I returned to the office and saw Hakiki chatting with the businessmen sitting in the corridor waiting to speak to the Minister. I can't be completely sure, but I think he was retelling the Golden Rule story because everyone laughed long and hard when he finished.

My three-month contract was coming to an end, and I had little interest in renewing. They probably felt the same way about me. I just couldn't understand how a project that was embedded in a Ministry could promote its own views on policy and legislation. I was hoping to find another job that would allow me to stay in Kabul, but the projects I contacted were fully staffed.

The last week before I was scheduled to fly out, Pierre, the team lead for the World Trade Organization project, caught up with me in the Ministry's busy foyer. Pierre was a direct-speaking Belgian who had heard that I was leaving.

"I understand you are finished with your project?" I nodded and explained it was only a three-month contract.

"Then come work for me," he said, opening his arms dramatically. "I need a legal person to review all the trade-related laws as part of Afghanistan's accession package that will be submitted to the World Trade Organization. We have been fast-tracked, and the review must be completed as quickly as possible—in less than four months. You'd be commenting on many of the same laws you've already reviewed. You are the perfect person for the job."

And just like that, I was a WTO advisor.

Folsom Prison Blues

My contract with the WTO project didn't start until September, so I had some time back in California, with my folks. My dad was dealing with new symptoms of his condition, specifically the onset of aphasia, the inability to speak. To encourage him, my mother hired Emma, a retired piano teacher, to come in once a week to play the old classic songs, the idea being that if my dad couldn't talk, maybe he could sing. He had always enjoyed singing and had a deep, rich baritone voice.

The rule was that when Emma was at the keyboard, everyone had to sing. My mother sang along when sweeping the porch. I'd sing along when baking cookies. Even the UPS package delivery person sang as he waited for a signature—and my mother held him hostage until he did. (Despite these efforts, there were days when my dad didn't say or sing anything. It was very discouraging.)

To cheer ourselves up we decided to see the movie *Walk the Line*, a biopic of the singer Johnny Cash. In the theater, my dad sat silently between my mother and me, completely unengaged. After the trailers for upcoming movies and advertisements for the concession stand, the feature movie started and Johnny Cash's signature rockabilly beat blared through the speakers. I felt the drum of my dad's fingers on our shared armrest, and he was nodding his head along with the music. (About a half-hour into the movie, the Johnny Cash character started to sing "Folsom Prison Blues," and so did my dad—in full voice.)

There were only a few other patrons in the theater, but they all turned around and shushed my dad. My mother, grateful to hear the sound of his voice, encouraged him, "Keep singing, Walt. You sound great."

An elderly woman, thin and bony with only a few wisps of hair on her head, stood and snarled, "Will you please tell him to be quiet?"

My mother folded her arms across her chest and shook her head. "No, I won't." My dad was into the second verse, completely oblivious to the ruckus he was causing.

I apologetically explained that we hadn't heard him speak for several days. "It's a new stage for us," hoping they would understand.

The wispy-haired woman shot back, "Well, why didn't you say so." She was clearly the ringleader and said to the rest of the patrons, "Let him sing, kids. It's not really Johnny Cash singing, anyway."

Miriam's Breast

[handwritten: always need approval]

My return to Kabul was delayed by an unexpected deterioration in the security situation. While I missed Roberto terribly, there were days that I was glad to be seven thousand miles away. As he explained on the phone, his school and clinic repair project had stalled, and the delay was making him grumpy. If approval wasn't received in the next few weeks, there wouldn't be enough time to complete the repairs before winter.

By the end of September, the security situation improved, and I returned to Kabul. On my first morning back at the Ministry of Commerce, I happened to run into Miriam, the elderly tea-lady from my prior project, in the busy foyer. She wore the same salwar kameez that she'd worn every day when she served me tea and said prayers in my office, but something was different. She didn't look well. She was thinner, paler, and if possible, smaller. Further, the typically reserved Miriam was highly agitated and speaking loudly in Dari. I held my hands up in the air to indicate that I didn't understand what she was saying.

Clearly frustrated by my inability to understand, she reached up, grabbed my hand, and placed it over her right breast. It was just a small pad of flesh under a threadbare tunic. Then she slid my hand to the other side of her chest where her left breast should have been—but wasn't there.

Standing in the busy foyer with my hand on Miriam's chest was extremely awkward, to say the least. Fortunately Amooz, the dapper head translator from my former project, walked through the front door and helped me out. Amooz explained that Miriam had breast cancer, and her left breast had been removed a few weeks back. She was desperate because she needed follow-up treatment, but her family couldn't, or wouldn't, pay for it.

I took my hand from Miriam's breast and looked through my backpack for some cash. Because of the higher rate of exchange they command, I only carried $100 bills. I took one and pressed it into her hand.

"Tell her this is for her medicine and whatever else she might need." She was so small that she couldn't reach my neck, so she grabbed me around the waist and hugged me until Amooz gently peeled her off. As he escorted her down the hallway, she turned back several times and bowed in my direction.

The next week I spotted Miriam entering the building. She was wearing a smart new salwar kameez, and the wisps of hair peeking out from under her scarf may have been colored. I just accepted that feeling good about yourself is also an important part of the healing process.

The WTO Project

My new project was funded by the World Trade Organization (WTO), an international organization established to supervise and liberalize international trade between nations. Countries must apply for membership in the WTO, and once accepted are required to follow established rules designed to increase the predictability of trade. I was hired to review all of Afghanistan's trade-related laws and to highlight the provisions that didn't align with WTO guidance. I would also participate in a large intergovernmental working group on the WTO accession process.

That first day I walked down one of the long corridors to the back of the ministry building and found the WTO project office. The door was open, but no one was at the front desk. Abe, a tall, slim Afghan,

190

probably in his mid-twenties, came out to greet me. He had an easy smile and strong English skills.

"Pierre hasn't arrived yet?" I asked.

"Oh, don't worry. You'll know when Pierre arrives," he mused. "The whole floor knows when Pierre arrives," he added good-naturedly.

"Is Abe your given name?" I asked, because it didn't have an Afghan ring to it. He gave me a curious look. "Is Abe what your mother calls you?" I tried to clarify.

"Oh no, it's a compromise for the Western ear. No one could pronounce my name, so I shortened it." He shrugged. "It's just easier."

Abe escorted me to the small adjoining room, which was completely taken up by a collection of small tables arranged in a huge rectangle.

"Your seat is over there." He pointed to a spot at the table. While I didn't expect my own office, as an attorney, I was usually given a separate desk. But in this job I would share a large square table with nine or ten Afghans who worked on a variety of trade-related issues. I could see there was no point in complaining.

Before I could sit down, I heard shouting from the hallway. Abe gave me a tight smile and said, "Pierre has arrived."

I hadn't seen Pierre for several months, but the time in Kabul had taken its toll. His white hair was wildly unkempt and his eyes watered with exhaustion. He was easily irritated. I would later learn that he had placed himself under extraordinary pressure by promising to secure Afghanistan's WTO membership within four months. This struck everyone as preposterously optimistic, especially since Nepal and Cambodia, the last two accessions, had each taken about ten years to finalize. Realistic or not, Pierre's timeline put a huge amount of pressure on me to get through the stack of laws that needed to be reviewed.

Except for Pierre's frequent outbursts, it was a very nice arrangement. The Afghans were a congenial, inclusive team, and even those that didn't speak English made me feel welcome. (As they became more comfortable around me, I sensed a subtle effort to convert me to Islam. It was rather touching.)

(Abe described the punishment infidels (nonbelievers) received after death. According to Abe, their heads were chopped off and boiling oil was poured down their necks.)

"That sounds really painful," I said, trying to keep a straight face.

"It's supposed to be," he responded incredulously.

"But how do you know this?" I asked softly, trying not to cause any offense.

"It's a fact!" He said it with such conviction that I just let it go.

(Infidel or not, I came to know the members of the WTO team quite well, as they invited me to lunch at a local restaurant at least twice a week.) Initially, the invitation had little to do with them wanting me along—they needed me for my gender. (There was one female Afghan on the team, and she could not go out to lunch with her male colleagues unless another woman was in the vehicle.) So as an accommodation to her, I went too. We frequented the same restaurant because they served excellent kebabs and had a curtained area for any groups with women. Ultimately, I was invited along even when the female colleague was out of the office. That's when I really felt part of the team.

Money for Sex

Every day we indulged in a few minutes of group conversation. (Once Abe lost interest in converting me, we discussed a wide range of social and economic issues affecting Afghanistan, including the need for girls to attend school, the poppy production in the Southern provinces, and the role of warlords in local government.) One day, Abe slapped a newspaper down on the table and announced, ("All women who have sex with men for money should be put to death.")

192

I thought back to those young women in Ukraine who laughed so hard about my ugly snow boots. How, realistically, they had no alternatives but to take on sex work to support themselves and their families. I didn't believe that those young women deserved to die. But Abe disagreed.

"What if the woman is having sex with men," I proffered, "because it's the only way she can support her family?"

"Makes no difference. She should be executed." I was surprised he was taking such a hard line.

By coincidence, that same week, a team member took some days off due to a family crisis. The woman's young female cousin had married an elderly man earlier in the year. It was an arranged marriage, and while the dowry had helped out her struggling family, he had treated his bride badly; she'd sustained a broken arm and fractured ribs. She was hiding in the home of our colleague.

If Abe had been just a little more open-minded, I would have pointed out that there was a fine line between a woman having sex for money and a woman being sold off to a husband she didn't know for the price of a dowry. To make things worse, in the latter case, it's the family, not the woman, who gets the money. But I let it go. I was there to review laws, not change the minds of my colleagues.

The WTO Delegation

The last week of October, a two-person WTO delegation arrived from Geneva to review the progress on Afghanistan's accession plans. They reviewed the accession package and spoke candidly with various stakeholders regarding the appetite for the reforms required to secure membership. Pierre made it clear that everyone on the team had to be on their best behavior—one of the delegates was a rival colleague. It was then that I realized that the short accession timeline demanded by Pierre probably had more to do with proving a point to the colleague rather than anything to do with Afghanistan.

(Just a couple of days into the visit, it became clear that Pierre's timetable was indeed unrealistic. In the end, Afghanistan wouldn't become a WTO member until 2016, eleven years later.)

Roberto's Birthday

(Under my contract, Pierre and I were supposed to share a driver and a United Nation's vehicle, but it didn't really work out.) In the morning, the driver picked me up at Roberto's compound, then drove a few blocks to pick up Pierre. But in the evenings there was always a reason why the driver couldn't take me home. Pierre had a meeting across town, needed to go shopping, or simply wanted to be alone. (So I just accepted that I had to take the United Nations staff van every night.)

The two-hour ride home allowed me to see more of Kabul than most other expats saw. I tracked the gradual change in seasons through the fruits and vegetables on sale in the open markets. The summer produce of watermelons, berries, and corn gave way to winter apples, eggplant, potatoes, and unusual varieties of squash. It was on one of these rides home that the idea of Roberto's perfect birthday gift came to me.

Roberto's birthday fell on a Friday that year, the day of holy worship in the Muslim world. I wanted to do something special, but being in Kabul severely limited my options. I knew he was homesick for Argentina. He spoke more and more about how much he missed his family and the animals on his property outside of Buenos Aires. He frequently mentioned his old horse and the long ride he'd take through the open fields around his home.

One evening the UN van was held up at a major intersection. The driver swore (I think) and complained (in English) about the stupid farmers and their animals. I peered through the front windshield to see a massive traffic jam caused by an uncooperative horse and wagon. But it wasn't just a horse—it was a magnificent black steed that reared up on its hind legs in defiance of the honks and calls by the frustrated drivers who couldn't get by.

Seeing that farmer standing tall and proud, with one foot on the buckboard and one hand on a whip in hand, gave me the idea. I would rent a horse and wagon for Roberto, and we'd drive around the deserted streets of Kabul on the morning of his birthday. I was sure he'd love it. I mean, who wouldn't?

Arrangements took a tremendous amount of back-and-forth between the project translators, who agreed to help me, and Roberto's housekeeper. Each was sure they had misunderstood the other. They couldn't comprehend why I would want to hire a horse and wagon for just a few hours. Ultimately, a price was fixed, and I was told the owners and animal would be outside our compound before six on Friday morning. I teased Roberto for days, dropping hints about his incredible birthday present. He was infuriatingly incurious.

A little before dawn on Roberto's birthday, I peeked out the container window and saw the housekeeper fly across the lawn carrying a small red carpet. I immediately had second thoughts—a lot could go wrong. What if the horse was too high-spirited for Roberto to handle? What if the wagon overturned and crushed us both? What if I was setting us up to be Taliban-bait?

As we left the container and headed for the security door leading to the street, I put my hand on Roberto's arm.

"I might have made a mistake," I said. "If you think this is too dangerous, just tell me."

"Now I'm really intrigued," he said, pushing open the security door. I wrapped my scarf around my head and followed him out onto the street.

Much to my relief, instead of the wild-eyed steed and wagon that

I had envisioned, (the housekeeper was standing next to an unusually small donkey hitched to a two-person cart made of worn planks) The donkey was decorated with dusty black tassels from some prior event, maybe a funeral, and had a row of pom-poms attached to the side harness. The owners, two teenage boys, dressed in traditional village attire, took turns shaking Roberto's hand, but touching me, even to shake my hand, was haram (forbidden).

"You got me a donkey?" Roberto, the animal lover, was already scratching the animal's nose and getting an affectionate nuzzling in return. He didn't seem to be particularly thrilled.

"Well," I explained, "It's supposed to be a black steed and wagon. But something got lost in translation."

Being a good sport, Roberto climbed onto the cart and took the reins from one of the smiling boys. Custom dictated that as a woman, I couldn't sit up front next to Roberto (again, haram), so I was relegated to the back of the cart like a milk jug. I'm still thankful to the housekeeper who thought to lay down a carpet on the splintering wood.

Roberto gently slapped the reins, and the cart jerked forward but then stopped again about five feet on. The two boys rushed to our aid. The taller one reached for a fork that was attached to the cart by a length of string. From where I was sitting, I could see droplets of dried blood on the tines. The boy pointed to a bare, wounded patch, about the size of a half-dollar coin, on the donkey's rump and made a jabbing motion indicating that Roberto was supposed to poke the donkey to get it moving. Roberto turned toward me with a look of disgust. I don't know who eventually did the honors, but the fork met the donkey's butt, and after a quick jerk, we slowly took off a second time.

Roberto guided the donkey down the first side street, and as I had expected, we had the road to ourselves. While not the exhilarating experience I had envisioned, the ride was pleasant enough. The donkey's hooves made a gentle clip-clopping sound on the pavement. A security guard wearing a singlet T-shirt and sweatpants was placing a kettle over a small fire. He slowly stood up and watched us clop down the street. We offered a shy wave, and he nodded back.

We were surprised to see a couple of families standing near the road on the next block. The men were looking our way, ready to take photos on their phones. The children, still in pajamas, rubbed the sleep from their eyes. Roberto turned and said, "They're expecting us. The guard from the first street must have phoned ahead." Again, we exchanged shy nods with the observers as if this was the most normal thing in the world.

The streets near the US Embassy were lined with people. We were greeted with a smattering of applause, which turned into clapping in unison. Young bearded men called out and saluted Roberto. The women grouped together and laughed behind their hands. Teenagers mimicked Roberto holding the reins and bouncing up and down. Even the donkey got into the spirit. He picked up his head and stepped up the gait. It seemed everyone wanted to be part of this admittedly crazy event.

I called up to Roberto, "I hired all these people to celebrate your birthday."

He turned around, finally smiling, and said, "Thank you, dear. This will be a birthday to remember. That's for certain." Even he had to laugh.

School and Clinic Repairs

After six months of negotiations, USAID finally approved Roberto's plan and budget for repairing the flawed roofs of the schools and health clinics. The approval came through in mid-November, and after that, the project consumed him. He spent his days canvassing Kabul for materials, calculating and recalculating costs, arranging transportation, and identifying viable delivery routes.

197

Timber was purchased in bulk and cut to specification in a large facility specially created for that purpose. The necessary pieces were assembled into "kits" that included all the fasteners and tools needed to complete the repairs. Roberto estimated that it took over a million specialized cuts to produce all the pieces. Carpenters came in from the provinces for a two-day seminar on how to remove and replace the faulty roofs. Working through translators, Roberto explained each step of the repair process and answered the endless technical questions.

On the designated day, a bumper-to-bumper convoy of over eighty trucks carrying repair kits rolled out of Kabul destined for villages in every corner of the country. Over the next two weeks, Roberto sat at a desk in front of four phones, with translators on either side, waiting to troubleshoot calls and answer questions from the field. In a couple of cases, he had to make on-site visits and take over the repairs. In less than a month, all the faulty roofs were repaired, well before the first winter snow. It was a remarkable effort.

Leaving Kabul

Winter descended on Kabul the first week of December and brought snow and a bone-chilling dampness that was hard to shake off. We kept up our walks on the weekend but had to navigate around dirty mounds of snow and slush. Most nights I slept fully clothed under my thick coat. The electricity was even more unpredictable than usual, and the city suffocated under a cloud of generator fumes, smoke, and gloom.

The Ministry stopped heating the building, and our offices were so cold that after Pierre left for Brussels, the local staff showed up for a few hours and then stopped showing up at all. There were a couple of days when I sat at the large rectangular table by myself, blowing in my hands to keep them warm. After that, I also decided to work from home.

Sadly, Roberto's satisfaction from completing the school and health clinic repair project was short-lived. Several schools in the more conservative provinces were blown up for allowing girls to attend. He swore in Spanish each time the news reported the destruction of another school.

But there was some good news. First, the Afghan Parliament adopted the Law on Foreign Direct Investment. So the Minister got his law despite the new Golden Rule as articulated by Patrick. Roberto and I celebrated over dinner at the Italian restaurant. Second, Roberto's company decided to send him to New Zealand to inspect a new type of construction equipment. He was scheduled to leave the first week in January, and as a mark of appreciation for all his hard work, his firm offered to send me along free of charge. I had one or two evaluations to complete, but my work on the WTO project was essentially finished.

I was careful to follow the United Nation's strict departure procedures. I made the trip over to the UN compound to return my badge and remove myself from the transportation and security rosters. I peered into the small kiosk window to see the woman processing stacks of paperwork. She was short and round and wore a woolen cap and man's jacket inside the office. She took my ID, let out a labored sigh, and said, "It's Jamie Bowman."

Just behind her, I could barely make out the figure of another woman, sitting at a desk piled high with untidy stacks of stapled forms. A tiny heater glowed an angry orange on the floor. The woman at the desk called back, "Tell her we tried to find her."

The woman at the window relayed the message, "We tried to find you."

"Well, I'm here now," I chirped. But, honestly, I couldn't have been that hard to find. I took UN transportation to and from work every day, and I was on the UN security roll call every night. So I was on some list.

"Is everything ok?" I asked. "I'm not in trouble, am I?"

"No, it's just that you're owed some per diem." It took a minute to sink in. She was talking about the daily allowance for meals and lodging. I had just assumed that it was included in my paycheck, which was automatically deposited in my account back in the States.

"But we can't give it to you in cash." She pushed some documents toward me for signature. "You have to come back tomorrow for a check."

I returned the next day and picked up a $9,000 check, which I cashed at the local bank branch on the UN compound. I spent the rest of the day searching the internet for interesting things to do in New Zealand. Since I was newly flush with cash, I booked us into the five-star Auckland Hilton on the quay and paid extra for a room with a bathtub. On the plane, I leaned toward Roberto and listed the things I wanted to see and do.

"We need to buy new clothes," I said. "People will think we are hobos. I want to visit the Maori museum and go to Waiheke Island for wine tasting. We should rent a car and visit some of the beaches."

Roberto turned to me and asked good-naturedly, "Do I have any say in our itinerary?"

I reached into my bag and pulled out the large stack of hundred-dollar bills. I fanned the cash in front of his face and said, "Let me tell you about the Golden Rule."

CHAPTER 6

Juba, Southern Sudan

2006–2007

Troubles in Rumbek

Things weren't going well. I should have been in the training room leading the afternoon review session, but under the circumstances, I stayed in my tent. I lay on the squeaky metal cot clutching my Nokia phone, hoping for a "ping" confirming my evacuation on the afternoon flight. I passed the time by ranking the worst days of my life. That day was definitely in the top ten.

It was late February 2006, and I was in Rumbek, the rural town serving as the administrative center for the new Government of Southern Sudan, or GoSS, for short. I lived and worked on a secured compound located across the dirt road from the airport. I hadn't seen much of Rumbek—but then again, I'd heard that there wasn't much to see. Just a few decrepit government buildings, some open-sided school rooms, an outdoor market that wasn't safe for me to visit, and lots and lots of goats.

I'd been hired by a USAID-funded project to revise a list of laws deemed to be a high priority for the GoSS. I was also supposed to train a group of inexperienced local lawyers—the drafting team—on how to write laws and regulations. I was working for Brian—the same Brian

201

who had managed the Kosovo project back in 2002. In fact, he was instrumental in getting me hired, assuring USAID that I could replicate the success of the Kosovar Assembly. When I arrived a few weeks back, I was fully confident that I was up to the task, but now I had my doubts.

(First off, I questioned the assignment. I was instructed to take the "old laws," the ones in effect before Khartoum imposed Shari'a-based provisions back in 1983, and replace the word "Sudan" with "Southern Sudan." Just an easy "search and replace" on a list of priority laws that would serve as the cornerstone of the country's new legal framework. Easy, right? *antiquated laws*

But that couldn't be what they wanted. (The "old laws" were *really* old—some dated back to the late 1800s when the British administered the Southern part of Sudan) The provisions were ridiculously out-of-date and inadequate for the promise of a new country) I had raised this issue with Brian the last time I was in the project's home office in Nairobi and had tried to convince him that much more than a simple "search and replace" was needed. But the project's legislative component was way behind schedule. He gave me a look of exasperation and said, "Just do it, *okay?*"

(To make matters worse, I was at odds with the drafting team— the people I was expected to train—and really, it was only partially my fault. I had taken over from another advisor, a woman who was, by all accounts, a truly wonderful person. I called her "Saint Pam)" She loaned money to the local staff and never asked for it back. She allowed them to use the project vehicle to run personal errands(Most importantly, she accepted that progress would be slow.)

(But I didn't have that luxury. In fact, I was under pressure to make up for the time squandered by Saint Pam.)I needed to "Just do it, *okay?*" and my insistence on regular review sessions that lasted more than an hour made me very unpopular with the drafting team.)

But the real trouble had started a couple of days before due to a personnel problem at an unrelated project. Lillian, the international team lead for a USAID-funded democracy project, was having issues with Solomon, a young local employee who missed deadlines, disappeared with the project vehicle, and skipped several days of work each month without prior approval. Lillian sent Solomon what I thought was a kind and encouraging email. "If you're having problems," she wrote, "come to the office, and we'll get it sorted."

(For reasons that are still unclear to me, Solomon reworked the original email and added language that was critical of the Southern Sudanese work ethic, then circulated the forged message to his friends, some of whom were on the drafting team.)

The phony email enraged certain members of the team, particularly Mr. Eddy from Blue Nile state, an older lawyer with a limited grasp of how the internet worked. He didn't understand how easy it was to forge an email.

("If you insult one of us," he cried, "you insult all of us!" He decided it was his responsibility to uphold Southern Sudan's honor and to prosecute the "slur" against the Southern Sudanese.)

Had Mr. Eddy undertaken even the most basic investigation, such as asking for a copy of the original email, he would have learned of Solomon's trickery, and the whole thing would have been a nonissue. Instead, he and another lawyer stomped menacingly around the compound. They threatened Lillian with jail time, which was frightening, considering the horrendous reputation of the Rumbek jail.

I tried to play peacemaker. I met with the drafting team and explained that Solomon had modified the original email. I added that I knew Lillian (we met over breakfast one morning), and that she wasn't the kind of person who would send a disparaging email.

It was the wrong approach and not well received.

"Of course, you white women stick together." Mr. Eddy curled his lip and snarled. If I had been sitting closer, I would've felt his spittle on my face.

Then one of the younger male lawyers, a notable hothead, stomped out of the office, yelling, "We know how to deal with white women."

I didn't take offense at the "white women" remark, but I knew I had to consult my home office. I texted Brian in Nairobi for guidance. After a discussion with USAID, it was agreed that I should be extracted from Rumbek *as soon as possible*. Unfortunately, in 2006, no commercial flights operated in Southern Sudan. All air travel had to be prebooked with the United Nations, and with all the aid workers in the country traveling between Southern Sudan's ten states, there was no guarantee when or if I could get on a plane.

As I lay in my tent waiting to hear back from Nairobi, I questioned my tenure in Southern Sudan. A big appeal of this job had been the prospect of working in the same country as Roberto. His employer was part of a larger consortium that had won an important road construction contract in Juba, the capital. So when he encouraged—no, insisted—that I take the job in Southern Sudan, I didn't know I'd be working in Rumbek, almost two hundred miles north of Juba—a six-hour drive—over some of the worst roads in Africa.

Just as I was about to give up hope of being evacuated, my phone pinged with a text message confirming that I had a seat on the UN flight, leaving Rumbek later that afternoon. I was already packed. I just had to walk across the dirt road and wait on the laterite airstrip. It took three separate flights, but I was back in Nairobi by early evening.

My Role in Southern Sudan

When I accepted the job, Southern Sudan was on the brink of becoming the world's newest nation. Consequently, its history and path to independence were constantly in the news. At one time, Sudan was the largest and most geographically diverse country in Africa, bordering Egypt,

Chad, the Central African Republic, the Congo, Uganda, Kenya, Ethiopia, Eritrea, and the Red Sea. In 1898, an Anglo-Egyptian force under Lord Kitchener proclaimed Sudan a "condominium" subject to British-Egyptian administration. For practical reasons, the North and the South were administered separately, resulting in the North aligning itself with the Islamic traditions of its Arab neighbors and the South becoming predominantly Christian due to the British influence.

In 1953, Sudan was allowed to commence an era of self-governance, which caused a wide range of problems due in part to the religious and cultural differences between the North and the South. Khartoum, the designated capital, reneged on a series of promises to the South, which led to the first civil war, which lasted seventeen years (1955–1972). After a relatively short period of peace, the imposition of Shari'a by the North in the early 1980s led to a second civil war, which lasted twenty-two years (1983–2005).

In addition to the conflicts over culture, religion, and politics, tension arose over control of oil-rich areas in the South. The revenues from these fields were crucial for keeping the notorious Omar al-Bashir in power in Khartoum. A campaign of displacement was waged by the North, leading to gross human rights violations against the Nuer and Dinka people, the two largest ethnic groups in the South.

In 2005, after a half-century of conflict and the loss of millions of lives, the North and the South signed the Comprehensive Peace Agreement (CPA), which ended the second civil war and legitimized the government of Southern Sudan. This was a huge achievement, but only an interim step. The CPA called for a referendum to be held in 2011, whereby the Southern Sudanese would decide whether they wanted to be an independent nation or remain part of Sudan. A well-functioning government, which provided essential services to its citizens, was key to increasing a favorable outcome on the referendum, and this required a solid legal framework. That's why I was there.

With the referendum just a short six years away, a blink of an eye in the legislative context, there was some urgency in getting the new laws enacted. A variety of donors were providing assistance, including the United Nations, the Japanese, the Germans, and the US government. USAID was funding several advisors, including my position in the Ministry of Legal Affairs—assuming, of course, I still had the job. Brian was an understanding boss, but it would be difficult, even for me, to put a positive spin on what essentially was an emergency evacuation.

"You Had Me at British Raj"

It was a relief to be back in Nairobi. On the car ride in from the Jomo Kenyatta International Airport, I peered up at the colony of gigantic marabou storks perched unapologetically in trees along the Uhuru Highway. Because of their black cloak-like wings, these grotesque-looking birds have the nickname "the undertaker birds." Stuck in evening traffic, a glob of bird poo splat on the car windshield. A fitting end to a very difficult day.

The Nairobi office was in the upscale Gigiri district, not far from the United Nations' African Headquarters. While waiting for USAID to decide what to do with me—it was unlikely I'd be going back to Rumbek—Brian suggested that I write a memo explaining my concerns over the "search and replace" approach to revising the laws.

I kept it simple and used the Penal Code as an example because it was at the top of the Ministry's legislative priority list. I explained that the Penal Code had been introduced by the British Administration and was based on the Indian Penal Code of 1860, a product of the British Raj. It failed to provide for an independent judiciary, which was a requirement of the Interim Constitution of Southern Sudan. But there were other problems. It prohibited women from accepting subpoenas or other official documents at their homes (a provision borrowed from

206

Shari'a), which violated the constitutional requirement that men and women be treated equally under the law. "In sum," I argued, "the Penal Code and the other laws on the priority list need more than a few cosmetic tweaks."

Less than five minutes after clicking "send," Ashok, a program manager of Indian heritage, rushed into my office with a hard copy of my memo in his hand. He must have read the pages as they came off the printer.

"You had me at British Raj," he beamed. "Now I understand." The memo was forwarded to the project manager at USAID, who spoke with Michael Mckuei, the Minister of Legal Affairs. It was ultimately agreed that larger, more comprehensive revisions to the laws were required.

I was redeemed and was told to start the legislative drafting process in earnest. But I wouldn't be going back to Rumbek. I'd be working in Juba, the new capital of Southern Sudan.

Afex Camp

There were no direct flights from Nairobi to Juba. Juba-bound passengers had to fly to Lokichogio, or "Loki," for short, a small town in the Turkana District in northwest Kenya, and then take an onward flight to Juba. The flight from Nairobi was loud, which made it difficult for me to talk to Brian, so I spent the time looking out the plane's small oval window. It was two hours of flat, dry, seemingly uninhabitable expanse, punctuated by the occasional settlement of round huts known as "tukels."

Loki itself was little more than a long single airstrip and a low-lying nondescript terminal. The onward flight was waiting for us, so we walked across the scorching tarmac and boarded the flight to Juba. Brian was disengaged. He'd lost that quality that made him such a good manager in Kosovo—the ability to see the irony in what we did. He spent most the time scrolling through old messages on his phone.

Turbulent crosswinds made for a wildly bumpy approach into Juba, and I leaned over toward Brian and yelled, "This is what it's like flying into Vegas."

"Trust me," he said, without a smile, "that's where the comparison ends."

As I deplaned in Juba, I was hit by a strong, hot gust that blew my skirt up embarrassingly high and left an unpleasant grittiness in my mouth. The temperature must have been in the high 90s, and I felt myself starting to melt. The immigration officials were abrupt and intimidating, so I stood back and let Brian deal with the passports and visas. (I wanted to stand closer to the monster air conditioners that sat in the corner, but was dissuaded by the AK-47-toting border guards who stood unsmilingly under the vents.)

Lemy, the project's head driver, greeted us outside the terminal. He was built like a boxer and had a smile worthy of a magazine cover. As it turned out, this would be one of the few times I'd be met at the airport. (If I wasn't traveling with Brian or Ashok, the drivers always had something more important to do. I'd have to bum rides from the other projects.)

On the ride from the airport, Brian pointed out various sites of interest, including the Ministry of Legal Affairs, where I'd be working. The Ministry was housed in an old brick structure, an architectural souvenir from the days when the Brits were in Juba. It must have been a beautiful building at one time. Sadly, it was in a bad state of disrepair due to years of neglect. The inelegant front steps were made out of blocky concrete. The windows were missing their panes and secured by chicken wire and plastic sheeting. Boxes, broken chairs, and other clutter sat in a jumble outside under blue tarps. I don't know what I was expecting, but it was a bit of a letdown.

(Turning onto the main road, which was just two lanes of unpaved red dirt, we passed a row of small kiosks cobbled together from a variety of discarded materials—bits of plywood, sheets of corrugated metal, and plastic tarps with the United Nations logo. Each kiosk seemed to be selling the same things as the next: notebooks, unrefrigerated sodas, the odd-lot tire, and small plastic jugs of fuel.

Goats were everywhere—on the road, sleeping under cars, on the top tree branches, and even perched on the tombstones in the cemetery. I'd read somewhere that there's an inverse correlation between goats and poverty. The more goats, the poorer the country. If true, Southern Sudan was the poorest country I'd ever encountered.

We eventually arrived at Afex Camp, my new home, just a little after three in the afternoon. While Brian had a private conversation with the office staff, Gatluak, one of the camp's young "concierges"—a Sudanese man in his early twenties—offered to take me on a tour. He must have been close to 7 feet tall, which was common for both Dinkas and Nuers.

Despite Gatluak's enthusiasm, the camp was basic at best. No boardwalks, no outdoor lighting, and the goat control was either non-existent or completely ineffective. The tour started, oddly enough, with the toilet block, which was tucked in one corner of the camp. Gatluak encouraged me to go inside and take a look around. There was a heavily stained sink, a smelly non-flush drop toilet, and a couple of moldy concrete shower stalls.

Next we walked through the residential area, which comprised several rows of green tents in different stages of sun-bleach. Gatluak explained that residents had two options when it came to tents: the luxury tent with an *en suite* bathroom, and the standard tent, whose occupants had to use the toilet block. We continued past the huge dining tent, and Gatluak noted meal times and other food options.

The tour ended at the "bar area," an open space on the bank of the White Nile. It was there that the magnificent beauty of Africa hit me for the very first time. Standing under a leafy canopy of ancient mango trees, I watched the afternoon sunlight dance on the fast-moving current. There was a dilapidated truss bridge a hundred feet upstream and the rusty remnants of a scuttled barge just offshore, but other than that, it was wide-open river and untamed greenery.

"You cannot go into the water," Gatluak cautioned. I'd read up on the water-borne parasite that carried bilharzia, a disease that can result in internal bleeding, cancer, and even death.

"Because of the parasites?" I asked, trying to sound informed.

"No. The crocodiles."

Roberto was going to love it here.

There was just one problem. There was no tent for me. Construction hadn't started on my new luxury tent—the concrete base hadn't even been poured—and the camp was full that night. While Gatluak assured me that everything would work out, I had little confidence that it would.

When Brian came and found me, he explained that the team lead from another project was making a field visit and had kindly offered me the use of his tent. It was one of the standard tents, which meant I'd have to use the toilet block. Showering wasn't so bad, but there was always something moving in that dark hole of a toilet.

My First Week

On Monday, I visited the Ministry, but the Minister was "up North," which in Southern Sudan meant only one thing—Khartoum. The Minister had left instructions for me to attend a daylong legal conference on the structure of the new judicial system, which was based on a complicated German model. It took some time for Lemy to find the venue, and for a good part of an hour, I sat in the room by myself. Just as I began to question whether I was in the right place, the other attendees straggled in.

Directly across the table from me sat a young Sudanese man, who was clearly unwell. His hands shook, he perspired profusely, and he seemed to have difficulty keeping his eyes open. The woman sitting next to me whispered, "He has malaria. Some forms are like the flu here."

"Shouldn't he stay home and rest?" I asked naively.

"For malaria…?" She clicked her tongue. "We'd never see him."

At the time, malaria was a huge problem in Southern Sudan. In severe cases, the patient may experience seizures, mental confusion, kidney failure, coma, and death. I was taking mefloquine, as prophylaxis, as a precaution. Unfortunately, even the best prophylaxis is not one hundred percent effective, so mosquito nets were recommended.

The conference ended early, and to my horror, the moderator decided to fill in the extra time by reading off the names of the attendees along with their titles from a sheet that had been circulated earlier in the day. Back when I was an irrepressible young attorney, I'd started the practice of listing my title as "Big Cheese." It was a harmless joke. And not thinking it through that morning, I mindlessly wrote Big Cheese as my title on the attendance sheet.

When the moderator came to my name, he read in a loud, clear voice, "Jamie Bowman, Big Cheese." A few attendees chuckled, which I appreciated. But I had completely mortified myself my first day on the job—and it got worse. I closed my eyes and blushed.

"Look, she is turning pink. Now she is red." I heard the scraping of chairs across the floor—the sound of attendees standing up to get a better look. Knowing people were staring at me only made it worse.

In the long run, that personal humiliation served me well. Whenever I bumped into someone from that conference, they would greet me good-naturedly, "Ah… it's the Big Cheese."

Afex Residents

Other residential camps would eventually open, but at the time, Afex was pretty much the only game in town. As a result, the camp's residential make-up reflected a good cross section of the diverse donors and agencies in Juba supporting the new government.

There was a group of Chinese construction workers who made it clear that they wanted nothing to do with us. The team from the Japan International Cooperation Agency, or JICA for short, kept their distance as well, but that might have been due to their limited English and our nonexistent Japanese.

As their name implied, the de-miners were in Juba as part of the massive effort to remove the countless land mines from Southern Sudan's roads and strategic locations. They were primarily white South Africans who had lost their jobs as "policemen" after the fall of apartheid. Unable to find other work, they were forced to take some of the world's worst jobs—mercenary jobs in Nigeria, security details in Iraq, and de-mining work in Southern Sudan. But as someone noted, "It's hard to feel too sorry for them. They were repugnant bastards when they were cops."

There was Alex, a white Kenyan who worked for the United Nations. Alex was a terrific flirt who felt it was his duty to tease the camp residents and staff. He called me "Sister" because I wore simple T-shirts, knee-length skirts, and loafers, which he said made me look like a nun.

Most of the other residents worked directly or indirectly for USAID. So if you needed to know what was going on in any particular ministry, it was just a matter of chasing down the right person at dinner or happy hour: there was John, who worked at the Ministry of Labor; Sinclair, who worked in communications; Leslie, a Scottish engineer and Chief of Party of the road construction project (Roberto's project); and Martina, who worked for the Ministry of Education.

Martina was a stylish blond Australian with a passing resemblance to Meryl Streep. She favored a pair of tight-fitting red jeans, which were a frequent topic of conversation at the de-miners' table. She was a good person to meet early on because she didn't take the difficulties as seriously as I did.

The Riek Machar Hand-Holding Contest

Every Friday and Saturday, the camp hosted a happy hour in the bar area, which attracted most of the camp residents—except the Chinese, of course. At one of these early happy hours, I learned about the Riek Machar hand-holding contest. Martina and I were sitting at a cluster of tables when we overheard a couple of twenty-somethings, working on a health project, giggling about their meeting with the Vice President of GoSS, Riek Machar.

I hadn't met Machar, but news articles spoke about his intelligence, commanding physique, savvy advocacy, and gentle manner. But that evening, the women were whispering about his well-known tendency to hold the hands of female consultants just a little too long for a professional situation.

The first woman thought Machar probably held on to her hand a full eight seconds, give or take. The other thought he held hers a bit longer. It was a gentle competition that fifty-year-old Martina could not resist.

"I don't mean to interrupt, but are you speaking about Riek Machar?" They nodded.

"Well, ladies, I hate to one-up you, but I had to remove my hand from his. He just wouldn't let go." That was Martina. We all laughed.

("You Look Bad")

A couple of weeks in, Nick, one of the senior advisors on the project, took scheduled leave and graciously offered to let me use his luxury tent while he was away. Hallelujah! The *en suite* bathroom meant I no longer had to make that scary walk to the toilet block in the dark, and if I dropped the soap in the shower, I wouldn't have to examine it for bits of lizard poop.

Even before Nick was physically off the Afex premises, my things were in his tent. I flopped down on the bed for a quick pre-happy-hour nap and sank into the softness of the comforter. But no matter how hard I tried, I couldn't get comfortable. The outside light seemed unusually bright, and I felt a little queasy and rather achy. About ten minutes later, my legs and feet felt cold, but my chest, neck, and head were hot. I worried about sweating on Nick's bed set. As my symptoms worsened, I realized this was no ordinary bug.

I dragged myself out of the tent and staggered over to the camp concierge desk, where Gatluak, the young man who had given me my initial tour of the camp, was on duty. He looked at me with alarm.

"Oh ma'amy, you look bad." He came out from behind the counter. "You must go see the doctor right away."

I found the doctor's tent behind the bar area and scratched weakly on the canvas. The flap opened and out stepped an extremely tall, Hollywood-handsome man. He had a magnificent head of dark hair, empathetic eyes, and a broad welcoming smile. I suddenly felt self-conscious about my appearance, and while I had barely enough strength to stand up, I slowly tried to rake my fingers through my hair.

"Good evening." He was British, not South African. "I'm Dr. Mark. You look… well, to be honest, you don't look too good." I smiled feebly. "Come on in, let's see what the matter is."

A quick test confirmed I had malaria.

He loaded me up with blister packs of Qualaquin (quinine sulfate) and antibiotics, which he promised would ease the joint pain and other aches. He warned me it would be a tough week, which was a monumental understatement. Over the following five days, I was either shivering with cold or sweating with fever, and sometimes both at the same time. I slept for eight- and ten-hour stretches and even that wasn't enough. I had no appetite and loathed getting up even to use the toilet. John, a colleague who hadn't been particularly welcoming when I'd arrived, barked through the tent two or three times a day, just to make sure I was still alive.

And suddenly it was gone. I was weak, that's for sure, but I was able to sit up. I helped myself to a soda from Nick's mini-fridge and took a couple of small, tentative sips, half expecting to throw it back up. Once I was confident the sip of soda would stay down, I took a long, healthy swallow. I waited for a bit and felt bubbles in my stomach force their way up until I expelled a long, loud burp that resonated in the empty tent.

"Feeling better then, are we?" The voice was coming from outside the tent. I looked through the mesh window to see incredibly handsome Dr. Mark peering back. After almost a week in bed, I looked and smelled awful, but I didn't have the strength to care.

I managed a shower and felt well enough to make my way to the dining hall, where they served me some of the broth usually reserved for the Chinese construction workers. I sat at a table with Martina and the two women we'd met in the Riek Machar hand-holding contest.

"Who was that attractive man at your tent earlier today?" they asked. I explained about the de-miner doctor.

Later that week, I walked over to the de-miners' area to drop off a small token of my gratitude to Dr. Mark. There was a line of three women waiting to see him. The news that a handsome doctor was in camp traveled fast.

The Minister

I didn't meet the Minister, Michael Mckuei, until his return to Juba, a couple of weeks after my bout of malaria. One of the consultants working on supporting the democratic process gave me an overview of his credentials. The Minister attended law school in Khartoum and served as a judge before joining the resistance movement against the North. During the conflict, he rose to the rank of Commander (Brigadier General), and served as the South's Secretary and Commissioner for Legal Affairs. After the adoption of the interim constitution, he was appointed the Minister of Legal Affairs.

The Minister cut quite a figure in his well-tailored suit. Standing more than six feet, five inches tall, he was remarkably fit, particularly for a man in his sixties. He spoke to me about Southern Sudan's future and the important role that I could play with the new legislation. As he spoke he handed me files on special projects that he needed researched. He was smart, fair, progressive, and most importantly, honest.

The only drawback of working at the Ministry was Mona, another American advisor employed by the United Nations. A tiny woman with a huge ego, I found her infuriatingly self-important. She wouldn't let you finish a sentence, a control technique that allowed her to dominate a conversation. She expressed opinions on matters she knew nothing about, often complicating my work. I usually try to squash the "Mona-types," but she had the Minister's ear. After the incident in Rumbek, I didn't need any more bad press. So I did my best to pretend that I cared about what she had to say.

My Luxury Tent

My luxury tent was finally finished, and I moved in even before the plumbing was fully hooked up. The tent had two sections, the living area and the toilet area. The living area was just large enough to accommodate a single bed, desk, chair, and a mini-fridge. The toilet area had a sink, shower and commode. I was delighted. I could now officially resign my membership in the toilet block club.

I put my project-issued trunk on my tent's narrow brick porch, and established a camp lending library. I scoured the camp for books. I badgered the short-term consultants into leaving behind their airplane reads, even if they were only half-finished. After a few months, I had a pretty good selection. But far and away, the most popular book was Martina's day-by-day astrology guide, which was two years out of date, but everyone still wanted it.

Laundry was done the old-fashioned way—a crew of local women placed your clothes in a bucket full of highly caustic detergent and used a long piece of wood to pound out the dirt. After drying on a line, each item, including underwear, was carefully ironed to kill any eggs laid in the damp wash by the notorious putzi fly. Putzi fly larvae are parasitic, which means they burrow beneath the skin and feed on tissue until they are ready to emerge several days later. If you're infected, you can develop boil-like sores that secrete pus and blood.

A different crew of women cleaned the tents. I had a cleaning ninja. She never interrupted my work but somehow always found the opportunity to tidy up and, when necessary, do a thorough cleaning. She spoke no English, so I asked the manager about her. Her name was Alma. She was from a very rural part of Southern Sudan and had eleven children—two boys and nine girls.

At breakfast one morning, the manager notified me that a different woman would clean my tent that day. One of Alma's sons was sick—very sick apparently—and she needed to take him to the doctor. Alma was back the next day, and I tracked down the manager to ask about the sick son. The boy was still seriously ill, but Alma needed to work to earn money to pay for the medicine. I dug into my backpack, found a fifty-dollar bill, and asked if it was okay for her to leave without penalty. The manager said nothing but waived his arms as if shooing her away.

Two days later, Alma and the manager returned to my tent. She held a crumpled piece of cloth in the palm of her hand, which she slowly unwrapped to reveal several dirty ten-dollar bills. I figured it was good news, and the boy must be better.

"No," the manager explained, "the boy has died. She is returning the money she did not spend on the medicine." Tears streamed down Alma's face. I was unaccustomed to witnessing that kind of immense sorrow.

"Please tell her to keep whatever is left over. She can use it for her son's funeral or whatever her family might need right now." I still tear up over her loss when I think about it today.

The Deputy Minister

At the beginning of April I was informed that I would report to the Deputy Minister, Majok Madding Majok. I'd still work on special projects for the Minister, but my day-to-day interaction would be with Majok. I saw Mona's hand in this arrangement, but in the end it made good sense. The Minister couldn't do everything, and the drafting of legislation was a nice chunk of work to delegate. Plus, the Deputy Minister didn't travel, which meant he was more easily accessible. Best of all, I didn't have to deal with Mona, who was growing more and more insufferable by the day.

Majok was well over six-and-a-half-feet tall and probably tipped the scale at 350 pounds—a big man, even in a land of big men. He was probably in his early thirties, but the extra weight made him look older. His face was patterned with the marks and lines of the scarification, a tribal rite of passage taking him from boyhood to manhood. He worked out of a small but elaborately decorated office, draped in heavy curtains to mitigate the heat.

I visited Majok twice each workday, in the morning and after lunch. At the time, the internet wasn't widely used by the Ministry, and the two daily visits were the only way I could keep track of what was going on. He'd beckon me into this office, even when he had other

218

visitors, so I could deliver and pick up assignments. His Arabic was better than his English, and on those occasions when he was annoyed with me—and there were a few—he'd forget to use his English and would say, "La, La, La, La, La." (No, No, No, No, No.)

Break in Nairobi

Juba was exhausting. The heat, the bugs, and living in a tent wore me out. Fortunately, every six weeks the project flew its consultants back to Nairobi for a few days of recuperation. It was an opportunity to take a long hot bath, stock up on supplies, replace clothes that had been beaten to smithereens by the laundry ladies, and have a meal prepared for one person instead of eighty, which was the case at Afex.

On one of my first trips out, I found myself stranded in Loki overnight due to a mechanical problem with the connecting flight. The project assistant in Nairobi arranged for me to stay at a lodge near the airport. As I made my way across the dirt road, I was delayed by a long procession of people, a tribe returning from a morning of collecting material for building huts. The procession was quiet and highly structured according to the status of each individual in the tribe.

The strong adult men were in the front, followed by the young male adults and children. Next in line were the young girls, women carrying infants, and the children who were old enough to walk on their own. Finally, the older men and women of the tribe brought up the rear. The women were bare-chested and sported elaborate, close-cropped hairstyles and broad collars of brightly colored beads, which gave them a majestic otherworldly appearance.

A young man, who I later learned was the camp chef, stood next to me and watched the group pass. "They are the Turkana tribe," he explained. "They are seminomadic and live from day to day. They are uninterested in the events of our world."

I tried to think of a way to test his statement and, looking around, noticed a luminous moon climbing in the sky. "Do they know that a man has landed on the moon?" I asked.

"Probably not. And they wouldn't care," he said. Then he added, "I'm not sure I care, to be honest."

The chef made me promise to eat dinner at the lodge that night. He wanted me to try his "authentic oxtail stew." Kenya and Sudan are famous for their cattle—the region supported an estimated ten to twenty million head. So I thought I'd give it a try.

I lifted the lid off the chafing dish and could tell the meal was indeed authentic because the sliced oxtail still followed the gentle curve it had while still attached to the cow.

When I finally reached my hotel in Nairobi, I called Roberto, hoping for good news about his arrival in Juba. He didn't have any updates, and in the meantime, he had taken a short-term contract in Dubai. He was living in an air-conditioned high-rise apartment near the center of town and had already made a nice group of friends. I tried not to sound annoyed, but I was.

"Why don't you apply for other jobs in Juba?" I asked.

"I'm sure the road project will come through," he assured me. "It will just take a little more time." It was not the answer I was hoping for.

The Drafting Team

Just when I'd developed a nice routine in Juba and was making progress on the legislation, the drafting team moved down from Rumbek. This was not a particularly good development for me. I hadn't seen the team since the "white woman" incident a few weeks earlier when I was accused of taking sides with Lillian the project manager who had been wrongly accused of making an ethnic slur.

My contract required that I work with the local attorneys to build their legislative drafting capabilities) The Deputy Minister instructed me to liaise with Mr. Eddy on the scheduling of training sessions.

The gamesmanship started almost immediately. Mr. Eddy made it clear to me that he was in charge of the drafting process. "We will decide the approach and the timing, not you." I nodded, hoping it would get me out of the room faster. "We will call on you only if we need you." I was fine with that too.

Over the next few weeks, a number of drafting sessions were scheduled, but I usually sat in the room by myself. The local attorneys would arrive late—sometimes one hour, sometimes two—and sometimes they didn't show up at all. This was "African time," I was told; it was part of their culture. I had to deal with it.

All this was very tedious, but it also made me nervous. The referendum that would determine the future of Southern Sudan would take place in fewer than six years. It was critical that a modern legal framework be drafted and enacted to help move the country forward. So time was of the essence. But I couldn't build the capacity of lawyers that didn't show up. To complicate matters, I couldn't explain the problem to the Minister without making the local lawyers look really bad. So I continued to work on the legislation by myself, hoping something would change.

Explosion at the Ammo Dump

That explosion-filled afternoon I spent sheltering with the lizards under the sink served as a frightening reminder of Southern Sudan's tenuous peace. It was probably no more than an hour from the first "pops" to the final explosion, but it seemed much longer. Finally, I heard voices coming from the entrance and figured it was safe to come out. I was brushing off the dust when Brian appeared at the front of my tent.

"You had no idea how much fun Juba would be." The old Brian was back. This was the Brian who saw the humor even in the most difficult situations. "Pack a few necessities, we're going to a location closer to the airport. We leave in about twenty minutes."

My first impulse was to pick up my Thuraya satellite phone and call Roberto to yell at him for insisting that I take the job in Southern Sudan and then not showing up. But then I thought about Martina, who had driven herself to work that morning. Her driver's unpredictability had become too much for her, so she was out there alone. I had every confidence that she could take care of herself, but I was worried.

I picked up the Thuraya but didn't know whom to call. The only business card I had with a satellite number was Leslie's, the team lead for the road construction project. He worked at the Ministry of Transportation not far from the Ministry of Education where Martina worked. I didn't know Leslie well, but I had no other option. So I pressed his number into the phone, and to my surprise and relief, Leslie answered.

He was aware of the explosions, and he and the transportation team were already in his truck driving back to camp. I explained that Martina was driving herself and wondered if there was any way he could look out for her. Then I realized it was too big of an ask. We really didn't know what was going on, and asking Leslie to go out of his way for Martina was a ridiculous request. But Leslie, as it turned out, was a hero. After conferring with his local team, he turned his truck around and went back for Martina.

I was transported to a predesignated location with easy access to the airport. As we drove to the meeting point, I looked at the faces of the frightened men and women along the road, who feared renewed conflict. Only later did we learn that the explosions were caused by Northern soldiers, who were sorting through ammunition to determine what was suitable to take back to Khartoum. Whether they were care-less or simply decided to detonate the ammo they didn't want to take back, we'll never know.

When the all-clear was given, we returned to camp to discuss the exciting events of the day. Martina told the story of how Leslie came to her rescue. He entered the Ministry of Education and found her sheltered in a basement with the United Nations staff. Taking control of the situation, he escorted Martina out of the building, and they safely convoyed back to the camp. Leslie wasn't just Martina's hero; he was everyone's hero. Well, everyone except Alex and some of the de-miners, who were a bit put out that they had missed their opportunity to prove themselves to Martina.

Brian's Departure

The explosion at the ammo dump wasn't the only bombshell that week. A few days later I learned that Brian was leaving the project. At happy hour one evening, someone made a toast in Brian's honor, thanking him for all his hard work on the project and assuring him he'd be missed.

Brian turned to me. "I was going to tell you," he said apologetically. "I was just trying to find the right opportunity." This explained his improved mood.

I completely understood. He had a wife and children, and from what I'd seen of Nairobi, it wasn't the best situation for a young family. There were too many risks. Just going to the market was danger-ous. But he was a decent person and felt some guilt for bringing me on, and then deserting the project.

I felt obliged to take advantage of his guilt. When he asked if I needed anything, *anything at all*, I requested and received a LaserJet printer for use in my tent. In less than a week, an enormous box arrived with a printer large enough to service a medium-sized law firm. Now I could really get some work done.

Greeting the Staff

I continued to visit the Ministry twice a day but slipped in and out of the building, going straight to Majok's office, thereby avoiding Mona and the local attorneys. Occasionally, Majok would ask about training sessions.

"Mr. Eddy is taking the lead on that," I said. "I'm waiting for his call." Which was true; I just left out the part that I hoped he'd take his time in getting back to me.

(Ultimately, Mr. Eddy realized he was being ignored and complained to the Minister that I didn't come to his office and greet him each morning in the Southern Sudanese custom. That became a big issue, and the USAID representative and Ashok had to fly in for a meeting.

I wasn't invited to attend, but Ashok recounted the highlights. The Minister complimented my work by saying, "I love everything she does. She finishes assignments not just the same week, but by the next day." (To be honest, it wasn't that remarkable a feat, as there was nothing else to do.) But then the Minister got to the crux of the problem, (But she doesn't greet the staff, which is our custom. She is rude.")

"She's an American," Ashok purportedly responded, as if that explained everything.

(Ultimately, Majok was put in charge of my fate. I reminded him that Pam, my saintly predecessor, had spent months working with the local lawyers but was unable to move any legislation forward. And laying it on a little thick, I reminded him that I was working on the legislation necessary to support a positive outcome on the referendum just a few years away.)

"Okay," he said. "But what about the other laws?" This struck me as a counter-offer of sorts.

World Bank

I said, "We have someone working on the Prison Law and the Police Law. The World Bank is interested in the Companies Act."

"No. The other laws." He tossed a copy of the interim constitution in my direction. I didn't need to read it; I knew what was in it. The interim constitution was riddled with references to commissions and activities that couldn't start operating without proper legal authority, which could only be granted by legislation.

"Start drafting the other laws while the Minister and I decide what to do about the training." He wasn't letting me off the hook. I flipped through the document to remind myself of all the legislation that needed to be drafted.

"Okay," I said. "I'll start on the commission laws."

"But we still need to find someone to help build the capacity of the local staff," Majok persisted.

"Gosh," I said, trying to hide a smile, "What about Mona? I think she would be very good at that."

Roberto's Project Delayed

One Friday, Leslie, still being hailed as a hero for saving Martina, showed up to happy hour looking very happy. Half a beer in, he explained that the funding that had previously been allocated to the large road construction project in Southern Sudan, Roberto's project, had been diverted to the war in Iraq. As a consequence, the road construction project was delayed indefinitely. Roberto would not be coming to Juba any time soon. It was like a sock in the gut.

I excused myself and walked back to my tent. The internet was out, again, so I couldn't email Roberto. It was too much. I lay down on my bed and pulled the pillow over my head and cried.

Walking in Juba

(With Roberto's arrival delayed, I did the only thing I knew to console myself: I threw myself into my work) I continued to visit the Ministry twice a day, and while I always had a ride to the Ministry, getting back to camp was a different matter. The local drivers, Lemy and Mabior, used the project vehicles as their own. Lemy was building a home on his family's property located about an hour outside of Juba. After the morning drop-off of consultants, he spent the rest of the day carting building materials up to the site. Mabior, the other driver, ran a private taxi service for friends and relatives.

(So I frequently had to walk the mile or so from the Ministry back to camp.) On the bright side, the exercise was good for me, and I saw more of the town than I otherwise would have.

(The danger from unexploded land mines was still significant, so I walked the well-worn trails used by the Southern Sudanese.) From the Ministry, I'd cross the main road and walk parallel to the dry riverbed. About a half-mile along, I'd cut across the impeccably swept schoolyards and listen to the children recite lessons in unison. If it was recess, the braver children would walk alongside me, escorting me to the edge of the yard. Those too timid to approach would call out, "Morning, morning," possibly the only English they knew.

(It was not uncommon for me to share the paths with the local women. Most were extremely young mothers, with sleeping babies secured on their backs by swaths of colorful pieces of cloth) On the narrower trails, I'd hold my hand up to indicate that they had the right of way, and as they passed, they'd reach up and grasp my hand in solidarity with another woman who was forced to walk. Emboldened by this connection, some would reach up and slide their hand down my shoulder-length hair. When they reached the end, they'd give my hair a good yank, presumably to see if it was real.

(But walking in Juba posed a number of dangers. One of the

government's first purchases was a fleet of powerful four-wheel-drive vehicles for the new ministers. While the ministers may have been fearless soldiers, they were inexperienced drivers, unaccustomed to driving high-powered SUVs. They sped past me and made me fear for my life. At least once a week, I'd see one of the new vehicles lying upside down in a ditch.

Further, Juba was rampant with ex-child soldiers who had traded in their weapons for motorcycles. They raced at recklessly high speed around town. I learned from one of the health advisors that a whole wing of the newly refurbished hospital was filled with these young men who had wiped out on the poorly graded, dirt roads of Juba. I had no confidence that they would see me, and even if they did, that they would stop before running me over.

The change in seasons from dry to rainy made things even worse. Enormous raindrops fell from the sky and softened the dry, hard-packed dirt of the unpaved roads. The dirt quickly turned to dense mud, and a misstep risked losing a loafer. The heavy vehicles left gouges in the road, in some cases making them impassable even on foot. We begged Leslie to grade the rough roads to make our commutes smoother, but he said it was too early in the season or some such baloney.

Freedom of Information Act

People assumed that all my legislative drafting responsibility meant I had some influence over the Minister and his legislative agenda. That wasn't the case, but I didn't see any need to tell anyone else. So consultants tried to lobby me to get their legal projects in front of the Minister. One afternoon Sinclair, our communications advisor, dropped by my tent and asked me to speak with two British consultants who supported the enactment of a freedom of information act (FOIA). A FOIA sets out the rules by which the public can access information from public authorities such as ministries, agencies, and associations. It plays a critical role in promoting government transparency and accountability; it's a cornerstone of the democratic process.

The British consultants gave me their pitch as to why Southern Sudan needed a FOIA. I agreed with them but noted it might be a little premature considering the current situation. An effective FOIA regime must be supported by a government-wide system of document collection, indexing, secure maintenance, and a stringent review process for determining what must be released under the provisions of the law. I didn't think Southern Sudan was ready for that.

They were prepared for my response and presented handouts identifying other developing countries that had successfully enacted their own FOIAs, and how these laws had contributed to the democratic process.

"Have you been to the Ministry?" I asked as I waved a fly from my face. "You would have passed it on the way in from the airport." Yes, they had stopped by.

"Did you notice anything about the windows?"

"No, what's special about the windows?" one asked.

"There are none. There's no glass, at least. Just chicken wire and mesh, which doesn't protect against the weather, the damp, or bugs. It makes it difficult to maintain proper files." They gave me a wary look, as if I was just being unhelpful.

"Would you like to see the first four laws passed by the new Parliament?" I asked.

"Absolutely. Are they back at the Ministry?"

"No," I replied. "They're in the mini-fridge in my tent, wrapped in a plastic shopping bag. Both the Parliament and the Ministry agreed that my tent was the safest place in Southern Sudan to store these important documents."

They understood, and I didn't hear from them again.

The Company Law Workshop

And just as I felt as if I had my head above water, someone had the idea of hosting a half-day workshop to highlight the need for a new Companies Law. The existing law dated back to 1910, which meant it had been written before World War I, before the invention of the personal computer, and before modern business practices. I sat quietly, listening to ideas being batted back and forth, gauging how much additional work would be involved. The Penal Code still wasn't finished, and Majok had been asking after the Code of Criminal Procedure.

In the end, everyone agreed to a half-day workshop. The Ministry was responsible for compiling the list of invitees and sourcing a suitable venue. USAID would foot the bill. While everyone spoke excitedly about the benefits of the training, my only hope was that it would fulfill a portion of my contract's capacity-building requirement. I spent the next few days in my tent preparing the material necessary for three hours of training.

Somehow, the initial plan snowballed from a casual afternoon training session into a two-day seminar with attendees from each of the ten states that made up Southern Sudan. This meant arranging for travel, overnight accommodations, and locating a venue large enough to hold fifty note-taking participants. It also meant I had to crank up my game and prepare two full days' worth of material.

I spent a week preparing colorful PowerPoint slides, listing the existing law's limitations, and outlining what a new law should cover. I had slides on business formalization, the duties of officers and directors, shareholders' rights, corporate governance, and winding up operations, among other things. But enacting a modern Companies Act wouldn't be easy. To put it in perspective, when the United Kingdom updated its Companies Act in 2006, it was the longest Act of Parliament in history—it had more than 1,300 sections and ran almost 700 pages.

229

(Our logistics people did a great job, and we had a conference room full of local officials eager to discuss the need for a new law.) The Minister gave opening remarks, and then the seminar was all mine. We reviewed the purpose of the Companies Act and the pros and cons of taking one approach over another. We discussed process, expense, registration, and renewal. (Someone brought up the issue of whether criminal records and bankruptcy should be considered in the incorporation process.) Occasionally, a participant would refer to me as "the Big Cheese," and everyone laughed. The first day was long. The second day was longer (But overall, it went remarkably well, and more importantly, it left everyone hopeful that the country could move forward.)

After all the "thank-yous" and "goodbyes" and promises of more workshops, which I had no intention of keeping, I had to walk back to camp because, as usual, our drivers were nowhere to be found. I was so tired from two full days of talking that I lay down on my bed to take a few moments for myself. I had prepared enough material, and the participants were both fully engaged and respectful of one another's opinions. Certainly that should count for something toward my capacity-building obligations.

Ashok swung by my tent with some good words, but of course, there was a problem.

"Good job. I think the participants got a lot out of it, and the Minister seemed happy." I waited for the other shoe to drop. ("But you know, you really should have invited Mona.")

Mona. I hadn't thought about Mona in months. The last time I saw her, she was going over one of the out-of-date laws with the local attorneys—building capacity on legislation that would soon be replaced. I was about to explain to Ashok that I had nothing to do with the workshops guest list, and it was the Minister's own staff who neglected to invite her. But I was too tired and let it go.

After Ashok left, I thought about the fit Mona must have pitched after learning she had missed out on an opportunity to show off at a Ministry event. I lay back down and had a good long laugh.

"I Okay, I Okay!"

The residential make-up of the camp was changing. The de-miners had moved to a larger camp in early May, and the Chinese workers relocated to their own compound the following month. For the most part, the vacated tents were taken by a rotation of short-term consultants conducting research and giving training.

The Japanese still had several tents, and most of their group did a remarkable job of ignoring us. But there was one team member—a short man with a large round head sparsely covered by a few strands of dark comb-over—who made an effort to be friendly. Whenever I crossed paths with him, he'd flash a big smile and give a short bow. We called him "JICA-guy" in reference to the institution that employed him.

One day at lunch JICA-guy started to cough—not choke, mind you—just a persistent "it-went-down-the-wrong-tube" kind of cough. Having looked for an opportunity to have some interaction with him, I walked up behind him, put my arms around his torso, and pretended to give him the Heimlich maneuver, the anti-choking procedure involving abdominal thrusts.

JICA-guy's arms shot up over his head, and he yelled, "I okay, I okay!" And while it may have been a kind of "you had to be there" moment, it was very funny to us and served as our connection. After that, whenever he saw me on the compound, he raised his arms and shouted, "I okay, I okay!" I'd laugh. It was a nice interaction.

JICA-guy disappeared for a while. I guessed he went back to Japan. But one afternoon I heard a noise outside my tent. There was that big smile that I'd missed. He bowed and handed me a tin of precious, individually wrapped cookies, stamped with ancient Japanese scenes of pagodas and cherry blossoms. Then he raised his hands and said, "I okay, I okay!" I risked it, and gave him a half hug. I shared the cookies with the other consultants on the project and was not very happy when people asked if they could take two.

Martina's Illness

About this time, Martina grew quiet. She frequently left dinner early or didn't show up at all. I asked if she was all right, and she assured me she was just busy finishing up a report. But, ultimately, she couldn't hide that she was sick—so sick that she had to leave Juba for tests at the Tropical Disease Clinic in Nairobi.

A big risk of working in Africa is catching a bug that you can't shake, or one of the diseases that can't be cured, only "managed." Martina spent two weeks going back and forth to the clinic, giving blood and other bodily samples. I flew into Nairobi for a break, and I accompanied her to the clinic, where everyone seemed to know her. She was worried that she might not get better. Finally, her doctor advised her that it would be unwise for her to return to Juba.

We ate dinner on our last night together in Nairobi, and she lamented her situation. "I really can't believe I'm saying this, but I'm going to miss Juba."

"Miss Juba? You're sicker than I thought," I responded only half in jest.

"I'm serious." She was tearing up. "I'm going to miss the Ministry and the work we were doing. I'm going to miss the sound of the rain on my tent, the baby crocodile that lives on the abandoned boat offshore, and the sight of you walking down the road when you couldn't get a ride." As I listened I began to understand how she felt. Despite all the challenges, Juba had a certain charm.

The American Dream

The months flew by, and before I knew it, it was 2007. One Sunday afternoon in February, I sat in the bar area reading some magazines left behind by a short-term consultant. A group of young Southern Sudanese men walked in and stood by the banks of the White Nile, hoping to get a glimpse of the baby crocodile.

After a quick greeting, one of them asked, "Ma'amy, are you British or American? I cannot tell from your accent."

"I'm from the US." All three of the men smiled broadly and nodded their heads approvingly in unison.

The tallest one said, "I want so much to go to the United States. I want my children to be raised American. I want them to go to college and support me in my old age. I want, what do they call it? I want that American dream."

"Living in the States is tough," I said.

"I am a hard-working man. I know I could do it," the same man replied.

After they left—the crocodile was nowhere to be found—I thought about the so-called American Dream and wondered if it still existed. Was it really possible for one of these men to emigrate and have the opportunities that would allow him to make a life for himself and his family? I just didn't know.

By coincidence, I had the chance to test the existence of the American dream the following week when I flew back to San Jose to visit my parents. My dad wasn't doing well, and my mother needed my support. I hailed a cab at the airport, and dangling from the rearview mirror was a green, yellow, and red air freshener in the shape of a marijuana leaf. The driver was from Ethiopia.

We chatted briefly about the weather, how much San Jose had changed since I was a kid, and then I asked, "Have you lived in the States long?"

"About five years. My whole family is here now," he said.

"Was it a good decision to come here?" I asked tentatively.

"Yes," he said emphatically. "I love this country. If you are willing to work hard, the United States allows you not only to make money but to make something of yourself. I drove a cab during the day and went to school at night. Next week, I'm starting as a project assistant with Apple Computers." Still looking at me through the rearview mirror, he asked, "Do you know Apple?"

"Yes," I laughed and held up my iPhone so he could see it in the rearview mirror.

"My story would not be possible in Ethiopia. I am so grateful to the United States of America."

Dr. Wesley Davis

At home, there wasn't much remaining of the kind man who raised me. My dad's recognition of friends and family was hit and miss. He rarely spoke, and just that week he'd stopped walking. I helped the caregiver get him ready for bed, which was a long delicate process. As I prepared to slip on his pajama bottoms, I noticed his right leg was swollen, almost half again the size of his left, and it was hot to the touch.

A scan at the emergency room revealed limited blood circulation in his right leg. He had a thrombosis, and there was a danger that a clot in the veins could break loose, travel through the bloodstream, and cause a pulmonary embolism. He was an old man with excellent health insurance, so he spent the next seven days in a single room on the fourth floor of the hospital.

At the end of my dad's week in the hospital, both my parents looked much better. My mother looked refreshed from her break as the primary caregiver. We were sitting in his room when a young clerk came in and brightly announced that my dad would be discharged at the weekend) I looked over at my mother, who had literally crumpled in her chair. I asked if it was possible for my dad to stay a few more days, so my mother could have a longer break.

"Sorry," the clerk snapped. "We need the bed."

Not ready to give up, I made an appointment with the supervisor to discuss options. She was probably close to thirty, but she looked about twelve. I made the plea that every loving child makes when trying to do the best for a sick parent. I talked about my dad's achievements, his kindness, and his years as a doctor; surely, that must count for something.

"The only person that can make an exception," the clerk responded, "is Dr. Davis, and I've already spoken to him about this case."

My mother sat up in her chair, tucked a well-used tissue up her sleeve, and asked, "By any chance, would that be Dr. Wesley Davis?" The clerk was surprised that my mother knew the name.

"Does Dr. Davis know the name of the patient?" she asked. "Does he know we're talking about Walt Bowman?"

"I'm not sure," the clerk admitted, "but it won't make a difference. I've worked with Dr. Davis for several years, and I've never seen him change his decision in these cases."

At my mother's insistence, the clerk left to speak with Dr. Davis. While we were alone in the room, my mother explained that back in the 1960s, obtaining privileges to work at my father's hospital required a vote of the medical staff. Dr. Davis, a young African-American doctor, was considered controversial because of his skin color. When a show of hands took the vote, my dad was one of two doctors in the room of twenty-five who voted to give Dr. Davis privileges. Dr. Davis was forced to pursue his career at another hospital but thanked my dad for his brave vote and show of confidence.

"I remember when all that happened," my mother said. "After the vote on Dr. Davis, your dad came home so disheartened. We talked about whether San Jose was the right place to raise a family, but we had just bought a house and we were up to our eyeballs in debt. So we stayed." She shrugged.

The clerk came back to the room, followed by a tall black man with a gray Afro that looked like a halo. About my dad's age, Dr. Davis was still practicing medicine.

"So sorry to learn about Walt's condition," Dr. Davis said. "We'll find a bed for him. He deserves that. We'll give you some extra time."

As my mother and I walked to the car, she patted me on the back and said, "You did a good job in there today."

"It had nothing to do with me," I said. "It's the karma Dad built up fifty years ago." I opened the car door for her, and she sat for a minute before putting on her seat belt.

"But you know, your father never wavered. I'm sure the doctors who voted against giving Dr. Davis privileges made your dad's life very difficult for a while, but he carried on as usual. He said something like, 'You have to do the right thing, even if it isn't easy.' Your dad was a good man." The fact that she used the past tense, acknowledging that he was mentally gone, made me tear up.

Final Drafts

(I returned to Southern Sudan at the end of February and worked furiously to finalize the key pieces of legislation. By March the drafts of the Penal Code and the Code or Criminal Procedure were complete. It was a relief to plop more than four hundred pages of text on Majok's desk.)

As usual, Majok had a number of people sitting on the sofas in his office. He leafed through the top pages of the drafts and asked for a summary of the most important revisions.

("Per the interim constitution," I explained, "the judiciary provisions have been transferred to a new law being drafted by the United

Nations. So Southern Sudan will have an independent judiciary." Everyone nodded in approval.

"Since the interim constitution bans torture, and whipping has been deemed to be a form of torture, I removed the penalty of whipping from the law. Finally, women are now allowed to accept subpoenas in their own homes, due to the requirement that men and women be treated equally under the law."

"Whipping?" Majok was genuinely perplexed. "Why would we remove whipping from the law?"

"Because Amnesty International has deemed it a form of torture," I responded.

"We're not removing whipping from the law." He shook his head while he spoke. "La, La, La, La, La." (No, No, No, No, No.)

The men sitting on the sofa discussed the issue quietly in Arabic.

"I'm not saying whipping can't come out," Majok added. "I'm saying that the Ministry of Legal Affairs will not be responsible for its removal. If the Parliament wants to take it up as an issue, let it be on their heads." I knew from my past experience with Majok that this was his final word on the matter.

"I have to think about the subpoena issue," he said with a frown. He then spoke in Arabic to the men sitting on the sofas.

An elderly man spoke directly to me. "What is the issue with women and subpoenas?"

"The existing law prohibits women from accepting subpoenas in their homes. It's an old Shari'a provision. If women are going to be treated equally under the law, as required by the interim constitution, this needs to be changed." I looked over at the men sitting on the sofas and then back to Majok.

There was some discussion in Arabic, and then the elderly man provided some explanation. "The fact that women can't accept subpoenas in their homes is not a discrimination issue. It's a practical one. Our

BIKE RIDING IN KABUL

women cannot read." There were nods and soft murmurs of support of his position.

("Well, if your women can't read, you need to teach them," I said, not really thinking through my recommendation. The room froze in awkward silence. Majok dismissed me but agreed to discuss it later.

As I walked past the window of his office, I could hear them laughing. I guess the idea of teaching women to read was too much for them.

The George Forbes Case

George Forbes was a forty-five-year-old Australian contractor who was in the wrong place at the wrong time. He worked in Rumbek and lived on one of the secured compounds. One evening, a Ukrainian flight engineer, who claimed he was being chased, sought refuge at Mr. Forbes's compound. Sadly, the next morning, the Ukrainian was found dead, hanging from a towel rack in his room.

Despite two autopsies (including one conducted in Kenya) both ruling the Ukrainian's death a suicide, Mr. Forbes and two of his Kenyan colleagues were arrested and charged with murder. The three of them were held in the Rumbek jail, which had a horrific reputation. Forbes's friends and colleagues delivered food and water to the jail, but it was quickly snatched away by other, stronger inmates. His health began to deteriorate, and there was growing concern that Mr. Forbes would not survive.

The case garnered international attention, focusing on the unfairness of the process. And despite the autopsy findings and other evidence that supported acquittal, Mr. Forbes and his Kenyan colleagues were eventually convicted of murder. Under Sudanese law in effect at the time, all three men could face the death penalty.

Over my months in Juba, I was frequently approached by consultants, entrepreneurs, and other self-interested parties with matters of

238

policy and other issues hoping I'd lobby the Minister on their behalf. But I never did. He was smart, well-educated, and knew what he wanted. It wasn't my place to try and influence him unless he asked my opinion. But then the George Forbes case came up, and it was impossible to just stand by.

I decided that on this one occasion, I would approach the Minister. Since Rumbek was in Southern Sudan, the mishandling of this case would be a reflection on the new country that was trying to distance itself from the brutality of the North. The following Monday, I asked for an urgent meeting with the Minister.

I entered his large office, kept cool by a combination of heavy draping on the windows and large air conditioners. He sat behind his enormous desk that was covered with documents pertaining to the monumental legal issues facing the country—boundary disputes, oil revenue reports, incarcerated Ugandans, procurement contracts, construction plans, and so on.

I thought it best to keep it short.

"Sir, have you been following the case of Mr. George Forbes in Rumbek? It's getting a lot of international attention." The Minister was busy, and he looked at me with some annoyance. But with George Forbes's declining health, and the blow of his recent conviction, he might not have too many days left.

"Southern Sudan will not be judged by the standards of other countries," the Minister said, in a loud, authoritative voice. I suspected he was giving me a speech prepared for a different occasion. I scrunched up my face so he could see I was unsatisfied by his answer. "We are a country of laws, and they will be applied consistently, regardless of the consequences." I slowly shook my head from side to side.

He drew in a breath but stopped short. He put his elbows on his desk and spoke to me in a quiet tone. "Okay. What do you have to say?"

"The treatment of these men reflects badly on Southern Sudan.

One of the articles in the press is calling the judicial system 'barbaric.' *Your* judicial system. This is not the image this new country wants to project to the world," I said.

He leaned back in his chair and studied the ceiling. Then he drew himself back to the desk. He gave me a hard look and said, "I will not overrule the courts." I grimaced. "But I might be able to accelerate the appeal process."

I can't say for sure what, if anything, the Minister did, but in early June, all charges, including the murder conviction, were annulled. Mr. Forbes was free to go back to Australia, and his colleagues returned to Kenya.

The Final Drafts

Majok advised me that the Minister had signed off on the drafts of the Penal Code and Code of Criminal Procedure "with minor changes," and the local lawyers were conducting a final review before submission to Parliament. I had spent so much time on those laws that I wanted to see those "minor changes" for myself.

I found two of the local lawyers in the conference room in the process of reviewing the drafts. They greeted me warmly and complimented me on the clarity of the laws. But they had some questions. So we sat down at the table and went through each line of the draft laws. They asked well-considered, insightful questions about a wide range of difficult issues. We compared the language to the articles of the interim constitution and discussed why particular words and phrasing were used. It was a really good capacity-building session—the type of session we should have had since the beginning.

Near the end of the document, I found the changes made by the Minister. His bold pen marks scrawled across the section titled "female circumcision," a term used by the United Nations, to describe (the practice of partial or total removal of external female genitalia.) It was widely practiced in Sudan and other areas of Africa. I added a new provision, which made it a crime to deliberately cut, injure, or change the genitals of a female without a medical purpose.

I had borrowed the term from the UN for consistency's sake. The Minister had changed the name of the crime from "Female Circumcision" to "Female Genital Mutilation," which is exactly what it was.

Time to Leave

That day I left the Ministry a little high on the adrenaline that comes from completing a large, difficult project. By the time I reached camp, post-project blues were already setting in. I was mentally fried and physically exhausted from the work, the environment, and the never-ending challenges of working in Southern Sudan.

Back at camp I pulled a plastic chair over to the river and watched the trash from upstream rush by: a bright red Omo detergent package, broken flip-flops, and countless pieces of unidentifiable debris. I no longer saw the beauty that hit me the day of my arrival. It was time for me to leave.

Another attorney had been hired, and I hoped he'd be better at dealing with local lawyers than I had been. Although mine had been a one-year contract, I had stayed for eighteen months. Other consultants stayed for years, and I honestly don't know how they managed it.

Roberto happened to be "next door" evaluating a project in Rwanda and took one of the recently inaugurated flights from Kigali to Juba to help me pack up. He was mesmerized by Afex, the White Nile, and Juba, just as I knew he would be, but admitted, "I didn't appreciate what you were dealing with here."

We flew to Nairobi and then on to Zanzibar for a few days of relaxation. Our hotel had a highly recommended restaurant, and as the evening's first diners, we were offered a lovely table in the garden. But after my time in Southern Sudan, I'd had enough nature to last a lifetime. We ate indoors in the air-conditioned room. About midway through the entrée, I put my fork down and stared out at the glistening sea.

"Are you all right?" Roberto asked as he squeezed my hand.

"I just realized how much I'm going to miss Juba," I said.

"Tell me, what will you miss?" he asked.

"The faded tents, JICA-guy, the Ministry, the canoers on the White Nile, Majok, and the long walk from the Ministry back to camp. I'm going to miss everything about it."

"And Mona—will you miss Mona?" he teased.

"I'll have to think about that."

CHAPTER 7

Kigali, Rwanda

2008

Happy Birthday to Me

It was the first week of August 2007, and I had big plans for my fifti-eth birthday. Roberto was flying in from Dubai, and we'd have three days together in London before I'd take that long flight over the pole to San Francisco. We had reservations at The Ivy, the iconic West End restaurant, and I was looking forward to a glass or two of champagne to celebrate.

The Parkwalk, my two-star hotel near Lancaster Gate, didn't have Wi-Fi, so I passed on the full English breakfast, grabbed a piece of toast, and hurried down to the row of internet cafés across from Paddington Station. A cheerful woman with a long ropey braid, dressed in a salwar kameez and an over-sized men's cardigan, arrived a few minutes late to let me in.

"You're up early," she said, as I helped her press the power buttons of the long bank of consoles.

"It's my birthday," I grinned. "I have a lot planned."

I logged on and saw the top two emails had the same ominous subject line: "Terrible News."

The first was from Roberto. It was something about his paperwork not being in order and the Emirati authorities not letting him leave Dubai until the following day. That was the story, at least. Roberto had a long, frustrating history of missing planes. He was sorry and promised to make it up to me, but honestly, you'd think this one day he'd show up on time.

The second email was from my brother. My lovely old dad, the man who had been so supportive throughout my life, had passed away. He'd suffered six years of steady decline from Alzheimer's, so his death wasn't unexpected. But that morning, I learned that no matter how prepared you think you are to lose a parent, it still hurts.

I sat frozen at the keyboard and tried to hold back my emotions. I bit my lip, trying to stop a quivering chin, but it was useless. Tears rolled down my cheeks faster than I could wipe them away with the sleeve of my cardigan.

"Not bad news, I hope," the woman behind the counter called out.

"My dad passed away." There, I had said it. "He was old and poorly. In some ways, it's a blessing." She emerged from behind the counter, placed both her hands gently on my shoulders, and gave me a comforting squeeze.

"You know, the same thing happened to a man just last week," she fretted. "I think this computer is bad luck. I'll have it replaced."

Alone in London on my birthday and dazed by the news of my dad, I walked through Hyde Park until I found a bench near the Serpentine Swim Club. Watching the goggled members glide through the cold, murky water, I thought of my dad. He'd been a swimmer—a good one—a star on the Berkeley High swim team and a member of the water polo team at the University of California, Berkeley. He liked to tell the story about how his swimming prowess gave him an edge in World War II and potentially saved his life.

In 1943 my dad was an eighteen-year-old private in the US Army preparing to be shipped over to Europe on the Queen Mary, the ocean liner that was repurposed as a troopship. In an effort to maintain morale among the troops, several units were brought together for a few days of athletic competition. My dad, a strong freestyler, won several races. When the brass learned he was only a private, he was immediately promoted to staff sergeant. My dad mimicked the officer's Southern accent for years, "We can't have some dang private winning all the medals."

The promotion entitled my dad to better accommodations on the Queen Mary. Instead of a hammock down in the cargo area, he was given a bunk in a shared cabin. He believed the stability of a real bed staved off the seasickness that hit so many of the men on board. As a result, he was at full fighting strength when the ship arrived in Europe.

Sitting on that park bench in London, I realized that I would never hear him tell that story again, and the tears started all over again.

That night I phoned my mother to commiserate. She came to the phone and said, "Happy birthday, dear."

Grief Triggers

My dad's passing took some time to sink in. My mother decided to delay his memorial, so there was no emotional closure. I had trouble sleeping, I found it hard to concentrate, and I cried unexpectedly. After a few weeks, I began to worry that my response was abnormal, so I called Doris, a friend from Southern Sudan, who specialized in counseling the young victims of war-torn countries.

"Grief is tricky," she warned in her soft Irish accent. "Everyone experiences it differently. You can't expect it to disappear after a specific period. And be aware that there are 'grief triggers' that can be very emotional. You might find yourself bursting into tears at the silliest thing, such as hearing the name of your father's childhood dog. That kind of thing can set you off."

"Whisky," I whispered.

"Whisky?" she questioned.

"The name of my dad's childhood dog was Whisky, short for Whiskers," I explained.

"If whisky is one of your grief triggers, it's a good thing you're not Irish." It felt good to laugh.

"Just be aware that these grief triggers exist, and try to avoid them if you can," she cautioned. "Be good to yourself. Your dad would have wanted that."

The Project in Rwanda

Over the following months, I learned that grief is like a bee sting—it's extremely painful, and everyone has a "home remedy" for dealing with the ache. Recommendations included reading Psalms, taking afternoon naps, staying hydrated, making a memory book, and walking in the woods. I chose to keep busy and accepted a series of short-term contracts that I really couldn't get into.

Finally, in June 2008, I received a solicitation for a project in Kigali, Rwanda. USAID needed a consultant to review a proposed business plan to establish a private credit bureau in the tiny East African country. I was familiar with credit bureaus from my time in the mortgage industry. They assimilate information on an individual's or business's use of credit—the amount borrowed, payment history, defaults—which helps creditors weed out the bad borrowers. A well-functioning credit bureau is a key component of a modern financial sector.

I wanted the job. At the time, Rwanda was the darling of the global development community. Under the direction of the President, Paul Kagame, the country was undertaking monumental changes and enacting a long list of major legal reforms designed to make Rwanda a financial hub of East Africa. Establishing a private credit bureau would play a key role in that effort, so it was an exciting project.

Further, Roberto was working in Kigali overseeing the construction of an elementary school for USAID. I hoped that being in the same city as Roberto, someone who loved me and cared about my welfare, would be good for my mental health.

I did, however, have a small reservation about taking the job. Rwanda was the site of one of the most prolific genocides in human history. In 1994, the decades-long tensions (fomented by Belgian colonizers) between the country's two major ethnic groups, the Tutsis and the Hutus, reignited. In a short three months, Hutu extremists slaughtered more than 800,000 Tutsi and Tutsi sympathizers. To the shame of the world, no country or humanitarian organization, not even the UN on the ground, intervened in the massacre.

Although almost a year had passed since my dad's death, I felt fragile. I still wasn't dealing with the grief as well as I thought I should. When I called Roberto to explain my concerns, he dismissed them as being "dramatic."

"No one in Rwanda talks about the genocide," he assured me. "People are moving on. I think you might benefit from being here." This last comment stung. But in the end, I signed the contract and booked a flight to Kigali.

Open for Business

Roberto met me outside of immigration at Kigali's tiny airport. I was wearing a new Indian-print dress that I'd bought in one of the large department stores in London. He told me I looked beautiful, and just seeing him made the long trip worthwhile. He was driving his company truck, a jarring burnt orange color that looked terrible on everything, but especially a truck.

"It's Chinese," he said as if reading my mind.

The weather was perfect. The temperature was in the low

80s with a slight breeze. There wasn't a cloud in the amazing light blue sky. The road from the airport was newly paved, and a series of well-designed roundabouts facilitated the smooth flow of traffic. Small shops and cafés sporting flags and bright banners announcing "Grand Opening" flanked the road. The message was clear: Rwanda was open for business.

Kigali's small commercial area was bustling with people doing their Saturday shopping. We entered a modern mall with several floors of small enterprises—coffee shops, trendy restaurants, a women's tailor, and jewelry stores. A short escalator ferried shoppers down to an enormous supermarket on the lower level, where there was aisle after aisle of tinned goods, a large meat department, and a variety of fresh fruits and vegetables.

As we waited to check out, I noticed two unusually dressed teenagers. One was wearing pinstriped baseball knickers and the other a graduation gown, complete with a mortarboard cap and tassel. I looked at Roberto, and he leaned over to explain.

"Rwanda imports second-hand clothes from the United States, which are shipped in huge bales. Since the bales are sold by weight, the wholesalers sneak in garments that aren't technically considered clothing. Last week I hired a kid wearing a tuxedo jacket."

After picking up some supplies, Roberto drove me to his lodgings that he shared with workers on his construction team. He occupied one of several side-by-side rooms that might have been animal stables at one time. I stepped inside and inspected the sagging bed, stained basin, and broken chair.

"I'm not staying here," I announced, trying to stay calm. I felt a twitch in my right eye.

"It's not so bad," he countered. It was the exact same thing he'd said to me in Kabul, and I'd ended up living in a converted shipping container for eight months. For some reason, it infuriated me.

"In Kabul, I lived in a shipping container, and in Juba, a recycled safari tent. I'm not going to live in a mule stall in Rwanda. I've done my time in...," I searched for the right words, "... substandard accommodations."

Ultimately, we checked into the Hotel des Mille Collines, the hotel made famous by the movie *Hotel Rwanda*. The movie portrays the gritty story of how several hundred Tutsis survived the genocide by taking refuge on the hotel's grounds and, among other things, drinking water from the pool.

After check-in, the manager took the time to give us a tour of the premises.

"Welcome to the Mille Collines." He swept his hand to draw our attention to the large, sunny lobby. It was furnished with quaint clusters of rattan chairs with pink chintz cushions. Small bouquets of delicate yellow flowers sat on each of the glass tables. He apologized that we had just missed afternoon tea, but we could still order something at the patio restaurant next to the pool. Now, this was more like it.

But the Mille Collines posed unexpected challenges. The small outside bar accommodated a rotation of very young, distressingly thin, female sex workers. Typically dressed in revealing tank tops and shorts, these girls took an aggressive approach to the international clientele. I made the mistake of leaving Roberto alone at the bar while I retrieved something from the room, and upon my return, found him putting up little resistance to having his hair and face stroked by one of these young women who had taken my seat.

That image gave me all the incentive I needed to intensify my search for long-term accommodation. We quickly moved into one of the new apartment buildings springing up around the city.

Bernadette

At the beginning of my first week, USAID arranged for me to meet Bernadette, head of the National Bank's Department of Financial Institutions. Her unit was responsible for the oversight and supervision of the country's banks, microfinance lenders, and insurance companies. I arrived early and brought a book in the expectation that I was back on "African time," a concept that Mr. Eddy had tutored me in so well back in Juba.

At ten o'clock sharp, the door of Bernadette's office swung open, and a robust woman in a well-tailored gray suit announced, "There is no 'African Time' at the National Bank of Rwanda. We insist on punctuality."

Smart, well-educated, capable, and dedicated to both her job and her country, Bernadette was the ideal local counterpart. Usually these introductory meetings involve a bit of professional background and a vague work plan—not so with Bernadette. She explained the specific issues my report should address to ensure it met the needs of the National Bank. I frantically took notes.

She explained that KreditKare, a private South African company that operated credit bureaus in other African countries, had been granted tentative approval to expand into Rwanda. As a first step, KreditKare had prepared a business plan covering the technical and financial aspects of the proposed credit bureau. USAID wanted confirmation that the proposed credit bureau would be financially viable before it committed any funds toward its establishment.

Bernadette was direct and concise. She handed me a batch of documents, asked if I had any questions, and then politely dismissed me from her office.

Life in Kigali

I fell in love with Kigali almost immediately. It was safe and clean, but still had the charming challenges that made living in Africa so enjoyable. The streets were virtually litter-free—swept daily by an army of women wielding long grass brooms. With the heat, dust, and car exhaust, it must have been a horrible job, but it provided the women with an income. As a guest in the country, I reserved comment.

The easiest and cheapest way to get around town was on the back of a motor scooter. Hundreds of them buzzed around the city, defying traffic laws and terrorizing pedestrians. I had to be particularly cautious at the busier intersections and the roundabouts, where the fast-moving cars and scooters either didn't see me or didn't care.

If I were lucky, I'd come across a group of school children and hold onto the collar of one of the older boys or girls, who would guide me safely across the street. This was great entertainment for them, and occasionally I'd have to be escorted back across the street by another student and then back again, just so the preteens could tell the story about helping a "muzungu"—a white person—cross the street.

Roberto and I spent our Sundays taking long walks through the small valleys created by Kigali's hilly terrain. We were greeted by parents standing in front of tidy shacks and followed by children who called out for "bonbons," or candy. One time we found ourselves walking behind a young woman in a knee-length skirt. Roberto elbowed me and silently nodded in her direction. The backs of her dark legs were marred by a series of slashing scars—machete marks. She was a genocide survivor. Over the next several months, I'd see similar injuries and disfigurements—living reminders of the trauma the country and its people had suffered.

KreditKare

The KreditKare business plan was only a few pages long and lacked the detail necessary to make a meaningful analysis. My biggest concern was the overall cost to users. If costs were too high, the smaller lenders—the ones that made loans in lower amounts but more frequently—would shoulder a disproportionate share of the costs. I mentioned this to Bernadette, who instructed me to direct all my questions to Lee Jacobs, the KreditKare representative who visited Rwanda every other month. As luck would have it, he was scheduled to arrive the following week.

Lee was a large barrel-chested force of nature. His dark lively eyes took in everything that was going on in the room. He had the confidence of a successful dealmaker and the impeccable manners of someone who was raised well. He would eventually become a legend in the African credit bureau industry, but in 2008 he was still establishing himself. We would have our differences, but there was never a time in all our dealings that I felt belittled or marginalized—he was too good a businessman to alienate someone who might be useful to him later.

At our first meeting Lee explained that KreditKare would operate as a monopoly for the first few years, meaning it wouldn't have to compete with other credit bureaus that might want to enter the Rwandan market. Granting monopolies is a way of enticing companies to conduct business in untested and emerging markets. He also informed me that KreditKare's approach had been approved at "the highest level" of the Rwandan government—a nice way of saying, "if you don't like it, lump it."

In fact, I didn't like it. An exclusive award of the type under consideration should be accompanied by a detailed business plan reflecting reasonable costs and consumer protections. Otherwise, there's a risk of overreaching by the monopoly holder.

Bernadette had already alerted Lee that I had concerns.

"I understand you have issues with the business plan," he said as he handed me his business card.

"I think it's expensive," I said. "It might run the smaller institutions out of business, and maybe some of the medium-sized ones as well. They just don't have the profits to absorb the added costs."

"Well, if the profit margin is that small, maybe those institutions shouldn't be operating," he offered.

"Maybe," I said, trying to sound agreeable. "But it's the kind of issue that needs to be brought to the attention of the Central Bank governor, so he can make an informed decision." I flashed an insincere smile.

Lee smiled back and reminded me that KreditKare's arrangement had been reached "at the highest levels." But he told me to stay in touch and agreed to respond to any and all questions I might have.

Roberto's School

Except for a couple of final details—the replacement of a warped door and the installation of a couple of drainpipes—Roberto's school was finished. It was a beautiful little structure comprising eight classrooms that cascaded down a gentle hillside. The freshly painted alabaster walls gleamed in the bright Rwandan sunshine.

The new school was the pride of the village, and a day of festivities was organized to celebrate its completion. Apparently it was a slow week for dignitaries, as I was invited to sit on a shaded platform with the young female principal and a Catholic priest—the other "honored guests." Parents, grandparents, and village members sat in clusters of chairs in the open courtyard while groups of students darted about meeting classmates and friends.

The program started with a long blessing from the priest. In a combination of French and Kinyarwanda, he thanked the Lord for the president, the country, the honored guests (me), the construction workers, USAID, the school, the principal, the teachers, the parents, the students (both existing and future), the community, the barbeque—and on and on. It took the best part of a half hour, but everyone in attendance felt included.

The blessing was followed by a number of speeches, most in Kin-yarwanda, and then a program of local entertainment. A large church choir sang a number of hymns, and a group of young adults per-formed some of Rwanda's exuberant traditional dances. The priest leaned close to me and explained that the dances contain strong life messages such as the benefits of hard work. "It's good for the children to see our dances."

At some point in the program I was joined by two young boys, about four and five years old, dressed in matching shorts and T-shirts. At first, they nonchalantly rested their slim elbows on the edge of the podium, nervously peering back in my direction to see if I would chase them off. The next time they caught my notice, they were both seated cross-legged on the platform. Then with ninja-like stealth, they were next to me. One stood beside me, and the other directly behind. More than once, I felt a small hand slide down the back of my hair, followed by the soft sound of muffled giggles.

Finally the barbeque was served in the early afternoon, the hottest part of the day. Everyone received a generous plate of goat ribs and kebabs, with side dishes prepared by the local women. Someone had forgotten the ice, so we drank warm orange-flavored Fanta sodas out of the can.

I was looking forward to a goat kebab, something I'd acquired a taste for back in Southern Sudan, but as an honored guest, I was pre-sented with a special plate—(a skewer of six goat hearts) I had eaten goat heart in a restaurant in rural France and loathed it. But every-one was watching, so I took a tentative bite and earned an appreciative round of applause.

The two boys who had kept me company during the festivities reappeared with barbeque grease around their mouths and new stains on their shirts and resumed their places next to me on the podium.

As I drew the goat heart skewer up to my mouth, both boys pressed against me. I was almost eye-to-eye with the younger one who stood on my right, and it was hard not to laugh. I lowered the skewer back to the plate, and they leaned back out. I picked up the skewer again, and they once again pressed against me, making sure I knew they were still there. As I put the skewer back on the plate, they leaned back. In the end, the pressure was too much. I asked the priest if it was permissible to give the goat hearts to the boys.

"Oh, yes. They have a sick grandma. All those rich vitamins will help her condition. I will instruct them to take the food to her." The priest spoke to them in a harsh tone, and they solemnly nodded. I handed over my plate, and they scurried off, never to be seen again.

Meetings with Stakeholders

As part of my evaluation, I needed to gauge the level of private sector support for the proposed credit bureau. Bernadette helped me arrange meetings with the large African banks that had offices in Kigali, the smaller local banks, and some microlenders. I also met with the banking association and the newly established microfinance association to make sure I covered all my bases.

The meetings were a pleasure. As the rest of the world plunged headlong into a recession caused by the subprime crisis in the United States, the Rwandan economy and its fledgling financial sector were performing well. New banks were entering the market, and there was an optimism about the future.

Most of the officers of the large banks had experience with international institutions, such as Citicorp and American Express, and understood the benefits of a credit reporting system. The smaller banks and microlenders were unfamiliar with the concepts, but after a brief overview they were quick to appreciate its advantages.

When I mentioned the potential costs that might negatively affect their earnings, I received two responses, "whatever is best for the country" or "whatever the president wants." There would be no pushback from the financial service sector. I was the only person not completely on board—and as Lee Jacobs intimated, who was I?

The Genocide Memorial

During my meetings with Rwanda's banks and lenders, I was frequently asked if I had visited the new Genocide Memorial that had opened just a couple of years earlier. In light of the memorial's importance to the Rwandans, Roberto and I set aside Sunday afternoon for a visit.

The memorial was perched on one of Kigali's many hills, overlooking the city and the surrounding countryside. It was a serene location and befitting what the memorial represents—the remembrance of the victims and the expectation that nothing like it ever happens again. The complex is made up of a small library and garden, but the main feature is a museum that provides the history of Rwanda that led up to genocide and details the brutality of the mass killings.

The exhibits were heartbreaking, but I held it together through the main rooms of photos and exhibits. The last room was dedicated to children of the genocide, and included the favorite toys of young victims. My eye started to twitch. I had reached my emotional limit, and I told Roberto I would wait for him outside.

I sat on a concrete ledge still warm from the afternoon sun and breathed in the fresh air of the early evening. I kept thinking about the extraordinary pain that Rwanda had suffered. I felt my father's death so keenly—but the Rwandans had lost fathers, mothers, siblings, aunts, uncles, cousins, and neighbors in such a violent way.

A couple of men stood a short distance away, talking about the "next interment." I hadn't appreciated that the memorial also housed a mass grave that held the remains of over 250,000 genocide victims. Bodies discovered around the country were still being brought to the memorial for a dignified burial.

A strange ache radiated up my right arm. Nothing too serious; I might have slept on it wrong. I gently massaged my shoulder, hoping to ease the pain. I made a mental note to pick up some aspirin on the way home.

Roberto came out of the museum and sat next to me on the concrete ledge.

"I guess if a country doesn't have oil reserves, the US has no real interest in coming to its rescue." Indeed, it was to the world's shame that no country intervened during the one hundred days of killing. The violence ended only when the Tutsi-led Rwandan Patriotic Front, led by then rebel leader and now President Paul Kagame, captured Kigali and forced the killers across the border into the Democratic Republic of Congo.

I had some understanding of why the United States had failed to act, but I didn't want to discuss it at the Genocide Memorial. At the time of the genocide, the United States had recently suffered a number of casualties in connection with a disastrous peacekeeping mission in Somalia. The photos of dead American soldiers being dragged through the streets of Mogadishu had made the United States wary of intervening in African crises and, as a consequence, the Clinton Administration declined to intercede in Rwanda.

"Well, it wasn't just the United States that failed Rwanda," I said. "It was the French, the European Union, the United Nations, and other African countries." I teared up but didn't know if it was because of the sadness of the memorial, the scorn of Roberto's tone, my continuing grief over my father, or the fact that the US had not intervened to stop the killing.

Realizing he might have gone too far, Roberto put a comforting hand on my shoulder, and I felt the new pain in my arm more intensely.

257

Visiting the Gorillas

For Roberto's birthday in the first week of November, I bought tickets to visit Rwanda's famous mountain gorillas. The tickets were expensive, but I was still trying to make up for the donkey cart ride in Kabul, which Roberto didn't enjoy as much as I thought he would.

The gorillas live in the Virunga National Park along the borders of Rwanda, Uganda, and the Democratic Republic of the Congo, a four-hour drive from Kigali on winding roads. Along the way, we enjoyed the beauty of the greenery and marveled at the steep hills terraced with small cultivated plots. Roberto pointed out the groves of the eucalyptus trees, originally planted as an anti-malaria project. Non-native to Africa, eucalyptus trees require an extraordinary amount of water, which they leach from the ground. In theory, the eucalyptus would drain the breeding grounds for mosquitoes and tsetse flies and help control the spread of malaria and sleeping sickness.

"Did it work?" I asked.

"Hard to say," Roberto shrugged. "There's still a lot of malaria in Rwanda."

We were escorted to the gorillas by a young guide and two men carrying automatic rifles, a security measure due to the proliferation of poachers. Our group was made up of eight people: a couple of impossibly thin twenty-somethings, a young honeymooning couple, a college English lecturer and his girlfriend visiting from the UK, and Roberto and me. While we hoped for a long congenial trek, Roberto and I managed to alienate everyone in the first hour, and as Roberto gleefully acknowledged later in the day, "We weren't even trying."

First we offended the two youngest people in the group. Hiking up the steep, slippery hill was exhausting. The grass was slick, and my smooth-soled shoes made it worse. I'd take one step up and slide two steps back. Roberto grabbed me by the hand, but we were stopped halfway up the hill by one of the twenty-somethings taking a photo of tourists acted badly

a baby goat. She turned toward us and tried to articulate the adorability of the kid.

"He looks so...so..." When she failed to finish her sentence, Roberto and I did it for her, and in unison, said, "...tasty." Then we clapped hands in a lazy high five.

Our hilarity upset the young woman, who we later found out worked for an animal rights association and was a longtime vegan. She and her partner refused to acknowledge us for the rest of the day.

Next, the honeymoon couple asked us to take their photo next to an infant gorilla they had managed to back into some thick brush. The little gorilla was shaking in terror. Roberto refused to take their camera and added, "You'd be ashamed of yourself once you saw the photo." Two more of the group refused to speak to us.

Relegated to walking next to the English couple, the only people still speaking to us, I learned that she was visiting him "to see where their relationship was going."

"You see," she explained, "we're not married, so it's difficult for me to get a long-term Rwandan visa."

For some reason, Roberto jumped in and began admonishing her partner, the lecturer, to "make an honest woman out of her." Of course, after Roberto's interference, they kept their distance from us as well.

After a couple of hours of walking, we arrived at the troupe of gorillas, nestled among the growth of the leafy vegetation. Several adult females, a collection of juveniles, and a couple of infants played in the early afternoon sunshine. The females groomed the younger ones with expert picking. They were eerily humanoid; the similarity in mannerisms and gestures is undeniable. It was the juveniles and infants with their nonstop rolling, tumbling, and wrestling that stole the show. They were joyfully hilarious in their carefree play.

Sitting on a ledge, in a strategic spot, was the impressive silverback. From his perch, he kept an eye on both the younger gorillas and the visitors as well. He occasionally emitted short grunting noises, less than gentle reminders that he could easily tear our heads off. It was magical.

With no one speaking to us, it was a long, quiet, slippery trek back to base. I asked Roberto, "Better than the donkey cart ride?" referring back to his birthday in Kabul.

"Much better."

The Assessment Report

My report on the proposed credit bureau was due at the end of November. I highlighted the positive aspects of the proposed business plan, and noted that despite the additional costs, which were still unquantified, the banks and other lenders supported the credit bureau without reservation.

"Country before profits. That must be a difficult concept for an American to grasp," Roberto taunted. But he was missing the point. If the credit bureau was too expensive, it wouldn't be used, defeating its purpose.

"Maybe if there was more of this attitude in the United States, the whole world wouldn't be facing a recession," he added. While there may have been some truth in that comment, I looked into his big blue eyes and thought, when did Roberto become so annoying?

Lastly, I turned my attention to KreditKare's projected financials. I needed confirmation that the bureau would generate enough income to cover expenses. So I emailed Dave, an old friend and Harvard Business School graduate, and asked if he would look at the numbers. Despite running a large software company in San Francisco, he responded almost immediately.

In that language that comes from studying vocabulary lists in prep school and honed in the dinner clubs of Cambridge, Dave explained

(that no investor in their right mind would invest in an entity based on the KreditKare financials.)

(It will take too long to recoup their investment," he explained. "It's a poor return. ")

"That doesn't align with what's going on here," I said, trying to hide my frustration. "These guys are really pushing this forward."

"Okay, then this is what is going to happen," he paused for dramatic effect. (Somewhere along the line, you're going to see a huge hike in fees. Four or five times what is in the current business plan. That's the only way this company will see a profit in a reasonable amount of time. I can almost guarantee it.")

So I added a paragraph questioning the profitability of Kredit-Kare's business plan, finished up the report, and sent it off to Washington for review and comment. (With any luck, it would be well received, and I might be hired to write the credit reporting law.)

France

(To celebrate the New Year, Roberto and I took a trip to France.) We flew to Paris, took the train down to Bayeux, where we toured the old city and visited the famous Bayeax Tapestry, the 900-year-old fabric masterpiece that depicts the Norman Invasion of England in 1066. We stayed at the Lion d'Or Hotel, formerly an eighteenth century coaching inn that also served as the British press headquarters after the D-Day Allied invasion of Normandy in June 1944.

Since we had a free afternoon, we signed up for a tour of the Normandy beaches. Our tour group included two American couples and an Australian graduate student, who, by coincidence, was specializing in studying the genocides of the world. (The D-Day invasion made by the Allied forces of Britain, America, Canada, and France was the largest seaborne invasion in history.) In school, we're taught that the invasion

was a turning point in World War II because it forced the Germans to fight on two fronts, contributing to the surrender of Nazi Germany in less than a year.

Our French tour guide, a woman in her early thirties, had a petulant attitude toward the invasion and expressed doubts over its effectiveness in shortening the war. She also complained that every American serviceperson who visits Omaha Beach, one of the major landing sites, took home a rock as a souvenir. As a result, the beach had lost much of its natural beauty.

While waiting in the van for our guide to pick up some passes, Bart, one of the American men, complained about the guide's attitude.

"It seems to me that young mademoiselle and her countrymen should be more grateful for America's efforts in the war."

Bart's comment made me think back to an incident I shared with my dad. In 1990, we were in Paris on vacation and had ordered a take-away lunch from a small cheese shop near our hotel. It was a nice day, and my mother wanted to picnic in the Tuileries near the Louvre. My dad's French was pretty good, much better than mine, but the teenage clerk still rolled her eyes and sighed heavily when my dad fumbled for a particular word. In those days, it seemed the French hated you if you didn't speak French and detested you if you did.

As we waited for our lunch order, a short round woman wearing a paper hat and striped apron, burst in from the back room. She surveyed the shop with her hands on her hips and unexpectedly called out in French to my father.

"You, sir. Are you an American?" The shop fell quiet.

"I am." I could see he was uncomfortable at being singled out. I moved closer to him and gently touched his arm so he'd know he had back up.

She took a deep breath. "I thank you. I thank your service." She had tears in her eyes, and her voice grew reedy with emotion. "These children…" she waved in the direction of the surly shop clerks, "… they do not remember, and they do not take the time to learn. I thank you for my family. Thank you for my life." She gave us our lunch free of charge.

Remembering that day, I said in response to Bart's comment, "Not all the French are like that. Some are truly grateful to the United States."

The Law on Credit Bureaus

In February, USAID Washington accepted my report. I received an email from the project manager in Washington, DC, saying it was far better than what he had expected. It was meant as a compliment, I think. Regardless, I was pleased because his approval came with a contract extension covering the drafting of the credit reporting law.

I knew a lot about credit legislation, but credit bureaus present different issues. At the time, it was an evolving area, and there were no established best practices to follow. So I contacted everyone I knew who worked in the credit reporting area and developed a detailed list of all the major issues that needed to be addressed in the law. I compared different laws to find the ones that were well organized and easy to follow. Knowing that Lee Jacobs would review it, I really wanted it to be good.

Lake Kivu

As I worked on the law, Roberto was trying to cobble together financing for a new sports stadium. Rwandans are huge soccer fans, and a new stadium would enhance the perception of Rwanda as a developed country. In the meantime, he worked with a local construction company on several small projects.

One Friday, he had to deliver building supplies to a project located across the border in Goma, Democratic Republic of the Congo. It meant a long five-hour drive. At the last minute, I asked if I could go with him. My arm ached nonstop, and I needed to take a break from working at the computer. He hesitated for what seemed like a very long time but ultimately agreed that I could tag along.

We drove in an uncomfortable silence, broken only by my complaints about Roberto's driving. It was on that quiet ride that I realized that Roberto's and my relationship had changed. I was the first to admit that I was not the same fun-loving person he'd met in Kosovo, but so much had happened since then. I had more responsibility and less support. Here in Rwanda, the law and the project raised complex issues, and I didn't want to let the Rwandans down. Plus I had a problem with my arm that would not go away. The pain was growing more intense by the day.

We stayed the night at one of the recently refurbished hotels on Lake Kivu. We struggled to get through dinner, and it was a relief when the day was finally over.

The next morning, we started the long leisurely drive back to Kigali. Saturday is market day, and the roads were lined with a constant stream of women—a reminder that Rwanda is one of the most densely populated countries in the world. Swathed in brightly colored material, most of the women had babies tied to their backs and carried baskets of produce to sell at the local market. Despite the long walk and the hilly terrain, there was a great sense of joy and excitement as we passed the women going to market.

When we got back into cell range, Roberto's phone started to ring, and it continued to ring every thirty minutes for the next three hours. According to Roberto, it was a secretary who worked for an important minister, a minister who might play a key role in getting funding for the sports stadium. He never explained how or why she had his phone number, and the matter started to eat away at me.

A few more miles down the road, I asked Roberto to stop at a market so I could get some aspirin. The pain in my arm was so severe I could hardly stand it. The shop didn't stock aspirin, so I bought the largest beer they sold. I drank as fast as I could, but it did nothing for the pain in my arm.

Stalling for Time

Lee continued to visit Kigali every other month for meetings with the governor, Bernadette, and some of the larger lenders. I was still concerned about the expense of the proposed credit bureau, but I seemed to be the only one. The officials from the banks continued to support "whatever was best for the country."

Since I couldn't figure out how to address my financial concerns, I did the next best thing—I stalled for time. I wrote long emails to Lee asking questions about every aspect of the credit bureau process: information to be collected, submission process, pricing, etc. Even if I already knew the answer, I asked the question and requested a written response "for the files." I probably wrote a million extra words trying to slow the timetable down. On the flip side, Lee responded quickly, with in-depth explanations. I'm sure he knew what I was doing, but he played along. And it worked. I bought Rwanda—and myself—a few extra months.

São Tomé and Príncipe

After our trip to Lake Kivu, Roberto couldn't say or do anything right. Our life together was one long argument. There were a lot of little things that singly were manageable but collectively annoyed me to the point that I doubted that our relationship would survive.

At the end of another tough weekend alternating between petty arguments and painful silence, I decided I wanted him out of the apartment. No, I wanted more than that. I wanted him out of the country.

So I sat down at my computer and made extensive revisions to Roberto's resume—I *Americanized* it.

He went from "team member" to "team leader," and when that didn't sound impressive enough, he became "manager." I highlighted his work on the roads in the Serbian enclaves, the work on the US Embassy in Kabul, and the school and clinic repair jobs. Then I turned my attention to language skills. He'd listed Spanish and English.

"Don't you speak Italian?" I called to him in the other room.

"Yeah, pretty well," he called back.

"What about Portuguese?" I continued.

"Only a few words. Why are you asking?" He poked his head into the room where I was working.

"Just curious." I smiled.

Then pretending to be Roberto's secretary, I forwarded his revised resume to every consulting firm soliciting for an engineer, as well as those that might need an engineer in the future. I made it clear that any offers or inquiries should be directed not to me, but to Mr. Roberto directly.

Three weeks later, Roberto signed a contract with a French firm to work in *Portuguese*-speaking São Tomé and Príncipe. I did my best to sound surprised when he told me about the job and stifled a laugh at his puzzlement that the firm believed that he could speak Portuguese. I was almost believable when lamenting his departure. I suggested he take everything out of the apartment. I might have tipped my hand when I wondered aloud if he might want to leave early. That's how much I wanted him out of my life.

Dark Tourism

Once Roberto was out of the country, my life improved significantly. I bought a gym membership at the Serena, the new luxury hotel a few blocks from my apartment that catered to the celebrities on their way to see the gorillas. I became a regular at the Serena's opulent Sunday brunch, where I handed a serving spoon to the likes of Ted Turner, the communications magnate, and Ben Affleck, the actor.

One Sunday a man wearing a Dodgers baseball cap approached me in the lobby and asked for directions to Sainte-Famille Church. Sainte-Famille is located near the Mille Collines, the hotel where Roberto and I stayed the first month after my arrival. I gave him directions and even noted some sights of interest on the way, but cautioned he might be too late for Sunday services.

"I'm not going for the church service," he explained, "I'm a 'dark tourist.'"

"Dark tourist?" My instincts told me not to pursue this conversation, but I couldn't resist.

"You know, dark tourism, black tourism, grief tourism? I go around the world visiting places associated with catastrophic human events. Auschwitz-Birkenau, Chernobyl, and now Rwanda." I knew from my reading that Sainte-Famille was one of the massacre sites of the genocide. According to one report, the priest helped the extremists take victims from the church to be slaughtered.

Suddenly my shoulder ached, much worse than ever before. I reached up with my opposite hand to massage the pain. I spoke slowly, "I'm having a little trouble comprehending this."

"Come on, we're all dark tourists to one degree or another." He spoke without a hint of defensiveness.

"I'm not a dark tourist. I don't go to places associated with 'catastrophic human events,'" I said, feeling inexplicably tired.

"Have you visited the American Cemetery in France?" He was trying to use me as an example.

"You're not trying to compare the events of D-Day with what happened at Auschwitz or here in Rwanda are you?" I could feel myself growing emotional.

("There's really no difference. They all commemorate a tremendous loss of life. Right?")

"Normandy..." I paused to collect myself. "Normandy is a memorial to sacrifice for a greater good. Even though my arm ached, I pointed at him for emphasis. "It cannot be compared to what happened here." Why was I even having this discussion?

"Well, I think you're splitting hairs," he said. I detested this person. He and his ugly hobby were despicable.

I went back to my apartment, and by the time I'd reached the door, my arm ached so badly that even taking off my T-shirt was torturous. The pain in my arm could no longer be managed with hot packs and over-the-counter painkillers. I needed to see a doctor.

The American Hospital

(I booked a flight to Paris and made an appointment at the American Hospital in Neuilly.) It was the same hospital that F. Scott Fitzgerald begged to be taken to in *A Moveable Feast*, and where Aristotle Onassis went to for treatment in his final days.

My flight transited through Addis Ababa, an airport that's in a constant state of disruption due to never-ending construction. My flight from Kigali was late taking off, and with the long queue at security, I was concerned I would miss my connection to Paris. I explained my situation to the passengers taking off their belts and removing their shoes. They graciously allowed me to jump the queue so I could catch my flight. As I walked up the line, each person gave me a loving push on my back as a sign of support. It was a reminder of the many niceties that come with living in Africa.

Dr. Renard, one of the orthopedic surgeons at the American Hospital, saw me in the early afternoon. I liked him. In his late sixties, he maintained a rakish air by turning up the collar of his white coat and sporting a short spiky hairstyle. Dr. Renard looked at the films from my MRI, first with his glasses off and again with them on. Then he called out to the receptionist for my file, or at least that's what I understood. The receptionist was away from her desk, and we sat there in an uncomfortable silence. I decided to ask Dr. Renard a question that had been bothering me for years.

"Doctor Renard, may I ask you a rather personal question?" He looked at me for an unusually long time and then responded with a rather unenthusiastic, "If you must."

"Can you please explain to me why the French people love Jerry Lewis?" I was referring to the American comedian whose zany antics had won the French over in the 1950s and '60s. Lewis played the lead roles in the original version of *The Nutty Professor* and other films I found too cringeworthy to watch. "We just don't get it in the United States."

The staid Dr. Renard leaned back in his chair and swiveled back and forth, with his hands tented in front of him. Then he leaned forward, placed his elbows on the desk, and in almost a whisper, said, "Jerry Lewis, il est magnifique." Jerry Lewis is magnificent.

Dr. Renard explained that after World War II, France was devastated, and the people were grieving for loved ones lost in the war. They were suffering. The economy was ruined, food was scarce, and inflation had skyrocketed.

"All we had were the 'meemes.'" (I corrected his pronunciation, "mimes.")

"Yes, mimes."

That helped put things in perspective for me. If you have to choose between the Nutty Professor and mimes, the Nutty Professor will win every time. Dr. Renard went on at length about Jerry Lewis's irreverence and slapstick antics, and how hard Dr. Renard had laughed as a boy.

Eventually the receptionist brought my file, and Dr. Renard flipped through the various sheets and pulled out the personal questionnaire I had filled out at the beginning of my visit.

"Your father is no longer living. When did he pass?" he asked.

"About a year ago," I answered. "Maybe a little more than a year ago." He shook his head at my response.

"You are not married. But I assume you have a boyfriend or a girlfriend?" He looked up at me expectantly.

"I had a boyfriend up until a few weeks ago. But I had him shipped off to São Tomé for a job," I answered.

"I don't understand exactly, but the answer is that you have recently broken the relationship with your boyfriend. Is that correct?"

"Yes," I answered. I started to see where this line of questioning was going.

"And alcohol consumption? Two or three or maybe four glasses a day? Am I right?" he asked. I slowly nodded.

"But I'm still in single digits," I lied. I was drinking much more.

"It's too much," he admonished.

"And you live in Rwanda where you have no support system for dealing with these personal matters?" All this sounded so sad—and it was my life he was itemizing. Tears started rolling down my cheeks, and he reached behind him for a box of tissues, which he dropped in front of me.

"Jamie," he sighed. "I am not a doctor of the mind, but I see problems here. You are not taking care of your mental health, and it is negatively affecting your body. If you do not do something, your arm will only get worse." I was still sniffling.

"I think it is unwise for you to stay in Kigali. I urge you to go to a place where death is not so..." he searched for the word, "...prominent." Then he smiled at me in a kindly way. "And I recommend a few doses of Jerry Lewis. He will make you laugh. I promise."

My Replacement

On the plane ride back to Kigali, I thought long and hard about what Dr. Renard had said. I was disappointed with my inability to channel the Rwandan resilience and move on from my sorrow. But I just couldn't, and the pain in my shoulder was the throbbing evidence of that.

I wrote to my firm with a status update. The draft law was close to final, and the report and explanatory notes would be finished within the week. I suggested that it was in the project's best interest to find a consultant who was more familiar with the technical aspects of the credit reporting system. Specifically, they needed someone who understood the hardware and software needs and who would be better able to check KreditKare's plans for that component of the credit bureau.

I was surprised that it only took a few days to find my replacement. Cal, an expert with the necessary technical expertise, would be on-site in less than a month. We exchanged emails, and it was immediately clear that Cal would take a different approach to the project. After reading my background notes, he responded that he was more inclined to let KreditKare proceed with their business plan.

"After all," he wrote, "hasn't the plan already been approved at the highest levels? Who are we to interfere?"

I found his attitude extremely annoying. What's the point of being a consultant if you're not going to push hard for what's best for the country?

Final Law and Cost Estimates

I did a last read of the draft law. Knowing that the law would eventually be translated into French and Kinyarwanda, Rwanda's other official languages, I kept the language as plain as possible. I was pleased that despite the complexities of the credit-reporting system, the draft law was clear and easy to understand.

Bernadette asked me to work with Lee to make sure we agreed on all the provisions before it was submitted to the Parliament. We sat in the library at the National Bank, and I watched him review each article, almost daring him to make changes. I have to admit he knew his way around credit reporting legislation. He made some tweaks that improved the draft.

In a final attempt to address the cost of the proposed credit bureau, I urged Bernadette to have KreditKare prepare fee estimates for each institution based on its current level of lending. It was a practical way to demonstrate how the proposed credit reporting system would affect the earnings of Rwanda's financial institutions. In response to Bernadette's request, Lee prepared the estimates which were presented at a meeting with the National Bank's senior staff.

Lee read through the fee estimates for each institution. It was alarming. The cost of running the credit bureau would be three to four times higher than the initial plan. Here it was, the hike in fees that Dave had predicted so many months back. Not only would this affect the struggling microfinance lenders, but some of the weaker banks would be hard hit as well.

The Banking Association

"Given the revised costs," I caught up with Cal in the stairwell, "we need to find a way to change the governor's mind about KreditKare's plan." I wasn't quite ready to give up yet.

"Lee Jacobs is a descendant of the people who beat the British in the Boer War." Cal was inclined to let things play out. "He's not going to let one little girl from California get in his way."

I didn't like what Cal was saying, but he was probably right. After all the report writing, meetings, and efforts to stall the process, in the end I would just have to accept that I would not be able to derail the KreditKare plan.

Walking back to the apartment with the stack of fee estimates under my good arm, I noticed a newly installed sign, "Rwanda Bankers' Association." I had met with an officer of the association several months before as part of my initial evaluation—but now I had real data. I walked in and asked to see the association's president.

Trying to be as unbiased as possible, I laid out the current plans for the credit bureau. I explained that it would be mandatory and that all lenders would be required to participate. I showed him the fee schedules, and he realized the magnitude of the issue. Several of the smaller lenders working to provide credit to women and other vulnerable groups could not afford to operate with the added expense of the credit bureau fees—and that was bad for the lenders, the borrowers, and for Rwanda.

"I need to discuss this with our members," he said.

"Yes, sir. I think you do." I said calmly.

"We need to speak to the governor of the National Bank," he added with a bit of panic in his voice.

"Yes, sir. I think you need to do that as well."

Meeting with the Governor

I wasn't in Rwanda when the Bankers' Association hosted the governor of the National Bank, but Cal told me about the meeting. CEOs from both the large and small lenders packed the room, and everyone agreed that the proposed fees and charges would increase the cost of credit for businesses and consumers and would likely hurt the availability and affordability of credit in Rwanda. The country needed a simple, inexpensive approach to data collection and distribution. The governor

273

understood, and the KreditKare proposal was rejected in favor of a simpler, more affordable system)

(Over the next several months, a small, low-priced credit bureau was established by the National Bank that, along with the other new legislation, helped to establish Rwanda as a financial hub.)

I couldn't have asked for a better outcome.

CHAPTER 8

Panjshir, Afghanistan

2010

The Obama Surge

After leaving Rwanda, I took some time off and skipped across the globe like a flat stone across a pond. I visited the monolithic carved-stone churches in Lalibela, Ethiopia; spent a week shopping in London; flew to Sydney to see Kate, my colleague from Kosovo; and then home to San Jose for my father's memorial service. The memorial was a poignant affair with a small group of my parents' friends. Each took a turn telling a story about my father's kindness and what he had meant to them.

The time off was a tonic. The pain in my shoulder that had been so debilitating in Rwanda disappeared. I felt better and stronger than I had in years. And just as I started to feel a bit restless, I received an email with the memo line "Call for Resumes—Afghanistan."

At the end of 2009, the war in Afghanistan was not going well. The Taliban had regrouped and were making territorial gains. In an effort to contain the enemy and turn the war around, President Barack Obama committed to what became known as the "Obama Surge." This involved the deployment of 30,000 more troops and an additional 3,000 US civilians to work in the Kabul Embassy and remote field outposts known as provincial reconstruction teams (PRTs). USAID was particularly interested in hiring experienced professionals: agronomists, engineers, economists, and legal advisors.

When I had left Kabul at the end of 2005, I swore I'd never go back. The lack of collaboration, the incredible waste of funds, and the excruciatingly slow progress were so disheartening. And who could forget Patrick and his boorish interpretation of the Golden Rule? But Obama had a reputation for being a careful man. So I wanted to believe that his administration would get it right. And on a personal note, there was something very appealing about playing some small role in helping to shorten a war growing more unpopular by the day. But I was still reluctant to apply for the job.

The next day I received an email from Roberto. He was going back to Afghanistan on an engineering contract. He still didn't know the part I'd played in getting him out of Rwanda, but that seemed like ancient history. The thought of seeing him again, even if it was in Kabul, tipped the scales, and I filled out the extensive application.

Pre-Deployment

Since the position might involve access to confidential information, I needed a security clearance. The background checks took forever, but finally, at the end of January 2010, I signed a contract with USAID, and I flew to Washington, DC, for two weeks of pre-deployment training.

The first week involved classroom sessions at the Foreign Service Institute in Arlington, Virginia. Instructors gave an abbreviated history of Afghanistan, its cultural mores, tips for living on a compound, and some advice on how to work alongside the US military. One session covered the roles and interrelationships among the main players operating in Kabul: the Department of Defense, the Department of State, and USAID. Ideally, these entities should have been working closely together to ensure coordinated support and development assistance. But interagency squabbles were not uncommon.

The second week we flew to a place called Camp Atterbury near Indianapolis for field training with the Indiana National Guard. The week proved to be a mixed bag. The young guardsmen (and women) who drove us around in old Humvees salvaged from Iraq couldn't have been nicer or more professional. But I had never experienced the biting cold of a midwestern January, and I was miserable most of the time.

The weapons training was more to my liking. We learned how to fire everything from a Sig Sauer to an assault rifle—the idea being, you could try to save yourself if security was "taken out." I thought I was a pretty good shot, but the instructor took me aside and diplomatically noted, "There's no shame in just playing dead."

Kabul Arrival

With two weeks of training under our belts, my class of advisors departed Washington's Dulles Airport the third week of February with high expectations and a belief that we were valuable assets in a noble cause. But immediately upon arrival, we morphed into logistic nuisances. USAID didn't have the personnel or systems in place to manage the huge influx of people, and the overworked staff made no secret of how much stress we were causing them. We had to be fed, housed, and transported, and most importantly, deployed—*anywhere*—as quickly as possible to make room for the next batch of advisors that would be arriving shortly.

My resume hadn't been picked up for a position in Kabul, so I'd be deployed to one of the provinces. I hoped for one of the bigger cities—such as Herat in the west, or Jalalabad in the east—where I might be able to use my banking and commercial law background, but that was unlikely. My law degree made it a near certainty that I'd be slotted as a legal advisor. That meant I'd be supporting the rule of law programming by working with the judiciary and promoting the central Afghan government agencies as a means of increasing the government's credibility at the local level.

I made an effort to track down legal advisors who were either transitioning through Kabul for vacation or were at the end of their year-long contracts and leaving for good (I wanted a better idea of what I was in for.)

Unfortunately, there was very little positive news to report. (The courts were slow, expensive, open to taking bribes, and limited in their enforcement capacity) As for the general work in the provinces, there was too much reliance on "quick-impact" projects—constructing schools and community centers—that did little to promote stability. The more I heard, the less I liked.

While I waited for my assignment, I explored the US Embassy/ USAID compound. (Essentially there were two sides—the embassy side and the USAID side—that straddled a highly secured road) The jewel of the compound was the embassy itself, which gleamed a warm mustard color in the bright winter sunshine. Someone explained that the embassy façade, made up of an eight-foot curtain of bulletproof glass, was inspired by a traditional Afghan carpet pattern. Taking photos of the embassy was prohibited, but somehow plenty of pictures ended up on the internet.

In addition to the embassy, there were the Marine Security Guard Quarters; an apartment complex for civilians; a "DFAC" (military-speak for dining facilities); and a cluster of more temporary structures with office space, gyms, and sleeping quarters called "hooches" reserved for transients like me. There was also a small store that sold alcohol and embassy souvenirs such as cups, mouse pads, T-shirts, and fleeces with the elaborate US Embassy-Kabul logo.

The USAID side was much less glamorous. The offices were little more than a series of unattractive, low-lying, temporary buildings jam-packed with cubicles and workstations. The only real bright spot on the USAID side was the Duck and Cover, the small bar that the ambassador was always threatening to shut down due to his concern that no one be impaired in a war zone. The bar itself wasn't much, but there was a nice wooden deck where people could sit outside and exchange stories and information.

Still hoping that there might be a way to stay in Kabul, I decided to introduce myself to Mick, the Director of USAID's Office of Economic Growth (OEG). OEG was responsible for overseeing several large projects covering areas well within my wheelhouse, including bank regulation, access to credit, and private sector development.

I caught up with Mick as he strode into the OEG office on his way back from lunch. Mick, a thirty-something economist, had the chiseled jaw of a Ralph Lauren model but just missed being handsome. There was something about his eyes; they were too small for the size of his head. I explained that I wanted to "put a face to my name," and I handed him a copy of my resume. I shamelessly pointed out certain skills that might fit well with the programming in the OEG office.

"You're more impressive in person than on paper." He had seen my resume during the recruiting process but didn't pick me up for a job in Kabul.

"Thanks, I think." I wasn't sure if that was a compliment.

"I don't have any slots available, but I'll keep you in mind," he promised. It was the best I could hope for.

That afternoon, I received notice that I would travel up to Bagram Air Base, the massive military hub about thirty miles north of Kabul, and the ultimate decision on where to place me would be made by the USAID/Department of State up there.

Passive-Aggressive Person

The night before my departure, I ate dinner in the DFAC on the embassy side of the compound. It was smaller and less chaotic than the USAID one. Except for the men and women in pixelated camouflage-print uniforms, a new pattern that had recently been adopted by the US Army, the embassy DFAC looked pretty much like a high school cafeteria. I indulged in a salad because I didn't know if fresh greens would be available where I was going. A nicely dressed woman sitting at a small table next to the windows nodded to the open chair across from her.

Her name was Barbara. She had finished her year at the embassy and was leaving for DC at the end of the week. She encouraged me to ask her anything about embassy life, and she promised to give me an honest answer. As I was thinking of a question, she leaned forward with a knitted brow and asked, "Have you ever dealt with a passive-aggressive person?"

"I'm not sure," I paused. "What is a passive-aggressive person?"

"It's someone who avoids direct communication or is unclear about what they want. When there's a problem, they make excuses or blame others. You need to be prepared because, in this job, you're going to meet a lot of them."

"Okay. How will I know when I meet one?" I asked naively.

"They'll be wearing State Department badges." I laughed, but it was clear from her somber expression that she was serious.

Bagram Air Base

The next day an enormous SUV picked me up at the front gate and transported me the short distance to that part of the airport reserved for helicopter traffic. The pilot, still handsome in middle age but clearly bored by the routine of shuttling consultants in and out of Kabul, silently stowed my bag and yanked my harness to make sure it was secure. After a last-minute scheduling hiccup—resolved by a long string of muffled invective over the radio—the helicopter whirred into motion and lifted off for the quick flight to Bagram.

We climbed above the dust and pollution of Kabul, and as we careened to the west, the tilt of the aircraft gave me a magnificent view of the rugged cliffs and green lowland of the valley, some of which was still covered in snow.

At Bagram, the pilot made short work of extracting me from the helicopter. Then, shouting directly into my ear to compensate for the constant roar of fighter jets, cargo planes, and surveillance aircraft taking off and landing on the twin runways, he assured me that "someone in a jeep" would come collect me.

There were no benches, so I leaned against the corrugated metal of the building. Not fifty feet away, a long line of young American soldiers, just kids really, boarded a large unmarked jet. Each carried a bulging, dust-colored backpack and a weapon. A couple of them stood out for being talkative and upbeat, but the majority trudged up the stairs in silence.

Just as I began to worry that I had been forgotten, a jeep roared up, and a specialist jumped out.

"You Bowman?" Clearly in a hurry, he was already lifting my bag into the back of the jeep. He jumped behind the wheel, but instead of driving off, we sat in silence, watching the long line of soldiers disappear into the jet.

"If I'm not mistaken, ma'am," he hollered, "those guys are going down to Marjah, in Helmand Province. They're the first phase of the Obama military surge, and it's gonna be rough." He looked at me and then back to the jet. "If you're the type that prays, ma'am, put those guys in your prayers." Then without looking, he backed up at high speed, made a hard turn, and stepped on the gas.

281

Support From Home

As we drove down Disney Drive, Bagram's main street, the specialist alternated between shouting out bits of Bagram history and acknowledging friends.

"Yo, Webler. You owe me ten bucks," he yelled at a soldier rushing across the street. Then back to me. "I'll catch up with that guy later. Anyway—Bagram was established in the 1950s to keep an eye on the Ruskies during the Cold War. Imagine being way out here back then. No internet. No women. Whew. That would have been some tough duty."

We drove by a line of soldiers waiting to order from a familiar fast-food restaurant.

("Almost like home," I said.

"Well, that's what they want us to believe," he grinned and poked me in the side with his elbow.)

After a couple of turns, we skidded to a stop outside an unattractive building. He pulled my bag from the back of the jeep and informed me that I could find the USAID/Department of State office on the second floor. "I gotta go track down that Webler," he said. "I've got plans for that ten bucks."

I trudged up the stairs but paused on the first landing in front of a bank of floor-to-ceiling shelves crammed full of an amazing array of "stuff." There were granola bars, pocket packs of tissues, microwave popcorn, fruit-flavored lip balm, sunflower seeds, Hershey bars, packets of hot chocolate, and every sundry you could imagine. The packages came from San Diego, California; Lexington, Virginia; Fort Collins, Colorado; Trenton, New Jersey; Austin, Texas; Lancaster, Pennsylvania; and Hood River, Oregon, just to name a few.

(I was looking at the abundance of items sent by the American people demonstrating their support for the troops. The packages were addressed to "an American soldier," "Our Troops," and "Our Heroes." They contained handwritten messages of support and gratitude from elementary school classes, church groups, Rotary clubs, Little League teams, women's associations, and every type and size of entity imaginable. (It was heartwarming. It was America at its best.) And for the first time since accepting the job, I felt some personal pride in being part of the Obama Surge.

As I stood there on the landing, feeling a wave of emotion, a soldier rushed down the stairs, two steps at a time, stopping briefly to fish out a couple of mini Mars Bars. After stuffing them into his breast pocket, he encouraged me to help myself. Halfway down the next flight of stairs, he stopped and turned back, "Oh, if you're looking for alcohol, cigarettes, or porn, you're out of luck—they're prohibited items."

"No worries." I smacked my duffle. "I brought my own." He gave me a strong two thumbs up and disappeared out the door.

My check-in with the USAID/State Department office provided another reminder that I was a big logistical nuisance. The tiny woman behind the desk made a big production of finding me a bed. She told me, a couple of times, that she had to call in a "huge personal favor" to get me a decent place to sleep (In the end, I slept in a Quonset hut with a dozen or so female soldiers). So I guessed that the personal favor she had called in hadn't been that big after all.

The MWR

I ate in one of Bagram's three DFACs, a colossal structure that easily accommodated four hundred men and women in uniform (I was one of the only diners that didn't have a weapon slung across my back). The hot dishes were served by Afghan men who wore paper caps and beard nets. (Although I felt as if I was eating in an enormous gymnasium, there was a touching sense of community. Soldiers called out to each other and squeezed together to make room for late arrivals.)

After dinner, I made my way over to the Morale, Welfare, and

Recreation (MWR) building, where they showed movies 24/7. I reached up to open the plywood door, and an enormous soldier, whose neck was about the same size as my thigh, poked his head out and looked down at me. His bottom lip bulged from a plug of chewing tobacco. I was glad he was on our side.

"It's *Saw VI*, ma'am. A movie not for the faint of heart." He spoke with a thick southern accent, maybe Alabama or Mississippi. Then he spit some tobacco juice into a Styrofoam cup and wiped his chin with the back of his hand.

"Is it okay if I come in and look around?" I asked. Without saying a word, he swung the door open just enough for me to squeeze in.

I paused briefly to acclimate my eyes to the dark. On the large movie screen at the far end of the room, a larger-than-life-size woman sat paralyzed with fear. She had some kind of trap on her head, which was rigged so that two bolts would drill into her brain if activated. I looked back at the soldier by the door and frowned. He laughed and said, "Cain't say I didn't warn you, ma'am," then spit more brown liquid into the cup.

Annexed to the movie house was a small, harshly lit room full of plywood cubicles and computer equipment. Most of the cubicles were occupied by young soldiers, both men and women, talking to loved ones back home in the States. Everyone was using headphones, so I could only hear one side of the conversations.

While there was the usual small talk and inquiries about friends and family, I also heard repeated complaints about the rules of engagement, which define the circumstances and manner in which a soldier may use force. The then-current rules were subject to significant criticism for being too strict and purportedly placing a higher value on the lives of Afghan civilians than the lives of American soldiers.

As I left the room, I heard one soldier say, "You don't get it, Ma. If they don't change the rules, I could be here a whole year without shooting anyone. It could be a complete waste."

Chapter 8: Panjshir, Afghanistan

"You're One of Us"

Ultimately, I was assigned to "Lion," a Forward Operating Base (FOB) in Panjshir Province, a long, narrow, mountainous valley in the Hindu Kush. Panjshir's high peaks and narrow valley allowed it to be monitored by local guards making it secure from insurgents. As a result, it was one of the safest provinces in Afghanistan.

But that hadn't always been the case. Back in the 1980s, Panjshir was the site of a series of battles known as the "Panjshir Offensive" between the Soviet Army and groups of Afghan Mujahideen under Ahmad Shah Massoud, known as "the Lion of Panjshir." Mujahideen groups carried out ambushes against Soviet convoys bringing supplies in from Uzbekistan, then part of the Soviet Union.

While there was a new road up to Panjshir, it passed through extremely volatile Paktika Province. So in the interest of safety, I would be helicoptered up to my new home. The specialist who drove me to the airfield instructed me to stand by the back door of the terminal and promised that someone would eventually find me. After an hour or so, I was approached by a tall, heavyset man in his early sixties who had a passing resemblance to the actor John Wayne in his *Rooster Cogburn* days.

"I'm guessing you must be Jamie, the new legal advisor for Panjshir." He held out a massive hand for me to shake. "I'm Curtis. I work with the military in an engineering capacity."

"Where are you from, Curtis?" I asked.

"Ohio. The Buckeye State. I hear you're one of those liberal lawyers from California." I laughed. Curtis had a folksy way of speaking and a tendency to rock back and forth on his heels, almost nervously, as he spoke.

"You know, you'll probably be sharing office space with me and 'Little Jimmy,' the agricultural guru. Jimmy focuses on ways of increasing fruit production. You're going to learn all about soil acidity, rainfall, and way much too much about pear varieties."

"So there's you and Jimmy. Who else is up there?" I asked, really just trying to make conversation.

"Well, there's Ron, who's with the Department of State."

"Don't tell me," I paused. "He's a passive-aggressive person. I was thinking back to my last dinner in Kabul with Barbara, who warned me about the Department of State people.

"If passive-aggressive is a fancy term for a guy who can't give you a straight answer and is only interested in getting his photo taken with the governor every month, then yes, Ron is extremely passive-aggressive." It was impossible not to laugh.

"But it's not entirely his fault," he said. "For decades, the Department of State has trained its people to watch and report back to DC. As a result they don't understand development, and from what I've seen, they're not the fastest learners."

He continued. "Of course, we have a military presence, and while in the other provinces civilians have to be escorted by the military, Panjshir is so safe, we really don't need to. If you pass a driving test you can drive yourself, provided you can find a translator and a security guard to go with you." Then he paused. "That might be difficult, you being a female driver and all." He waited to see if I'd take the bait.

"This is Afghanistan, Curtis, not Ohio," I said. "They're more open-minded about women up here." He laughed long and hard.

"Okay, I can see you're one of us and will fit in nicely. I think we're going to have some fun."

Someone called out our names, and we boarded the helicopter, along with a soldier toting two sawed-off shotguns in his backpack.

The flight gave us a bird's-eye view of Panjshir, with its snow-peaked mountains and plunging valley. It was breathtakingly beautiful. The roar of the helicopter made it too noisy to talk, so every so often, Curtis would punch me on the arm to point out a sight of beauty or give me an encouraging "thumbs up."

FOB Lion

My new colleagues on FOB Lion came out of the main building to greet me. I think it was Dee Dee, the gender expert, who commented, "We're already so crowded up here, I can't believe they sent someone else." Yet another reminder that I was a big logistical nuisance. I looked over at Curtis, who did nothing to hide his amusement.

Someone gave me a quick tour of the compound. FOB Lion was little more than a collection of temporary buildings scattered at the base of a small hill. There was a main administrative office known as a Tactical Operations Center (TOC), a DFAC, a poorly equipped, overused gym, separate housing for men and women, and some other nondescript buildings. It would be a long three months until my first scheduled leave.

I bunked in with Kiera, the only female soldier assigned to the military police. About five foot two, blond, and impeccably coiffed in that way that only female soldiers and gymnasts can manage, Kiera was a lifesaver. While she wasn't particularly talkative, what she did say was important. She explained FOB Lion's workings and alerted me to particular issues as they arose. Occasionally, I'd see her at work, walking side-by-side with eight or ten enormous male soldiers who obviously liked and respected her.

Meeting the Judiciary

I was relieved to learn I had an assistant, a young local lawyer named Mohammad. Always sporting a blazer and suit pants, Mohammad may have been the best-dressed man in Panjshir. Then again, his only competition were the Afghan men in salwar kameez and the soldiers in pixelated camouflage-print uniforms. He was a gentle soul, the youngest of three sons, responsible for taking care of his elderly mother. He had a good sense of humor, and once we got past the awkward introductory phase, we worked well together.

287

That first week, we drove to Bazarak, the central city in Panjshir, to interview our first judge. Bazarak's main commercial area looked like a small slice of Kabul. There were butcher shops with the obligatory skinned lamb carcasses hanging outside; stores selling Islamic items such as Kaaba-themed clocks and prayer rugs; tailor shops with bolts of sun-bleached suit fabric on display in the windows; and several auto repair garages.

The judge's chambers were housed on the second floor of an unheated building that probably hadn't been cleaned since the Russians left in 1989. Ghostly dust bunnies floated down the halls.

We found the correct office, and a skinny male assistant, wearing what appeared to be a woman's tweed coat, escorted us into the judge's chambers. The judge, a tall man in a long white robe, knitted cap, and a dark blue parka, welcomed us with hearty handshakes. Then he barked something in a loud voice. I wasn't sure how to react, but soon the skinny assistant, still wearing the tweed coat, brought in a tea service.

As we chatted, it became clear that this judge was no country bumpkin. He was a war-tested professional who had been actively involved in the long campaign to drive the Russians out of Afghanistan. He peppered his remarks with brief anecdotes about his prior service. He deserved respect for his profession and status as a war hero.

I explained that one of my goals was to promote the government in Kabul at the local level to increase the government's credibility. As Mohammad translated, the judge's expression soured. He leaned back in his chair, crossed his arms, and said something in a low intense tone. Mohammad translated, "He says he will not deal with those bandits from Kabul. His job as a judge is to keep corruption out of Panjshir, not invite it in as our guests."

I made a show of drawing a line through that item on my agenda. He understood that I accepted his position, and his mood improved considerably.

(I raised the possibility of USAID providing computers and other office equipment to help the courts run more efficiently. The judge warmed to the point and grew rather friendly.)

"Not just computers," he explained through Mohammad. "We need a reliable source of electricity, computer training for the judges and the staff, printers, supplies of paper and folders, case management software, and internet access." He was right. There was little point in providing computers without the rest.

We said our goodbyes, and as we exited the building, Mohammad's phone buzzed, and he stepped away to answer it. When he returned, he said, (That was one of the judges who works in the court at the far end of the valley. He wants to know when we intend to visit him and discuss the possibility of computers.")

"That was quick," I said.

He smiled, "There are no secrets in Panjshir."

On the ride back from Bazarak, I thought about my introductory meeting with the judge. He was only interested in getting computer equipment, something a procurement clerk in Kabul could easily handle. I was reminded of the words of the young soldier back at Bagram—(I could be there a whole year without accomplishing anything. It could be a complete waste.)

Lashkar Gah

At the end of my first week I received an email from Roberto, who had been deployed to Lashkar Gah, the capital of Helmand Province. The same Helmand Province where the military side of the Obama Surge was just gearing up. With me in northeastern Panjshir, and Roberto in southwestern Lashkar Gah, it would have been almost impossible for us to be farther apart and still in the same country.(So much for rekindling our relationship.)

Helmand was responsible for growing as much as seventy-five percent of the world's poppies, and had a reputation for being a hotbed of insurgent activity. Everyone talked about Kandahar, but Helmand was consistently ranked as the most dangerous province in Afghanistan. Since the heroin that came from Helmand ended up on the streets of London, the British were taking the lead military role, but there was a big US Marine presence in Helmand as well. It took me a couple of days to get through, but I finally reached Roberto on his new cell number.

"So what are you doing in Lashkar Gah?" I asked.

"More road work. I'm inspecting the roads for wear and repair." His soft accented English sounded so far away.

"What...? You're inspecting roads in Lashkar Gah? Isn't that dangerous?" I asked.

"No. I'm surrounded by a bunch of Marines. Good guys. Kids really. They walk in a circle around me. I wear a flak jacket and a helmet," he said matter-of-factly.

"Wait, what? You're walking the roads in a volatile province with a bunch of US Marines?" I was horrified. "So what's the story? They found an Argentine and are making him do one of the most dangerous jobs in Afghanistan?" I was fuming.

"Oh, no," he said cheerfully. "I volunteered." I lost the connection before I could respond.

The National Anthem Loop

By March, the Obama Surge was in full swing, and civilian advisors had been deployed around the country. Someone in Kabul organized a massive conference call to disseminate updates and other news. Instructions on how to dial in were provided, but there were technical difficulties.

Little Jimmy, the agricultural guru, put the phone on speaker and dialed the number. After several clicks, which sounded like transfers, a recording of a woman's voice came on and encouraged us to stay on the line. Another series of clicks followed, then a wobbly tape of the Star-Spangled Banner played. Being patriots, Jimmy, Curtis, and I stood up for our national anthem, but ten seconds later, the music abruptly stopped, and we all sat back down. I went back to my computer.

After a few more seconds, the recording encouraging us to stay on the line repeated, as did the wobbly Star-Spangled Banner. I looked over, and Jimmy and Curtis were standing up again. I couldn't be the only person in the room not standing for the national anthem, so I got to my feet. We all stood for another ten seconds until the music abruptly stopped again, and we sat back down. After a few more seconds, the scene repeated itself; once more, we stood for the few seconds that the anthem played.

I'm almost embarrassed to admit that our jack-in-the-box respect for our national anthem continued for at least thirty minutes—until the three of us were laughing so hard at the ridiculousness of the situation that we couldn't stand up. We never did connect with the conference call.

You Don't Belong Here

Over the next few weeks, I tried to make the best of being placed in a province with limited commercial activity and no apparent credit system, my areas of expertise. Mohammad and I visited each of the courthouses within an hour's drive of FOB Lion to interview the judges and ask questions about their staffing, workload, and means of operation. I also worked with the two advisors supporting the local police and started drafting some broader governance proposals.

There wasn't much to do in the evenings, so after dinner I spent my time in the office, reading reports and watching movies. One evening

Curtis walked in, sat backward on one of the chairs with casters, and wheeled himself over until he was just a little too close to me. Then he rested his arms on the back of the chair and stared at me. It was very weird.

"You okay?" I asked tentatively.

"You know, you don't belong here," he said in a soothing voice. "And I mean that as a compliment."

I looked up briefly from my movie. "Where exactly don't I belong?"

"Panjshir. It's okay for me and Jimmy and Dee Dee." He rolled his eyes. "We'll limp along, but with your background, you belong in Kabul."

I was way ahead of him. I was actively waging a campaign to get reassigned. I frequently wrote to Mick back at the OEG in Kabul, demonstrating my keen interest in their programming and offering suggestions that might make his office look good. I wrote with the passion of a prisoner begging for early release.

The *WaPo* Article

A couple of nights later, I was catching up on old news reports and came across an article on Kabul Bank, Afghanistan's largest financial institution, published in late February by the *Washington Post*, familiarly known as *WaPo*. Kabul Bank was promoted by both Afghan and American officials as an example of how Western-style banking was transforming a war-ravaged economy.

The article was disturbing. It alleged that the officers of Kabul Bank had engaged in a massive misuse of funds in the form of multi-million-dollar loans to members of President Karzai's family, his government, and his supporters. The loans were allegedly used to purchase luxury villas in Dubai.

My first job out of law school was with the Federal Home Loan Bank Board, the agency responsible for regulating the savings and loan industry. During my tenure, the United States experienced its first savings and loan crisis, so I knew quite a bit about the complexities of dealing with a failing financial institution. Fortunately, there was a team of US contractors embedded in the Afghan Central Bank working to improve the bank supervisory capacity of the local staff. No doubt they were losing a lot of sleep over the allegations.

One thing was certain: if the allegations were true, the solvency of Kabul Bank would be put in question—and if that were the case, it would be a huge setback for the Afghan financial sector and the country as a whole. I read the article a second time, and for once, I was glad I was in Panjshir, far away from the problems in Kabul.

Sites Around the Valley

Panjshir had one main road, which was wedged in between the majestic cliffs and a crystal-clear, fast-moving river. I passed the driving test, but I rarely drove. As a passenger, I was better able to take in the breathtaking beauty of the valley. As the social customs were more relaxed in Panjshir, it was not unusual to come across women walking with their light blue burqas pulled up above their heads—an unheard-of practice in Kabul and the Southern provinces. The women usually had a baby balanced on their hip and a toddler in tow. We'd smile and exchange a friendly wave.

By far the oddest sight was the war tourists from Europe, Russia, and the United States who came to view the remnants of the Panjshir Offensive (the 1980s battle between the Mujahideen and the Russians). Easily identified by their expensive hiking clothes and broad-brimmed hats, I'd see them wandering about in the vehicle graveyards dotted around the valley, inspecting what was left of the old bombed-out tanks and other vehicles abandoned by the Russians. They were experts at finding the most dangerous curve in the road to inspect the battlefields sites through binoculars, but were always extremely apologetic for causing a near miss.

The Prisoners

(In early May, Ron mentioned that the local prison officials were looking to the United States for financial and technical assistance to build a modern prison.) I'd worked part-time for a criminal defense attorney while I was in law school. Some of our less fortunate clients went to prison, but I knew nothing about how they operated. And despite my protestations of ignorance, (I was dragged along on a group visit to the old prison, located just a few miles from the FOB Lion.)

(The warden, a man with a heavily lined face and constant frown, gave us a tour of the facilities.) The structure was so old and poorly maintained that it was hard to believe it was still in use. The walls were crumbling from damp, and there was a powerful smell of sewage. (I walked around the building with a sleeve covering my nose to avoid gagging.)

The warden provided the usual prison statistics: the average number of prisoners per year, the types of crimes, the typical length of sentence, etc. Then someone asked, "How many prisoners do you have right now?"

("Today, I have twelve prisoners," he said through a translator, "but I should only have four. Something must be done so the other eight can go home to their families in the northern district."

The eight men in question were stuck in the Afghan prison version of a Catch-22. After their respective arrests in the northern district on minor infractions, the local courthouse had closed due to either unusual snowfall or budget cuts—both explanations were offered. Under Afghan law they couldn't be released until they'd been arraigned, which couldn't happen until the courthouse in the north reopened. As a stopgap, they'd been transferred to Panjshir's prison, where they'd been languishing for months. As a result, eight families in the northern district were suffering because their breadwinners were incarcerated.

Once I understood the problem, I thought it would be a snap to get the prisoners released. But that wasn't the case because in Afghanistan, things have to happen a certain way, or they don't happen at all.

Getting the right decision-makers in a room at the same time involved a high level of secrecy and extreme logistical gymnastics. For reasons not entirely clear to me, an official appointment with the various officials could not be scheduled. The meeting had to appear to be serendipitous and take place outside of normal office hours. Transportation raised additional issues. We had to avoid all appearances of US involvement, so the USAID vehicle could not be used. The warden would not drive at night, and the judge from Bazarak did not have a car. In the end, Mohammad volunteered to drive the judge to the prison.

And just when I thought every eventuality had been addressed, Mohammad quietly mentioned, "We need to feed the judge before he visits the prison."

"What if I don't feed the judge?" I asked.

"He won't go."

So I invited Mohammad and the judge to dinner at FOB Lion, where we reviewed our plan over a fried chicken dinner and a selection of desserts. After they left FOB Lion for the prison, I paced around the compound like an expectant father. So many things could go wrong. Finally, Mohammad called me later in the evening.

"Was the warden surprised?" I asked.

"No, he was waiting for us outside the prison when we drove up." I had to laugh. "He knew we were coming. He was annoyed that we were late. It was the extra dessert."

"I know, I know," I said. "There are no secrets in Panjshir."

Now it was a matter of waiting to see whether that initial meeting would bear fruit.

Kabul Bank

One afternoon on the drive back from the courthouse at the far end of the valley, I noticed a sign for Kabul Bank. This was the Panjshir branch of the large institution that was the subject of the disturbing *WaPo* article alleging widespread fraud. I was curious to know more about the bank's operations in Panjshir, so I asked the driver if we could stop.

It's likely that I was the branch's first (and only) Western female visitor, and the all-male staff didn't know how to react to me. The branch manager ran out from his back office and was in such a state that he had to adjust and readjust his turban. I asked him about Kabul Bank's loan programs in Panjshir.

"We don't have loan programs," Mohammad translated, "we just take deposits. Many, many deposits."

This made no sense to me. Panjshir was one of the safest provinces in Afghanistan, so the war-related reasons for not lending didn't apply. In the United States, there's a law that incentivizes depository institutions to lend in the communities in which they take deposits. In my next email to Mick in OEG, I suggested a similar law might be helpful to address the limited lending in Panjshir and other provinces.

Prisoner Release

I had made it through my first three months in Panjshir, and at the end of May, I was eligible for my first leave. I couldn't wait. The last couple of weeks had raised some troubling issues. A rare IED exploded near a US convoy on patrol, raising the concern that it had been specifically targeted. In a separate incident, one of our military teams smashed their vehicle on the windy road, rendering it unusable, and then smashed the USAID loaner, depriving me of any transportation.

But there was also some good news. Two days before my departure, Mohammad came to the FOB Lion to tell me that the meeting between

296

the warden and the judge had been successful) (After a province-wide judicial conference, the eight prisoners had been released and transported back to their home district. The judge thanked me for my assistance. So at least for those eight families, I had accomplished something.

Munich

After three months is rural Panjshir, I wanted to spend time in a large city. So Roberto and I met in Kabul and flew to Munich for a week of vacation. We stayed at the upscale Kempinski Hotel near Munich's city center. We ate lots of pork, which wasn't served in Afghanistan, and drank the best beer on the planet. We took long walks in the woods, visited the city's oldest farmers' market, and were mesmerized by the cuckoo clock in Marienplatz, Munich's central square. Best of all, we spent time together.

Throughout the week, Roberto collected pens. He took the sleek white pen that the maid placed next to our phone each day, and any other pen that he could get his hands on. When checking out of the hotel, Roberto asked the clerk if he could take the pen I used to sign the bill. The young blond woman asked if he'd like another.

"Roberto, why do you need so many pens?" I asked.

He spoke both to the young clerk and me, "As part of my job in Afghanistan, I walk the roads in Lashkar Gah, inspecting their condition. Along the way, I meet children who beg me for pens. I have some pencils, but they insist on pens. So I'm collecting as many as I can to hand out to the kids I meet along the roads. It's a small thing," he shrugged.

The young clerk asked us to wait, and a few moments later, her supervisor appeared and handed Roberto two full boxes of pens. I'm sure there are children in Lashkar Gah still using the sleek white pens provided by the Kempinski.

Office of Economic Growth

When I returned to Kabul from Munich, I learned I wouldn't be going back to Panjshir. The emails I'd sent to Mick offering suggestions for new projects paid off. I was reassigned to work in the OEG in Kabul. Hallelujah!

(I would be overseeing a soon-to-be-awarded $108 million financial sector project designed to support small and medium-sized enterprises.) The procurement team was still evaluating the bids, but I was assured the project would be awarded within weeks—a month at the most.

USAID in Kabul was a hive of activity. The staff oversaw hundreds of contracts and grant agreements supporting a variety of technical areas, including agriculture, education, rule of law, women's empowerment, health, and of course, economic growth.) The dollar amount of these projects was huge. Clark, who sat across the aisle from me, was overseeing a $100 million project supporting lending in rural areas. Tony, who sat just down the hall, was managing the $92 million project designed to build the capacity of the local staff in the Afghan Central Bank, the country's financial regulator.

I wondered about putting Tony in charge of the Central Bank project. Bank regulation is both technical and challenging, especially in a politically charged environment such as Afghanistan. Tony was a young, smart twenty-something, but he had no financial sector experience—none. His lack of experience meant that he had to rely, almost exclusively, on the American contractors embedded in the Central Bank, the same contractors he was supposed to be overseeing.

(To make matters worse, some of the contractors had been working in Afghan Central Bank, on and off, since US government assistance in Afghanistan commenced in 2001—nine years earlier.) Such long-term associations can lead to overconfidence, complacency, and misplaced loyalties.) Tony's lack of experience meant he didn't know enough to be aware of these and other matters that affected the quality of the contractors' work(The arrangement was less than ideal, but accepted as an inevitable consequence of the limited staff that was willing to work in Afghanistan.)

Industry Rumors

Theo, the registry expert from the 2004 project in Moscow, came to Kabul to make a presentation on secured transactions reform to the staff of the Afghan Central Bank and some of the larger lenders. A small team from USAID attended the presentation, as did some of the contractors embedded in the Afghan Central Bank.

I introduced myself to Betty, the American legal advisor on the Central Bank team, a short, heavy-set woman several years my junior. In an effort to make small talk I asked how the officials at the Afghan Central Bank were dealing with the allegations laid out in the *WaPo* article. I was prepared for an "I can't comment" or "It's under investigation." Instead, she waved a dismissive hand and snapped, "There are always rumors in the financial service industry."

I snickered. Okay, it was more of a snort, but I couldn't help it. Her answer was preposterous.

It's one thing for a disgruntled employee to float rumors of improper conduct at a bank—that's just part of the business. As a regulator, you take those kinds of complaints with a grain of salt and make a note in the file to look into them during the next scheduled exam.(But when the "rumors" are thoroughly researched allegations of massive fraud made by world-class investigative reporters, they deserve some serious follow-up) I would have called the reporter and grilled him about the bank and what else he might know.

(Two days later, Mick came by my cubicle to advise me that the contractors in the Central Bank had filed a complaint against me.) He wouldn't let me see it, but I assumed it had something to do with my conversation with Betty. Mick had too much going on to deal with petty complaints. He instructed me to limit my contact with the contractors in the Central Bank to what was absolutely necessary. I was completely fine with that.

I called Roberto about the complaint.

"You would think," he said, "that those contractors would have more to do than waste time filing complaints, especially in light of the *WaPo* article."

The Interest Rate Cap

As it turned out, that was only the first of several complaints that the contractors in the Afghan Central Bank would file against me, which seemed strange considering I had nothing to do with their project. If it wasn't for my work with the smaller lenders, I would have left them entirely alone.

A second complaint was filed after an exchange with Reggie, a contractor I'd worked with in Southern Sudan. The Afghan Central Bank had instituted an interest rate cap of fifteen percent on all new loans. It was a move designed to appease influential parliamentarians who thought interest rates were too high. Politically, interest rate caps are a good move. They make the politicians look as if they're really doing something for their constituents. In practice, however, interest rate caps work to decrease the availability of credit and foster higher up-front fees, driving marginal borrowers back to the informal sector where they have to deal with cutthroat moneylenders.

I called Reggie to ask about the interest rate cap, and he was exceptionally unhelpful. He believed the Central Bank had a "gentleman's agreement" with lenders to cap interest rates. I couldn't make him understand that the interest rate cap would wipe out the small gains being made in lending to micro, small, and medium-sized businesses and put the good work of USAID in jeopardy. It was hard to hide my frustration.

So I wasn't surprised when Mick advised me that another complaint had been filed against me. It was so petty. Really, really petty.

The Elections Expert

The DFAC on the USAID side of the compound was more crowded than usual, (an indication that yet another batch of Surge advisors had arrived and was waiting to be deployed) I made my way down the long line of tables and found a seat directly across from a mustachioed man who extended a welcoming hand toward an open seat. We introduced ourselves and our respective areas of work.

Del was conducting an in-depth analysis of Afghanistan's 2009 presidential elections, which reportedly suffered from widespread ballot stuffing and other forms of electoral fraud) He was compact and powerfully built—not an ounce of fat on him. He asked how things were going in the Office of Economic Growth.

I sighed and thought about my answer. "Well, there are a lot of things that don't make any sense to me. But I don't want to bore you with the details." I shrugged and picked up my fork.

"You won't bore me," he smiled. "Before moving into the elections area, I was a director of the largest credit bureau in South Africa. I'd love to hear what's going on."

To avoid violating the US government rules on sharing confidential information) I spoke in general terms. I told him about my interaction with Betty, who dismissed the *WaPo* article about Kabul Bank as "industry rumors." With that, Del put his fork down and gave me his full attention. I told him about the interest rate cap, and he agreed it would stifle any development lending in Afghanistan. Then I mentioned how exasperating it was to have complaints filed against me, especially by contractors who didn't seem to be doing a very good job.

"You're being bullied," he said in a quiet voice. "When you're on the small side, like I am, you learn to spot it right away. They're probably worried that you'll bring attention to their poor performance, and they're trying to discredit you. It's a classic technique."

"Okay, how do you handle it?" I asked.

He smiled and said, "I have every confidence that you'll find a way."

Bigger than My Puny Job

With the complaints rolling in, Mick may have been regretting his decision to bring me into Kabul, but I was thoroughly enjoying being there. A lot was happening. The effectiveness of the Obama Surge was under constant scrutiny, which brought a raft of high-profile officials and celebrities to Kabul. John Kerry, the head of the Senate Foreign Relations Committee, was a frequent visitor. A very young Ronan Farrow passed through, as did a number of high-profile journalists.

And I was enjoying the work. I continued to lobby against the interest rate cap that, as expected, had stifled all lending to small and medium-sized businesses. I helped Clark deal with issues raised by the rural lending programs. Eventually, I became the go-to person for questions about USAID's work in the financial sector. I spent a couple of days briefing the Asian Development Bank on various programs, explained the principles of bank supervision to a Cornell grad student, and spent an afternoon discussing microfinance with the daughter of a *New York Times* reporter.

My favorite part of the job was answering questions from advisors in the field. They'd stop by my desk or catch me at the Duck and Cover when transiting through Kabul on their way to or from leave. They wanted information on specific USAID credit programs and asked whether it was possible to expand them into their province.

One afternoon Barry visited me; I hadn't seen him since our

weapons training class at Atterbury. He was working in Jalalabad, one of the places I had originally wanted to go to (I listened to him talk at length about his work improving cross-border trade)

"So there's a Kabul Bank branch up there, right?" I asked. "What kind of credit programs are they offering? Are they supporting trade, manufacturing, what?"

"Not that I know of." He shook his head "None of the businesses we deal with have a loan from Kabul Bank. I honestly don't think they're lending."

At lunch that day, I told Del about my conversation with Barry.

"How is that possible?" I asked. "How is it possible that I can't confirm the existence of one loan made by the largest bank in the country?" I was baffled "First, there was no lending in Panjshir, and now none in Jalalabad. Last week I spoke with a guy in Herat—no lending there either. Doesn't that strike you as odd?"

"Very odd," he responded, digging into his lunch. "There should be some reports on the bank somewhere in your department. Maybe you should take a look at its balance sheet." I nodded. It was a good idea. "On another matter," he continued, "any complaints filed against you this week?"

"Not yet, but it's only Tuesday. But I have an idea on how to handle the contractors in the Central Bank. I'm thinking about writing a memo detailing all the problems I see with their work: the cavalier attitude toward the *WaPo* allegations, the interest rate cap, the new mortgage law—it's a long list. But, it will memorialize all the deficiencies and—"

Before I could finish my sentence, Del leaned toward me and said, "Do it." His dark eyes bored into me. "Write the memo."

"Well, I'm just a little worried that the contractors might find a way to make my life even more miserable," I said. "I might end up losing my job."

"So what?" Del almost spat the words at me. "Protecting the reputation of your government is *your* job. It's *your* duty to bring these deficiencies to the attention of the ambassador and USAID. It's much more important than your puny job."

I raised my hands in resignation. "I'll do it," I said. "I'm just saying it won't be easy."

"Jamie," he said almost angrily, "it's the right thing to do, and you need to do it, even if it isn't easy."

The hair on my arms stood up. It was almost the exact quote my mother attributed to my dad back when he voted to give Dr. Davis privileges at his hospital. I saw it as a sign. The next day I started pulling together the information I needed to support my allegations.

Kabul Bank Meeting

In early August, USAID announced its intention to introduce a credit guarantee scheme, a pool of funds used to "insure" a portion of a loan, another means to encourage lending to small and medium-sized enterprises. As part of the preparatory work, USAID in Washington needed a list of viable financial institutions that met certain minimum criteria. I was volunteered to help out.

Due to its size and extensive branch structure, Kabul Bank was an ideal candidate for the credit guarantee scheme. But we needed to be cautious. There was the February *WaPo* article alleging fraud and other improprieties, and even if the contractors in the Afghan Central Bank didn't take the allegations seriously, I did. Chris, the lead on the credit guarantee program, contacted the Treasury consultants to see if Kabul Bank should be included on the list of possible partner institutions. They had no objection, so we scheduled a meeting with two of the bank's senior officers.

After dealing with suspicious security guards, Chris and I were escorted into a large office where we met the bank's Chief Audit Officer and another high-ranking official. They took turns detailing the bank's remarkable history: the number of branches, the increase in deposits, and the successful lending programs. Then the Chief Audit Officer added, "And you know, we don't have any delinquent loans."

His statement, "*We don't have any delinquent loans*" stirred the old bank regulator in me. (It was highly improbable—no, it was *impossible* that an institution the size of Kabul Bank could operate without incurring bad loans.) It just doesn't happen. I gave him a doubtful look.

"Oh, it's very true. Not one bad loan." He was all smiles and nods.

Over the years, I've been lied to by financial institutions, loan agents, borrowers, and boyfriends, and I knew this guy wasn't telling the truth. I tried to choose my words carefully, but I wanted him to know I wasn't buying his story.

"Then," I said cautiously, "there's something very wrong here."

I prepared for some serious blowback. I can assure you that if the roles were reversed and some visitor had the temerity to question the soundness of my bank, they'd be shown the door. But to my surprise, the mood in the room grew upbeat, almost friendly. The tea-wallah was called upon for a tray of golden raisins and pistachio nuts, and when the officials learned that I liked kebabs, someone was sent out to the street to buy me an order.

There was a great deal of interest in me personally. Where was I from? Was I enjoying my time in Kabul? *How long was my contract?*

I was being played.

FDIC Dennis

That evening, I scoured the USAID office for reports and filings on Kabul Bank. I rifled through the dusty stacks stored above the mailboxes and through the forgotten packets under desks. I hunted down all the quarterly reports and organized them in chronological order.

In the process I came across Kabul Bank's recent financial audit, and the language on the front page said it all. It was "qualified," meaning the bank had limited the auditor's work or the information provided. That's a huge red flag. In the States a qualified audit would have led to additional scrutiny of the bank's operation and soundness. This is the document that should have been walked across the embassy compound to the ambassador's office and presented with the words, "Mr. Ambassador, there's a big problem with Kabul Bank."

I copied a few pages of the financials, blocked out names, and faxed them to my friend Dennis, a senior examiner at the Federal Deposit Insurance Corporation (FDIC) in San Francisco. I first met Dennis back in the late 1990s, when I worked for a large bank headquartered in Southern California. My institution had been going through a big transition, and at the same time, we had applied to acquire a new branch. As the country's deposit insurer, the FDIC had been very interested in how all the pieces would fit together. Despite the occasional unfavorable decision, Dennis and I became friends and stayed in touch. He was always willing to help out when I needed advice about financial institution supervision.

The fax cover sheet to Dennis simply read, "What do you see?"
He responded by email, "Whatever I'm looking at, it's not a bank."
"What if I told you it *is* a bank?" I emailed back.
"Then there's fraud—a massive amount of fraud."

"Kabul Bank is Failing"

I spent the next few days drafting and redrafting the memo, knowing full well it might subject me to more complaints and possible termination. That self-satisfied look on the Chief Audit Officer's face, coupled with the qualified audit, convinced me that the information in the *WaPo* article was fact, not rumor, and I worried that things could go south very quickly. Suddenly, my memo wasn't just about the poor work of the contractors in the Afghan Central Bank. It was about the real possibility the Kabul Bank could go under.

I tried to keep it simple, so readers unfamiliar with banking could understand that there were real problems at the Afghan Central Bank and its oversight of the industry. I boldly stated that despite what we read in the success stories, the "financial sector was functioning at a very low level," and then I laid out ten full pages of problems and poor practices.

I completed the memo on August 15 and sat down with the Deputy Director of the OEG to walk him through the issues. But my poor relationship with the contractors in the Afghan Central Bank was well-known. I'm not sure how much he actually listened.

I grew anxious and had difficulty sleeping. I was too nervous to watch a full movie and took to pacing around the compound. A week passed, then two, and nothing happened. I began to doubt my instincts. I must have misread the situation, and now my "Chicken Little" memo about Kabul Bank was out there, memorializing that I was a hysterical alarmist. A large bank failure? Girl, get a grip!

On the first of September, I was scheduled to take leave. I was meeting Roberto in London for a week. After he raised concern over a faulty irrigation plan, Roberto's contract hadn't been renewed. He was on his way back to Buenos Aires. I was looking forward to seeing him and getting out of the fishbowl of the embassy compound for a while.

As I rolled my suitcase to the front gate, I heard someone running behind me. Tom, my one buddy at the Department of State, was part of the small group that had concerns over the quality of work coming from the contractors in the Afghan Central Bank.

"Have you heard the news about Kabul Bank?" He was a big guy and panted as he spoke. He grabbed my arm to stop me. "It's happening right now. The chairman and CEO of Kabul Bank were forced to resign Hundreds of Afghans are gathering outside Kabul Bank offices all over the country, trying to withdraw their savings. The police are having to beat back mobs. Kabul Bank is failing."

Principles vs. Paychecks

When I returned to Kabul from my week-long break in London, insiders told me about the long, painful conference calls between Kabul and Washington. News articles reported that Kabul Bank had falsified its books to hide hundreds of millions of dollars in unsecured loans to politically connected business executives. As a result, there was an estimated $1 billion in losses.

There was a flurry of press releases questioning how the Afghan Central Bank and its high-priced contractors had missed the fraud in Kabul Bank. I was sure USAID would take action, and I waited for the five contractors at Afghan Central Bank to be "perp walked" to the airport. But nothing happened—they kept their lucrative jobs. It was too much to take, so I decided to leave.

Del tried to talk me into staying, but there was no point. In 2002, I had left a job I liked in Kosovo because I didn't want to appear to be supporting the toxic management style of Terry Jones. I couldn't stay in Kabul and watch the ineffective Central Bank contractors deflect blame.

As I finalized my departure paperwork, the woman behind the counter passed me a card with my personal and other information already filled in. Under the heading "reason for leaving," someone had penciled in the word "stress." I picked up a pencil and modified the answer to read "stress due to my government's refusal to hold its contractors accountable for poor performance."

Walking back to my quarters, I was stopped by Lance, an agronomist whom I had met at Camp Atterbury. "I hear you're leaving. You lucked out with a job in Kabul. What's the problem?"

"I'm leaving because no one is being held responsible for the failure of Kabul Bank," I said, trying not to sound sanctimonious. "I know it sounds hokey, but if you don't have principles, what do you have in this world?"

"Um, a paycheck?" he responded, completely missing my point. But his comment cemented by decision to leave.

El Camino

After leaving Kabul I spent some time in Washington, DC, and then flew back to San Jose. (I'd been right about the contractors in the Afghan Central Bank, but there's no satisfaction in being right if you're too late to do anything about it.) I just wanted to put the whole affair behind me. (I had no job, nothing in the pipeline, and probably didn't have the frame of mind to take on something new. I felt a little lost.)

I was checking my Facebook feed, and an advertisement appeared. "Lost? Find your way. El Camino." It was as if those algorithms read my mind. Creepy.

("El Camino" referred to the Camino de Santiago, or the Way of Saint James, a major Catholic pilgrimage route since medieval times.) There are nine routes, but the most popular is the Camino Frances, which runs along Northern Spain and finishes at Santiago de Compostela, the purported burial place of Saint James. I thought a big dose of spirituality would do me some good. All I needed was someone to walk with me. Preferably someone who spoke Spanish.

After a series of emails, alternating among pleading, cajoling, and making promises I had no intention of keeping, Roberto agreed to walk 100 kilometers of the Camino Frances with me.

The Congressional Aide

Roberto and I met up in Madrid and spent a few days enjoying the museums and tapas in the small bars around the city. While checking the weather reports online, I received an email from a woman named Sarah who worked for one of the US Congressional committees. She wanted to ask me some questions about the Kabul Bank scandal.

I was hesitant to speak with her. After all, I was making the pilgrimage to forget about Kabul Bank. Plus, there are strict rules against disclosing information, even when the other person has a security clearance. I reluctantly agreed to take the call. When the phone rang, Roberto pulled his chair up close to me so that he could listen in.

Sarah explained that she was finalizing an investigation for her committee and wanted to ask me some questions about who knew what, when, and more importantly, had people on the US government payroll been doing their jobs?

"I wrote a memo on some of those issues," I said. "USAID probably has it." Roberto stood up to face me and made the gesture of drawing a knife across his throat. He wanted me to tear the Central Bank contractors apart. I put my hand over the receiver and whispered to Roberto to stop it. He sat back down next to me and put his ear close to the phone.

"The Committee has your memo, Jamie. But I have to tell you, we all found it very disturbing."

"Disturbing?" I echoed. I wasn't in the mood to defend my work. I was regretting taking the call.

"It's disturbing that with all the staff and consultants that have been in and out of the Kabul mission, you're the only one that actually took the time to sit down and articulate the problems of USAID's support of the Afghan Central Bank. Thank you for your service. You're a credit to your country. A patriot." I thought back to my dinner with Blaine in Kosovo, over ten years earlier, and how he encouraged me to be a credit to my country. I guess I had in some small way achieved that.

Roberto stood in front of me and gave me a thumbs up while mouthing the word "patriot." I wiped a tear from the side of my face.

("But I wanted to ask," she continued, "how were you so sure that there would be a bank failure? Was it the *WaPo* article that convinced you?")

I told her about my visit to Kabul Bank, the assertion that they had no bad loans, and how when I questioned them, they tried to buy me off with a street kebab.

"The committee is going to *love* that story." We chatted a bit longer, and then she said she had another call. "Thanks again, Jamie, for all your hard work—and good luck."

The next day, Roberto and I caught the overnight train to the town of Sarria and stumbled off the next morning in the predawn darkness(Our plan was to walk eighteen to twenty-five kilometers a day and arrive at the Cathedral de Santiago by the end of the week.)As we walked, Roberto asked me to repeat the phone conversation with Sarah over and over, "A credit to your country. That's my Jamie."

"But it's not enough," I sighed. "There's no accountability(Those guys who should have known about the situation at Kabul Bank bear some responsibility, and they're still employed. It's soul-crushing.")

The El Camino was just what I needed. We spent four and a half days walking a mostly dirt path through some of the most beautiful scenery in Spain. Since we had started before Easter, we had almost the whole route to ourselves. If we happened to meet other pilgrims, we'd exchange stories about our experiences and share a chocolate bar, if we had one. Frugal Roberto enjoyed the nine euro "pilgrim meal," which consisted of three courses and a small glass of wine.

(We arrived at the cathedral in late March.)Sitting in that enormous structure, tired and sore from our walk, listening to the crystal-clear voice of a nun singing near the apse(I felt the spirituality that so many pilgrims report in their blogs)I insisted we climb the short flight of steps to the shrine of Saint James and embrace the bejeweled statue of the apostle in accordance with pilgrimage custom. I wanted the full experience.

We checked into the Parador Hostel, a beautiful building that originally served as a royal hospital to accommodate pilgrims traveling to Santiago. Roberto went to use the internet, and I lay on the bed, thinking about what I would do next in my life.

Just as I was about to doze off, Roberto burst into the room with a piece of paper in his hand.

"I had the hotel print this out for you. It's a *Wall Street Journal* article from a couple of weeks ago that I think you'll want to read." I raised my eyebrows. "It's about your buddies in the Afghan Central Bank," he said.

I propped myself up on one elbow and gave him my full attention.

Roberto continued, "USAID's Office of Inspector General released a thirty-two-page report on the Kabul Bank failure. It speaks to the inadequacy of the contractors in the Central Bank. And get this, it says the program was 'not capable of developing sufficient capacity to detect the fraud at Kabul Bank.'"

"I could have told them that." I said sarcastically.

"Here's the good part," he continued. "It says here that the American government has terminated the $92 million contract supporting the technical advice in the Afghan Central Bank." He looked up, smiling. "Those guys who filed complaints against you have lost their jobs. Now tell me, is that enough for you?"

I rolled on my back, looked up at the ceiling. By walking the El Camino, I had hoped for the same thing as the millions who had walked before me—some spiritual relief from the hardships and challenges of everyday life. In my case, the challenge had been my time working in Kabul and dealing with the bullies in the Afghan Central Bank. A day after completing the trek, I had learned that the contractors lost their jobs in a very public and humiliating way. The connection was almost too easy for me to make.

I looked back at Roberto and laughed, "Yes, actually, that's enough for me."

Paris, France

April 2011

We stayed a few extra days at the Parador Hostel, in part to explore the quaint town but mostly to give our blistered feet a rest. We made a day trip to Finisterre, literally the "end of the world," and passed the rest of the time getting lost in the ancient streets and dining on the large plates of charred octopus, the regional specialty.

The French firm that hired Roberto for the São Tomé job back in 2009 wanted to speak to him about a new project in Cambodia. So we traveled back to Madrid, where we had started the trail, collected our luggage, and took the overnight train to Paris. As we sped through the dark Spanish countryside, I realized that the walk had restored my spirit, and the $92 million contract cancellation had partially restored my faith. I wasn't quite ready to excuse my treatment in Kabul, but somehow it mattered less.

Roberto went to his interview, and I met up with Martina, my friend from Southern Sudan and the winner of the Riek Machar hand-holding contest. She was in Paris visiting a French journalist she'd met on a project in Libya. I hadn't seen Martina since Nairobi, back when she was gaunt and pale, frustrated with the doctors at the Tropical Disease Clinic who couldn't give her a specific diagnosis. Fully recovered, she looked great, still wearing the red jeans that had caused such a stir in Juba.

(I wanted to treat Martina to a nice meal to thank her for all her support while I was in Kabul. She was one of the few people who truly understood my fear of losing my "moral compass." Unfortunately, the dining options were limited. The tourist season was ramping up, and the nicer restaurants were full of large tour groups. In the end, we settled for a tiny crêperie near the Pantheon. The tables were so close together you still had to turn sideways to maneuver through the room.

Despite the shabbiness of the restaurant, it hosted a rather well-heeled international clientele. A man dressed in a bright blue agbada, the elaborate garment favored by Nigerians, sat one table over, reading a guidebook with a photo of the Eiffel Tower on the cover. A middle-aged woman with an unflattering, feathered haircut, sat at the table next to the window (She was reading an English language newspaper, and I could just make out some of the headlines—the continued hunt for Osama bin Laden, the demands for President Obama's birth certificate, and civil war in Syria.)

Trying to make the best of the crummy little restaurant, Martina suggested we have some champagne. She signaled the waitress and ordered "deux coupes de champagne" in her breathless, "Jackie Kennedy" French. Moments later, two disappointingly small glasses arrived along with a basket of sliced baguette.

"Okay, I have to ask about Roberto," Martina said reaching for a slice of bread. "Are you two back together? He did fly halfway around the world to walk a pilgrimage with you. That's almost an engagement in most people's book."

"Honestly, I don't know if we're back together. He surprised me by coming to Spain. We were together for two weeks, ate every meal together, and slept in the same bed (but we never once talked about the future.) I shrugged, slightly embarrassed I didn't have a better answer.

"Okay, what about work?" she asked. "Are you applying for jobs?"

I sat back in my chair and slowly rotated my glass of champagne by the stem.

"I'm not sure what I want to do next. I'm to the point that I'm questioning whether I want to continue working internationally." Just saying it aloud made me feel sad.

"Don't say that," she said. "You just need more time off after your time in Kabul, that's all."

"Afghanistan certainly didn't help, but it's more than that," I said. "I still enjoy the challenge of working in difficult places, the travel, and meeting new people, but there are certain issues that bother me more and more."

"This sounds serious," she reached for her champagne.

"Growing up in the States, there wasn't a lot of discussion about America and its role and responsibility to the rest of the world. As one of only two superpowers, we *were* the world stage—or at least half of it. I don't remember ever thinking about how America's policies or actions affected other countries because who could dare fault us? We were the 'good' in the battle between 'good and evil.' It was easy being an American back then."

"And now you've discovered that America has its critics," she offered.

"No, I've known we've had critics. But I love my country and want other people to love it too. Our countries are like our families. It's fine for us to find fault with our own, but I don't like it when other people feel free to criticize my family and expect me to agree and join in the condemnation."

"And do people condemn the United States—to you, I mean?" She asked with genuine interest.

"Yes." I nodded. "When I worked in Kosovo—"

"I loved my time in Kosovo," she said.

"Me too. It's where I met Roberto."

"The first time you saw those blue eyes," she said.

"The first time I saw those blue eyes," I confirmed. "Anyway, when I was in Pristina, I met a Polish banking advisor who complained about the salted butter in the food packages her family received from the United States after World War II."

Martina interrupted. "Who eats salted butter?"

"Well, that was the problem," I laughed. "Apparently, the Poles don't, and she had to make a point of it forty years after the fact. Bear in mind that those CARE packages contained a collection of tinned meat, sugar, salt, and other foodstuffs supplied to keep people from starving."

"Ingrate," Martina said. I could always count on Martina to take my side. "She could have said 'Thanks for the Spam, ma'am.'" We both laughed. It was nice to see her again.

"I don't think I was expecting a 'thank you,' but her criticism of the effort took me by surprise. I looked into it, and the shelf life of salted butter is longer than that of unsalted butter," I said. "So it was more an issue of American ingenuity—trying to make the butter last longer—rather than American blundering. But that's my point (Instead of mentioning the good, she complained about the bad.)

"You were right to be annoyed," she said. "She was wrong."

"In Afghanistan, in 2005, a British woman told me that America deserved the 9/11 bombings. Over three thousand innocent people died—and she said we had it coming."

"Now, *that* would definitely bother me," she agreed. "If someone had said something like that about the bombings in Bali, where most of the victims were Australians, I would have been livid."

"I didn't take it well. Roberto and I had a bit of an argument over it. (He said something like, 'Americans will always have enemies because they're full of themselves, privileged, and hypocritical.')

"I'm not going to comment on that," she said, sitting back in her chair.

"But you know, I've seen instances where tough criticism of the United States is warranted. Sometimes, we're our own worst enemy. It's as if we leave our values and even our common sense back home."

"Give me an example."

"There was a guy named Patrick in Kabul, who told a conference room full of Afghans his version of the Golden Rule—*he who has the gold makes the rules*. And he was sitting in an office on the embassy compound when he said it." Martina put both hands over her mouth to stifle a laugh.

"Did that really happen?" She laughed some more. "So much for supporting a democratic government in Afghanistan."

"I know. It was absolutely the worst message to come out of the embassy," I agreed. "And just before I left Kabul this last October I had a discussion with another consultant who believed it was better to choose a paycheck over principles. It was so disheartening. And yes, while it's okay for me to knock our performance, it's still hard to hear people from other countries criticize the States."

At that moment, a man wearing a Roman collar, a member of the clergy, hustled into the restaurant and sat with the woman with the feathered haircut. After kissing her on the cheek and apologizing for being late, he picked up the newspaper the woman was reading and skimmed the headlines. In a loud, pulpit-worthy British accent, he announced, "Oh, it looks as if our American friends are having more troubles. What did my mother always say? 'The Americans have more dollars than sense.'"

I leaned over to Martina and whispered, "It's almost on cue. Now a man of God is dissing my country."

The woman piped up, "Why would anyone want to go to America? Shootings, bad weather—and really, what is there to see?"

"New York, maybe," he responded. "And there is that big hole in the desert that's supposed to be impressive."

I leaned in close to Martina and whispered, "That 'big hole'—I think he means the Grand Canyon, one of the world's most spectacular natural wonders." She smiled almost apologetically.

The waitress made her way to their table, took the man's order, and she quickly returned with a glass of red wine. Martina and I ordered a couple of crêpes.

When it came time for the table next to us to pay the check, the woman with the bad haircut took the opportunity to bring the young waitress into her anti-American discussion. "Would you visit the United States? Would you want to go over there?"

The waitress looked very uncomfortable at being put on the spot.

I leaned toward Martina again. "This is exactly the kind of anti-American baloney that I've lost my patience with."

I felt emboldened by the champagne and thought about interjecting myself into the conversation, but the couple paid the bill and left. I looked at Martina and shook my head, and said, "How irritating."

The Nigerian put his book down and spoke to anyone who might be listening. "Was that woman asking about going to America?" He twisted around in his chair and faced our table. "Well, I want to go."

"As a young boy in Lagos, I was taught by Peace Corps volunteers. Because of their instruction, I became the first person in my family to graduate from college. I want the opportunity to show my teachers the man I have become." He nodded, hoping for a response.

"I agree," Martina said supportively. "Some of my very best friends are Americans." I laughed.

"I have been to America," the waitress responded in her heavily accented English. "I studied a year at a university in West Virginia and lived with an American family. They made sure I saw as much of the country as possible. I'd go back tomorrow if I could afford it."

That day in the restaurant, I didn't defend my country. I didn't have to. The waitress, the man from Nigeria, and Martina did it for me. I felt my face flush, and I wasn't sure if it was from the pride I felt in my country or the champagne—but whichever it was, it felt good.

I walked back to the hotel, hoping to sober up a bit before meeting Roberto for dinner. The time by myself gave me time to think over what Martina and I had discussed at lunch.

I was the first to admit that my work in development was no noble calling. As a financial attorney, I didn't feed the poor, tend to the sick, or educate the masses. And it wasn't glamorous. No president had ever called me for advice—but some fairly influential people had taken time to yell at me.

Despite the frustration and inconvenience, the work was both challenging and fun. And I was confident that I had actually accomplished some things. Maybe I did have one more project left in me.

Roberto was waiting for me in the hotel lobby, just as he had all those years ago in Moscow. He stood up and hugged me.

"I got the job in Cambodia," he said. "I start in a month or two."

"Congratulations," I said as I gave him a kiss. I was genuinely pleased for him.

"Any interest in going to Phnom Penh?" he asked. "I mean with me?" I leaned into him, and he put his arms around me. "It won't be for a couple of months."

"Then how about we first go to the United States," I said. "There's a big hole in the desert I want you to see."

A NOTE TO READERS

Thank you for reading *Bike Riding in Kabul*! If you've enjoyed this book, we hope you'll take a few moments to leave a review on Amazon and/or Goodreads. Your review means a lot to the author, publisher, and everyone who had a hand in bringing this book to you.
Thank you!

Acknowledgments

Bike Riding in Kabul was my COVID lockdown project. Friends and colleagues worldwide were subject to stay-at-home orders, and I shamelessly prevailed upon them to help me with my stories. And while they had no obligation to read my manuscript—they did. I am so grateful for their time and collective insights, because each reader brought something unique to the final book.

I am incredibly grateful to those friends who saw me through the initial few months of writing. My deepest thanks goes out to Martina Nicolls and James O'Neill who read and reread the early drafts. Those pages were extremely rough, prone to questionable grammar and creative punctuation. But they took the time to correct errors and comment on the growing chapters. Thank you, Martina and Jim, for your time and endless encouragement.

As the book came together, and the pandemic raged on, I prevailed on more friends. I received invaluable editorial assistance and a mid-manuscript boost from a special group of people who put aside their own work and interests to help me out. This group includes Holly I. Melton, Jessica Vapnek, Eva Knight, Roy Dalle Vedove, Timothy

Ham, David DeVoss, Sophie Rojas, A. Glibbery, and Ms. A. Gomez. Thank each and every one of you.

And thank you to those people who were willing to read specific chapters for accuracy and, in doing so, provided me with additional encouragement. Thank you to Piro Rexhepi, Sheela Rahman, Everett Wohlers, Beverly Bensalam, Kathleen Montgomery, John Wheeler, Sue Tatten, Dale Lampe, R. Jerome Anderson, Chris Hardaway, and DJ Durtal. Again, thank you.

Thanks to the terrific team at Boyle & Dalton, including Emily Hitchcock, who made the publication process both manageable and enjoyable.

Finally, a special thanks to Pepe Castilla, whose in-depth knowledge of *everything* was instrumental in helping connect the historical dots that gave each chapter its context. I would also like to thank the staff and patrons of the Bell and Crown in Canterbury, United Kingdom, who helped me formulate several of the underlying themes. There would be no book without their willingness to debate.

About the Author

Jamie Bowman is a born storyteller with plenty of stories to tell. For the past twenty years, she has worked as a legal consultant in some of the world's most challenging environments. As part of the bargain, she has lived in buggy hotel rooms, converted shipping containers, and recycled safari tents. She is a California native, a graduate of the University of California, Berkeley, and a member of the State Bar of California. Jamie currently lives in Washington, DC, but she spends a few months each year in her favorite city, Savannah, Georgia. After a long career of writing legal documents, reports, and a variety of laws, *Bike Riding in Kabul* is Jamie's first book.